To Barbara & Dennis

May the dialogic endure

[illegible]

S0-ALD-664

Fluid Signs

FLUID SIGNS
Being a Person the Tamil Way

E. Valentine Daniel

UNIVERSITY OF CALIFORNIA PRESS
Berkeley Los Angeles London

University of California Press
Berkeley and Los Angeles, California

University of California Press, Ltd.
London, England

Copyright © 1984 by The Regents of the University of California

Library of Congress Cataloging in Publication Data

Daniel, E. Valentine.
Fluid signs.

Bibliography: p. 303
Includes index.
1. Tamils. I. Title.
DS432.T3D3 1984 306′.089948 84-163
ISBN 0-520-04725-7

Printed in the United States of America

1 2 3 4 5 6 7 8 9

For Vanessa

Contents

Acknowledgments

During the course of this study I have accumulated many debts. Grants from three sources funded the fieldwork on which this study is based. The National Science Foundation met the greater part of the expenses of the project, the Danforth Foundation, some of them. A grant from the Amherst Memorial Fellowship fund enabled me to carry out some essential ancillary field research in Sri Lanka among Āru Nāṭṭu Veḷḷāḷa expatriates.

To Lee Schlesinger I owe my successful experiment in gathering and interpreting maps drawn by villagers, which was to subsequently lead to my discovery of the *ūr* concept. I also owe thanks to James Lindholm, who along with Lee taught me the value of asking those crucial questions whose quintessence lies concealed in their apparent simplicity. To Nick Dirks, who patiently read over selected portions of various drafts of this manuscript and who proved to be an invaluable source of helpful suggestions, I am grateful.

Among my teachers at the University of Chicago, A. K. Ramanujan helped sharpen my awareness of the aesthetic dimension of Tamil culture through his poems and informal musings, luring the simple qualities of commonplace recognitions to inhabit snatches of words. Victor Turner introduced me to the rich possibilities of comparative symbology, and Terry Turner showed me so many different ways of seeing the forest for the trees during times when I was trapped in the thicket of my field notes. My greatest intellectual debt is owed to McKim Marriott, my principal adviser, mentor, and friend, whose high standards of meticulous fieldwork remain paradigmatic and whose skill at critically reevaluating the most convincing idea and interpretation has been unfailingly sobering. Others whose comments, criticisms, and editing of various portions of earlier drafts of the manuscript have enhanced the clarity of the final product are: Bernard Cohn, Veena Das, Dianne Mines, Ralph Nicholas, Paula Richman, Michael Silverstein, and my colleague Jean-Paul Dumont. Peg Hoey's good taste and good judgment have contributed enormously in converting many passages of good Sri Lankan English into good American English. To her and to Larry Epstein, who perused the galleys, I express my thanks.

To R. Srinivasan, my research assistant in the field, who willingly toiled with me through both happy and trying times, I owe thanks. To all my friends and informants in Kalappūr and its neighboring villages, to all my friends in Tiruchirapalli, and to all my Āru Nāṭṭu Veḷḷāḷa friends in Sri Lanka, who gave so much of their time and put up with all my prying and rude questions, I shall ever be grateful. I must single out A. Devadas, at whose suggestion Sherry and I chose to work in Kalappūr and without whose help our fieldwork might not have been possible.

Special thanks are owed to my sister, Indrani, and to my nieces Rowena and Vero, who generously gave of their time and love during the preparation of this book, in typing, in taking care of Vanessa, and in assuming many of the household responsibilities, thereby freeing Sherry and me to devote ourselves to its completion. The greater part of the child care was assumed by my father and mother, who lovingly and happily gave long hours of their retired life for Vanessa.

To three individuals from the University of California Press I owe a special word of thanks: Stanley Holwitz and

Shirley Warren, the kindest of editors, let so many deadlines slip by, and Sylvia Tidwell made the incomprehensible comprehensible in countless ways. Need I add: they were patient.

Finally, and most important, I owe the most special of debts to Sherry, who unstintingly gave of her time, energy, and intellect to help me work through almost every page and idea of the second, third, fourth, fifth, and seventh chapters of this book, who cleared up my thinking whenever I was unable to do so myself, who lifted up my spirits with sober encouragement in times of despondence, and who saw to hundreds of details, great and small, which have helped make this study an accomplished fact.

Where I have erred, the blame is mine.

I dedicate this book to my daughter, Vanessa, who has taught me more lessons than I could number, foremost among them being those of faith, hope, and charity.

Note on Transliteration

1. Long vowels are distinguished from short ones by a dash over the appropriate roman letter substitute of the corresponding Tamil character.

Vowels		*Approximately as in*
Short	*Long*	
a	ā	*u*p; *a*sk (Brit. Eng.)
i	ī	*i*n; *e*at
u	ū	p*u*t; b*oo*t
e	ē	*e*gg; *a*le
o	ō	s*o*laire (Fr.); poke

Most Tamil vowels are pure, with no diphthongs.

2. Long, or stressed, consonants are differentiated from short, or unstressed, consonants by a doubling of the roman letter representing the appropriate sound. For example,

Stressed	*Unstressed*
mullai ("grassland")	mūlai ("corner")

3. Retroflexes are indexed by the placing of a dot beneath the letter. These occur only in the following forms: *ṭ, ṇ, ḷ,* and *ṛ*. The retroflexes are to be phonetically distinguished from the dentals, *t, n, l,* and *r,* which roughly correspond to the sounds of the italicized letters in the English words pan*th*er or fa*th*er, cu*nn*ing, ca*ll*, and in the Scottish *r*oll.
4. The voiced sounds like *b, d, j,* and *g* are not represented as such but are represented by *p, t, cc,* and *k*. Whether a sound is to be voiced or not is determined by its position. The above consonants are voiced after nasals; *p, ṭ,* and *t* are voiced between vowels; k is pronounced as an *h* or a *g*. The sound of *s* is represented by *c*.
5. Where *ś* or *ṣ* occur, they indicate Sanskrit words or words in Tamil whose Sanskritic origins are still "fresh," so to speak.
6. The *tch* sound in the word *catch* is rendered by a double *c,* as in *paccai* ("green").
7. Names of persons and places have been spelled in the text without any diacritical marks, to conform to the manner in which these names have come to be written in English in India. Diacritical marks are provided for the names of deities, *jātis,* and the pseudonym of the village where this research was carried out, Kalappūr.

1
Introduction

An Overview

If one were to seek out the principal theme that binds most sociocultural studies of two generations of South Asian anthropologists, the one that is bound to surface over and over again is caste. I do not intend to review in any way this literature on caste, except to allude to its somewhat paradoxical nature. By focusing on the caste system, scholars who consider it a uniquely Indian institution (Bouglé 1971; Dumont 1970) and those who see it as an extreme manifestation of its rudimentary or vestigial counterparts found in other cultures (Berreman 1960; Watson 1963) have both in their own ways subscribed to the creed that to understand caste is to understand India. Caste studies, by becoming autonomous, closed systems of inquiry—ends in themselves—have prevented scholarly inquiry from escaping its confines and taking into account symbolic constructs more pervasive and regnant than caste, and more natural to the cultural matrix of South Asia than the "naturalized" one of caste.

This is not to deny that several principles have been identified as underlying or generating the caste system, the most popular being that of purity versus pollution (Bouglé 1971; Dumont 1970; Dumont and Pocock 1959; Moffatt 1979). Unfortunately, these present but half the truth, inasmuch as they are chosen from within an artificially enclosed analytic system called caste. The inability to go beyond or beneath caste arose from the failure to see that jāti, meaning "genus" (the source concept of the ill-translated "caste") is not applied to human beings only, but to animals, plants, and even inorganic material, such as metals and minerals, as well. What is more, jāti itself is a development from a generative system of thought that deals with units at both the suprapersonal as well as the infrapersonal levels. There is no better term than *substance* to describe the general nature of these variously ranked cultural units. In other words, differentially valued and ranked substances underlie the system known as the caste system, which is but one of many surface manifestations of this system of ranked substances.[1]

Having said this much, I must hasten to say that the ranking of substances itself is among the least of my concerns in this book. Steve Barnett has written two commendable essays using ethnographic data gathered in Tamil Nadu which deal directly with the issue of rank and substance[2] (1976, and with Fruzzetti and Östör, 1982). My

[1]The first notable exception to the traditional approach described above came in working papers written around 1969–1970 by Ronald Inden and Ralph Nicholas on Bengali kinship (published in 1977). Somewhat later, between 1970 and 1972, Inden's Ph.D. dissertation at the University of Chicago on marriage and rank in Bengali culture and Marriott and Inden's joint essay on caste systems were written (published in 1976 and 1974, respectively). Susan Wadley's study of Karimpur religion (1975) as well as Kenneth David's dissertation on bound and unbound castes (1972) also point to inadequacies in the "purity-pollution" paradigm, and so does the excellent essay "From Varna to Caste through Mixed Unions" by S. J. Tambiah (1973).

[2]In this regard, Barnett's insistence on the difference of his use of "substance" —derived from, and faithful to, Schneider's analytic terms (biogenetic substance and code for conduct)—from the more culture specific usage in this and other recent studies (Marriott and Inden 1974, 1977; Inden and Nicholas 1977) is hereby recognized. (See Östör, Fruzzetti, and Barnett 1982: 228.)

interest focuses on certain other properties of substances, namely, their ability to mix and separate, to transform and be transformed, to establish intersubstantial relationships of compatibility and incompatibility, to be in states of equilibrium and disequilibrium, and to possess variable degrees of fluidity and combinability.

I intend to trace these properties of substance[3] not through studying some esoteric form of ethnochemistry but by looking at certain phenomena in the cultural world of the Tamil villager, phenomena that are part of daily, ordinary, routine life. These phenomena are a Tamil's attempt to cope with the substance of his village, or ūr, his house, or *vīṭu*, his sexual partner, and his own body under conditions of sickness and health, and finally, to search for *the* substance from which all these various substances derive.

The last-mentioned quest for the one undifferentiated, primordial substance of perfect equilibrium may be an extraordinary one, but the awareness of such a substance is neither extraordinary nor esoteric. This is made clear by the following creation myth, told to me by an elderly villager in the presence of a number of other villagers who threw in their own versions, corrections, and modifications as the narrative unfolded. The myth is intended to serve the function of a prolegomenon to the thesis developed in this study.

> God (Kaṭavuḷ) was everything. In Him were the five elements of fire, water, earth, and ether [*ākāsam*], and wind. These five elements were uniformly spread throughout [the three humors] phlegm [*kapam*], bile [*pittam*], and wind [*vāyu*]. They were so evenly distributed that even to say that there were phlegm, bile, and wind would be wrong. Let us say that they were in such a way that one could not tell the

[3]My use of the singular *substance* as well as the plural *substances* somewhat interchangeably is intended. It is in keeping with the Hindu world view (to be discussed later) that the various substances are but manifestations or permutations of a unitary, primordial substance.

> difference between them. Let us say they were nonexistent. Similarly, the three primordial qualities, or dispositions (*kuṇams*), or *rajas, sātvīkam,* and *tāmatam,* neither existed or did not exist. That is why we still call God *Kuṇātītan* [He who transcends all qualities]. Even the question as to their existence did not arise. Then something happened. The five elements started to move around as if they were not satisfied, as if they were disturbed. Now, as to who disturbed these elements or why they were disturbed, no one knows.

At this point, a second villager interrupted the narrator to suggest that the one who caused this mysterious disturbance was Kāmam, the god of lust. The narrator found his suggestion unacceptable, because Kāma had not even come into existence at that time. But his friend insisted that Kāma himself was distributed throughout Śiva's body, as are the humors, the elements, and the kuṇams. After considerable debate, it was agreed that it did not make sense to speak of Kāmam existing when he was as evenly distributed throughout Kaṭavuḷ's body as floating atoms (*aṇus*). Then the narrator continued.

> Let us say that what disturbed them was their *talai eṛuttu* [codes for action or literally, "head writing"].[4] When the elements started moving around, the humors started separating from one another and recombining in new proportions [*aḷavukaḷ*]. These new combinations resulted in the three kuṇams. Now the kuṇams and humors and elements all started to move hither and thither.
>
> Then came the separation, as in an explosion, and all the jātis of the world—male jātis, female jātis, vegetable jātis, tree jātis, animal jātis, Veḷḷāḷa jātis, Para jātis—were

[4]Tamils believe that at the time of birth Kaṭavuḷ writes a script on every individual's head and that the course that each individual's life takes, to the very last detail, is determined by this script. This script, or writing of God on one's head, is known as talai eṛuttu. In the present narration, my informant ascribes "head writing" even to the particles that constituted the primordial being (Kaṭavuḷ).

> formed, and they started meeting and mating and procreating. This is how the world came into being.

I then asked him, "What happened to Kaṭavuḷ, then, in this explosion?" He replied:

> Oh, He is still here. Not as before, but He is still there, more perfect than any of us. He has more equilibrium [*amaitinilai*] than any of us. In Him the humors are more perfectly and uniformly [*camanilaiyāka*] distributed. That is why He does not fall ill, as we do. Our humors keep moving, running from here to there and there to here, all over our bodies and out of our bodies and into our bodies. . . . But even in Him the elements, the humors, and the kuṇams move around, try as He might to keep them in equilibrium [*ōṭāmal ātāmal*]. That is why He is unable to do the same kind of thing for too long. If He meditates for more than a certain number of years, the amount of sātvīkam begins to increase. So then Kāmam comes and disturbs Him, and then He goes after Śakti[5] or Asuras.[6] This results in an increase in His *rajasa* kuṇam. When rajasa kuṇam increases beyond a certain limit, He must return to meditating. But most of the time, He is involved in *līla*.[7] All our ups and downs are due to His līlas. But that is the only way He can maintain a balance [*camanilai paṭuttalām*].

This creation myth, in drawing on the world view of the villager, reveals several central cultural beliefs.

1. All differentiated, manifest substantial forms evolved or devolved from a single, unmanifest, equilibriated substance.

[5]That is, seeking the goddess Śakti to indulge in sexual pleasure.

[6]He goes after the Asuras ("demons") to make war.

[7]*Līla* may be translated as the play or the sport of the gods. One villager translated *līla* by the phrase "doing something for the heck of it" (vēra vēla illātatāla cummā irukka muṭiyātatāla ceivatu).

2. What triggered the "first"[8] movement (action, or *karmam*) of the generative process is an unknown, hence presumably inner property, such as the codes of and for action that are "written" into all substances. This is like the "dissatisfaction" of the five elements that one informant equated with desire, which replicates at a higher level of organization the inception of other disequilibriated entities.
3. Different entities in the manifest world have different degrees of substantial equilibrium. Kaṭavuḷ's bodily substance is in a more equilibriated state than is the bodily substance of human beings.
4. As a result of disequilibriation, men and even gods must continue to strive to restore equilibrium to their bodily substance. This equilibriated state within the body is the key to health and well-being.

Seen in the light of the above myth, much of a villager's activities takes on a new meaning and a new purpose. These activities, including the most ordinary and routine ones, are aimed at restoring lost equilibrium. The restoration of equilibrium among the multitude of qualitatively different substances (or rather, qualitatively different substance complexes, compound substances, or composite substances) in the phenomenal universe is not easily accomplished. The process is invariably complex. At times, certain substances attain equilibrium with respect to other substances only when they are qualitatively different; at other times, qualitative similarity is required for bringing about equilibrium; yet again, there are times when two substances are able to achieve equilibrium between themselves only if one is higher in some respect than is the other, and not vice versa. Thus a balanced (equilibriated) meal in a South Indian home must consist of all six different flavors,

[8]Strictly speaking, given that Hindu ontology is based on cyclical time, there is no absolute first event. The choice of an event as "first" is an arbitrary one, one of convenience. For a similar myth obtained in rural Bengal, see Davis (1976).

whereas a marriage will be harmonious (in a state of equilibrium) only if the partners in marriage belong to similar, if not identical, jātis; however, the male in any marriage must be older than the female (i.e., rank higher with respect to age) if healthy (equilibriated) sexuality is to be achieved, and so on. Clearly, these are but a few of many more possible ways in which states of intersubstantial equilibrium are attained.

While I hope that someone will undertake the compelling task of enumerating and delineating precisely the various types and dimensions of possible modes and means for achieving intersubstantial equilibriums, in this study I do not intend to embark upon such an enterprise. Part I and Part II are divided according to two broadly differentiatable types of action. In Part II, action will be directed toward bringing about (or restoring) a state of ultimate, perfect, and unlimited equilibrium of substance. Orthodox Hindu concerns with salvation as release from *saṃsāra*, the cycle of births and deaths, the merging of the individual soul (*ātman*) with the universal soul (*brahman*), are all closely related to the ethnography of Part II. In Part I, by contrast we shall encounter people's actions aimed at restoring substantial equilibrium between substances in domains or contexts that are limited by time, space, and place, among other things. The concerns of Part I implicate equilibrated states of a lower, less inclusive, marked order, whereas those of Part II implicate an equilibrium of the highest, unmarked, and most inclusive order. Stated differently, concerns with intersubstantial equilibrium in limited, lower-order, and less inclusive contexts stand in a metonymic relationship to the all-encompassing equilibrium attained in salvation—salvation being not unlike the equilibrated state described to us as having existed in the primordial being at the beginning of time in the creation myth above. From the more inclusive perspective, then, context-specific, equilibrium-directed actions are mere rudiments or facsimiles of actions aimed at achieving the ultimate equilibrated order that transcends all contexts.

More specifically, insofar as the above-mentioned lower-order, less inclusive states of intersubstantial equilibrium are concerned, I focus on a particular expression of this equilibrium, that of intersubstantial "compatibility." The preoccupation with *limited* equilibrated states is evidenced in almost all of a Tamil's daily activities. Such preoccupations are most often expressed in terms of compatibility. For example, be it with respect to the food one chooses to eat or not to eat or the way one chooses to build one's house or not to build it or the kind of partner one opts to marry or not to marry or the day and time of the year one selects to perform a certain ritual or not to perform it, concern with equilibriums or equilibrated states is expressed in terms of compatibility. "Will this food be compatible with my body?" one asks. "Will this house, if built in such and such a way in such and such a place, be compatible with my horoscope?" "Will the time of the day that I set out on a given business venture be compatible with my mental state at that time or not?" The Tamil word most often employed in such instances, which I have translated as "compatible," is *ottuvarutal* which also connotes fitness or appropriateness. This concern with compatibility of substances is complemented by specialists' as well as laymen's knowledge of numerous fine distinctions made of the phenomenal universe, distinctions characterized by differentially ranked and valued substances, be they Brahmin and Parayan, male and female, bitter earth and sweet earth, bile and phlegm, or consonant and vowel. Disequilibrated or incompatibly conjoined substances are "ill," or "imperfect." This knowledge I have referred to operates at every level of existence and aims at restoring intersubstantial compatibility, if not ultimate equilibrium.

The knowledge required for the attainment of ultimate and perfect equilibrium is of a special kind. In contradistinction to the knowledge that is at the service of states of limited equilibrium, this knowledge blurs all categorical distinctions until the very distinction between self and other is transcended. The process of this transcendence will be illustrated in Part II, whereas the four chapters of Part I that follow this Introduction will be concerned with relationships of compatibility and incompatibility between and among substances encountered in everyday life.

Apart from this broad organizing principle, the arrangement of the chapters of Part I and Part II was basically motivated by a whim, a certain pretension to some measure of architectural finesse. It is not new. Brenda Beck has already written an ethnography on South India, which is basically a replicate of the Chinese box principle (1972). Mine was intended to portray a series of enclosures, concealing the "person" at its core, where I wanted ultimately to arrive. The organization of these chapters in this manner was not intended to be a simulacrum of any cultural reality. Almost fortuitously, however, this organization facilitated understanding of the fluidity of enclosures in Tamil conceptual thought, whether the boundaries of a village, the walls of a house, the skin of a person, or the sign vehicle of a sign. Another related benefit was my ability to appreciate the cultural reality of the *nonindividual* person. Or to put it in terms that anticipate the next chapter, one begins to know a person by knowing the "personality" of the soil on which he lives. So to the question, Wasn't the person at the core the real person? the answer is like "the exhortation of the Majorca storytellers: *Aixo er y no era* (it was and it was not)" (Ricoeur 1977: 224).

Chapter 2 concerns a person's compatibility with territorial substance (ūr). The territory that affects a person's bodily substance is the village in which he is born and, to a lesser extent, the village or town or country he chooses to live in. These effects are manifest in significant events as varied as the ups and downs of personal fortune, happiness, state of health, or anxiety about the afterlife. We shall also see that *village* is too flabby a term to render a culturally, though cryptotypically, crucial distinction between an ūr and a *kirāmam*, the former denoting the quality or disposition of a territorial unit, especially with regard to its effect on and effect by its inhabitants, and the latter denoting a territorial unit, usually a village, which has clear demarcating boundaries. Kirāmam would lend itself with ease to distinctive feature analysis, whereas ūr calls for a pragmatic analysis (à la Silverstein 1976) in order to unpack its meaning.

In chapter 3 I close further in on the core person by attempting to understand, in cultural terms, the nature of the relationship between houses and those who own or build them. Once again it will become evident that this relationship, as in the case of villager and village, is understood in substantial terms. The inhabitants of a house or an ūr are concerned as to whether they are compatible with that house or that ūr; furthermore, there is sufficient evidence that this compatibility is expressed in the idiom of compatibility of substance.

Chapter 4 will sketch the way in which a male and a female exchange substances in sexual intercourse as well as sketch the formation of the nature of the fetus that results from the combination of these sexual–fluid substances. A healthy child is the result of a mixing of compatible substances, not only those of male and female but also of other substances, such as the gaze of auspiciously positioned planets at the moment of birth. Furthermore, it will be shown that not only is the health of the child determined by the compatibility of the sexual fluids but the health of the sexual partners is likewise determined. In the final chapter of Part I, we will focus our attention not on interpersonal exchange of substances but on certain very essential intrapersonal substances whose equilibrated state is quintessential for the well-being of a person. In this chapter we will learn how action, or karmam, itself operating as a substance, mixes with a person's prior kuṇam[9] substance and qualitatively alters the balance of kuṇams for better or for worse. This intrapersonal flow of substances will be ex-

[9]Provisionally defined here as "quality" or "disposition."

plored through the analysis of a popular rite of divination.

In Part II, the knowledge of diversity is replaced by the knowledge of unity, and the quest becomes one for perfect equilibrium and conjunction through a transcendental experience of the undifferentiated tranquillity of inner unity. A pilgrimage of villagers in which the anthropologist partook becomes the ritual means to effect this experience. For most pilgrims this experience proves to be only a moment's revelation; for some, it leads to a permanent release from the differentiated, manifest world and a total immersion in one's essence, which is the universal essence, the undifferentiated primordial substance. From previewing the organization of the text and outlining its main argument, I would like to move on to consider the theoretical matrix in which the text is embedded.

This book was not born with a great title but had to struggle through several intolerable ones before settling on the present one. The last abandoned title read, *Kalappūr: From Person to Place Through Mixed Substance. The Semeiosis of a Culture*. The trouble with that title, apart from its ponderousness, was that it failed to include some of the other, even more interesting, topics discussed in the book, such as houses and boundaries, disputes and color symbolism, marriage and compatibility, sex and divination, sickness and health, food and flavors, ghee and semen, and much more. While all the key terms in that abandoned title spelled out the major abstractions that have helped frame the book, the omitted details—some large, some small—are the ones that have given the volume life. Hence the present compromise, a title that neither says too much nor too little, constructed with the hope that even the reader who fails to see the whole point of the exercise in abstractions will, after having read this book, feel adequately acquainted with life and living in a tiny Tamil village in South India and will be able to partake in the imagination of its people and the genius of its culture. Before we steep ourselves in the ethnographic description that perfuses the main text, it is only proper to delineate some of the major theoretical terms and assumptions that constitute the discursive context of the text. The reader may, however, choose to skip over the rest of this introductory chapter save the last section, entitled "About This Research," continue to read from chapter 2 through the end, and then return to these unread pages and read them as postface.

The Culture Concept Revisited

The first concept to be considered is "culture." Weber understood culture as "the finite segment of meaningless infinity of the world-process, a segment on which human beings confer meaning and significance" (Weber 1949: 81). There are at least two anthropological theories of culture that influence this study: the first comes from the writings of David Schneider, and the second comes from those of Clifford Geertz, both, of course, belonging broadly to the Weberian tradition filtered through Talcott Parsons. I follow Geertz and Schneider, as well as Ward Goodenough, in understanding culture not to be an adaptive mechanism accounted for in behavioral terms. "Culture" is to be clearly distinguished from its use by those whom Keesing has characterized as adaptationists (Keesing 1974). "Culture," as it is employed in this study, also needs to be distinguished from its understanding in what has come to be known as cognitive anthropology, which found its earliest formulations in the writings of Conklin (1955), Goodenough (1956, 1964, and 1965), Frake (1961 and 1962), and Wallace and Atkins (1960). For the cognitivists, culture is not unlike the semantico-referential grammar of a language (see Silverstein 1976), Chomsky's "competence" or de Saussure's "langue," a set of codes to be learned and lived by. The cultural domain of the cognitivists corresponds to Schneider's "norms," which are like patterns and templates in that they are "more or less complete, detailed,

[with] specific instructions for how the culturally significant parts of the act are to be performed, as well as the contexts in which they are proper" (Schneider 1976: 200). To be sure, the present study, as any cultural study ought to, will have a great deal to say about norms and rules of and for behavior. This is not to be equated with culture, however.

Culture, or more precisely, a culture, is understood herein to be constituted of those webs of relatively regnant and generative signs of habit, spun in the communicative act engaged in by the anthropologist and his or her informants, in which the anthropologist strives to defer to the creativity of his informants and self-consciously reflects upon the *différance* inherent in this creative product of deference. This definition requires parsing, and to this task I now turn.

The notion that culture is a web of significance we owe, once again, to Max Weber, whom Geertz paraphrases in his semeiotic definition of culture when he says that "man is an animal suspended in webs of significance he himself has spun" (1973: 5). I emphasize the communicative act in order to underscore the proposition that culture is public. This is, however, not to say that it may not exist in someone's head as well, a posture that Geertz seems to take in his dissent with the positions of Goodenough, Lévi-Strauss, and Schneider, when he says, "Culture . . . does not exist in someone's head" (1973: 10). Schneider's rhetorical response, "For if culture is not internalized by actors, where can it be, except in the heads of observers?" (1976: 206), is equally one-sided. Insofar as culture's manifestation is to be found in the communicative act, verbal or otherwise, it is a function of "private" semeiotic structures to open up, to engage with other "private" structures, in public. The moment of cultural creation is one in which the private and the public, the internal and the external, become mutually immanent. I shall postpone my discussion of the anthropologist's part in the communicative act of culture making until I have explicated my use of *signs* for the usual *symbols* that occur in most definitions of culture.

Signs in Culture

At the very outset it behooves me to explain why I have substituted *signs* in place of the customary *symbols* that cultural anthropologists prefer to employ in their definitions of culture. In the preparation of this book, I have sought to use as systematic and analytically coherent a semeiotic terminology as I possibly could. The semeiotic terminologies employed by symbolic anthropologists have proved to be either inadequate or riddled with needless inconsistencies. The writings of David Schneider (1968 and 1976), Clifford Geertz (1973), and Victor Turner (1967 and 1978) represent the former, while Leach (1976) is an example of the latter. Fortunately, we have in the writings of Charles Sanders Peirce, the father of modern semeiotics, the most thorough, coherent, and comprehensive classification of signs available to date. As will become evident, I shall use but a very select portion of his semeiotics in the present work. In my opinion, even this limited use of a systematically developed semeiotics is preferable to the use of an unsystematic one.

In Peirce's scheme, a symbol is but a kind of sign, the icon and the index being among the better known of his other sign types. Before we explore further Peirce's more detailed classification of signs, however, let us examine the semeiotic sign in general, as Peirce defined it for us: "A sign, or *representamen*, is something which stands to somebody for something in some respect or capacity. It addresses somebody, that is, creates in the mind of that person an equivalent sign, or perhaps a more developed sign. The sign which it creates I call the *interpretant* of the first sign. The sign stands for something, its *object*" (2.228).[10]

The most obvious feature of the semeiotic sign is its triadic structure. When it is juxtaposed with de Saussure's

[10]All references to Peirce's *Collected Papers* (vols. 1–6, edited by C. Hartshorne and P. Weiss, 1932; vols. 7–8, edited by Arthur Burks, 1958) will appear in the text accompanied by the conventional volume and paragraph number.

dyadic sign, the difference becomes even clearer. De Saussure understood the sign to be a dyadic relation between a signifier and a signified, a concept and a sound image (de Saussure 1959: pt. 1, chap. 1). Milton Singer (1978) has analyzed in some detail the distinction between what he calls the semiological (de Saussurian) tradition and the semeiotic (Peircean) tradition in the study of signs, symbols, and culture. He makes the point that by adopting the semeiotic perspective of the sign, we are, thankfully, precluded from executing a cultural analysis that neglects the empirical subject as well as the empirical object.

More significant, the *symbol,* used in its non-Peircean, dyadic, de Saussurian sense, yields a view of culture as a hermetically sealed, "autonomous entity of internal dependencies" (Ricoeur 1978: 110). This phrase of Ricoeur, which was used to characterize structuralism's view of language, is even more devastatingly appropriate when applied to semiological studies of culture. The semeiotic sign, including the symbol, defies any such closure. We shall have more to say about the openness of the semeiotic process. Let us turn now to consider the semeiotic constitution of reality.

The Semeiotic Constitution of Reality

In the definition of the sign by Peirce which we have already presented, it is clear that the sign is one correlate in an indivisible triad: *sign, object,* and *interpretant.* "Nothing is an object which is not signifiable; nothing is a sign which is not interpretable as signifying some object; and nothing is an interpretant that does not interpret something as signifying an object" (T. L. Short 1982: 285). Apart from establishing the indecomposability of the triadic sign, this view of the sign contains within it elements that are likely to disturb the idealist as well as the materialist. This is good: At best, such a disturbance should be enlightening, at worst, sobering. This disturbance is thrown into clear relief in another, somewhat later formulation of the definition of the sign: "A

Sign, or *Representamen*, is a First which stands in such a genuine triadic relation to a Second, called its *Object*, as to be capable of determining a Third, called its *Interpretant*, to assume the same triadic relation to its Object in which it stands itself to the same Object" (2.274). From this definition it becomes clear that the representamen—the artifact, sign vehicle, or event, which we commonly identify as the sign—is the First, and the object is not the First. This is what makes Peirce's realism a semeiotic realism, the only kind of realism, in my opinion, that is capable of preventing anthropology from falling victim to either behavioristic positivism or to ungrounded idealism. For the best synthesis and explication of Peirce's complex and at times confusing thesis, I refer the reader to the study of Peirce's scholastic realism by John F. Boler (1963).[11] For the purposes of the present study I shall content myself by quoting from Boler and Peirce on Peirce's position. Boler claims that Peirce's realism is in fact a synthesis of epistemological realism on the one hand and epistemological idealism on the other. Epistemological realism maintains that "we cannot think whatever we want: something forces our opinion and is, at least to that extent, independent of our minds" (p. 10). "We find our opinions are constrained; there is something, therefore, which influences our thoughts, and is not created by them" (Peirce 8.12). This is "the real," the thing independent of how we think it (Boler 1963: 14). As for his epistemological idealism, we find Peirce maintaining that "since an idea can resemble or represent only another idea, reality itself must be 'thoughtlike' or of the nature of an idea" (Boler 1963: 11; see also Peirce 6.158, 5.310, and 8.151). Peirce eventually comes to define reality as what will be thought in the ultimate opinion of the community (Boler 1963: 15; see also Peirce 5.311 and 5.430). Thus, in his

[11]More recent, splendidly lucid, and critical evaluations of Peirce's realism are to be found in the following: Robert Almeder (1980), Bruce Altshuler (1982), Karl-Otto Apel (1981), and Thomas Olshewsky (1983).

definition of reality, Peirce's epistemological realism is present in the insistence that an individual's thinking must comply with something other than itself; his epistemological idealism is likewise maintained in the notion that the "other" is the ultimate *thought* of the community (7.336, 5.316, and 5.408).

It must be made clear from the outset that Peirce's community is a community of inquirers—not any defined community of inquirers but an indefinite community of inquirers. Furthermore, this notion of the community is inextricably linked with his concept of truth and the increase of knowledge. Since he was a scientist himself, this community of inquirers, for Peirce, was for the most part a community of truthfully, faithfully, charitably, and open-mindedly communicating scientists. I say, "for the most part" because there are passages in Peirce's writings where he formulates his vision of a community in such a fashion that it transcends all manner of anthropocentrism, including that of human scientific inquiry. The following passage is a striking example.

> The catholic consent which constitutes the truth is by no means to be limited to men in this earthly life or to the human race, but extends to the whole communion of minds to which we belong, including some probably whose senses are very different from ours, so that in that consent no predication of a sensible quality can enter, except as an admission that so certain sorts of senses are affected. (8.13)

For the cultural anthropologist whose primary interest is in understanding the culture wherein he or she carries out field research, the community of inquirers or believers is a far more limited community, a historical community. The "community's thought," in Peirce's language, is a partial isomorph of the anthropological concept of culture.

The fusion of epistemological realism and epistemological idealism of a Peircean sort may also be found in Marshall

Sahlins's discussion of value in the context of his critique of historical materialism. Sahlins writes,

> No cultural value can ever be read from a set of "material forces," as if the cultural were the dependent variables of an inescapable practical logic. The positivist explanation of given cultural practices as necessary effects of some material circumstance . . . [is] false. This does not imply that we are forced to adopt some idealist alternative, conceiving culture as walking about on the thin air of symbols. It is not that material forces and constraints are left out of account, or that they have no real effects on cultural order. It is that the nature of the effects cannot be read from the nature of the forces, for the material effects depend on their cultural encompassment. The very form of social existence of material force is determined by its integration in the cultural system. The force may then be significant—but significance, precisely, is a symbolic quality. At the same time, this symbolic scheme is not itself the mode of expression of an instrumental logic, for in fact there is no other logic in the sense of a meaningful order save that imposed by culture on the instrumental process. (p. 206)

In the triadic structure of the sign, the *object* is a Second. The *object*, though empirical, need not be a material thing. Peirce uses the term in its Latin Scholastic sense, meaning, that which is "thrown before" the mind, that toward which one's attention is directed.

The *interpretant*, as already implied, is the third correlate of the sign. More precisely, it is a correlate of one sign to which the represented object is addressed and by which its representation is interpreted. In general terms, the interpretant is the locus of interpretation, that by which a sign is contextualized, that which makes signification part of a connected web and not an isolated entity.

Without an interpretant, the First and the Second, the *representamen* and the *object*, will forever remain unconnected, existing apart from any *meaningful* reality. Equally true is that without an *object* and *representamen*, there will be nothing to connect and ergo no interpretant. In other words, for a sign to function as a sign, there must be present in it all three correlative functions. Objects may exist in the universe as individual empiricities or existent facts, but they do not become real until and unless they are represented by a sign, which representation is interpreted as such by an interpretant. This process of signification is as real in nature as it is in culture.

The Texturing of Culture

Another theoretical implication of the triadic structure of the sign and its role and place in culture concerns texture. What I do have to state with regard to cultural texture will, by necessity, be a brief prolegomenon, intended as a seed for future research. Let us for this purpose invoke that familiar image of culture as constituted of signs, held together as in a web. Admittedly, such an image remains inadequate for capturing the dynamic and processual aspect of culture. At best it is a representation of a captured instant in the cultural process. While in this captured, or arrested, state, if we were to take a semeiotically primed analytic microscope to one of these web's most elementary and irreducible units, it would look something like figure 1.

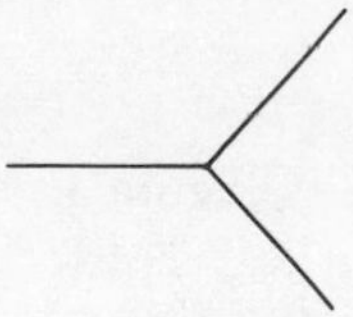

Three correlates
(a triad)

Figure 1

Terrence Deacon (1978), from whom I have adapted this schematization, uses it to illustrate the three correlates of a sign that make it a single triad. When four or five correlates are entailed in the sign relationship, they may be schematized as in figure 2, constituting a relationship of two or three triads. When five or more correlates are entailed, the complex of triadic structures may take more than one form, not unlike those of chemical isomers or polymers. This is illustrated in figure 3.

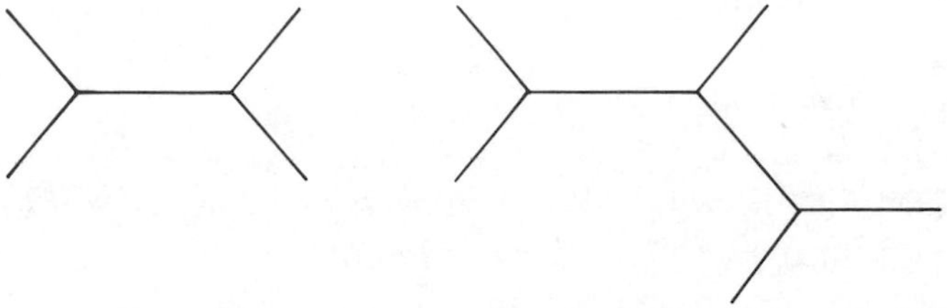

Four correlates (two triads) Five correlates (three triads)

Figure 2

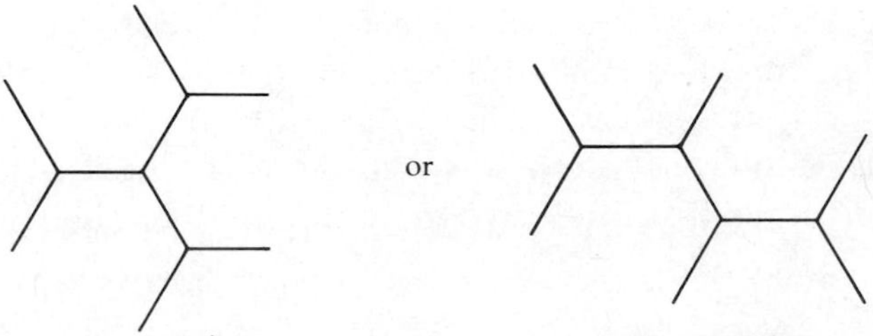

Six correlates (four triads) Six correlates (five triads)

Figure 3

Two points emerge from this: one, that all complex forms can be decomposed into a triad, which is the irreducible structure of the sign, and two, that even when as many as five correlates are involved in a sign relationship, their interdetermination need not be of the same configuration—which is another way of saying their overall significant effect can be quite different. The textural complexity of semeiotic relationships is something that semeioticians and cultural anthropologists have not even begun to systematically explore. A large portion of such an exploration must, by the nature of things, go beyond semantics, even beyond pragmatics, and must implicate and include the aesthetic dimension of culture. The extremities represented in the diagram as endpoints are, in fact, heuristic fictions. For no polyadic relation has reachable end points. For this reason, every semeiotic study of however small a cultural aspect must, by definition, remain open and incomplete. This brings us to the next theoretical point that may be abstracted from the triadic structure of the sign.

The Dialogic Sign

The sign, or representamen, addresses somebody. In the definition already cited, we saw Peirce elaborating on this opening statement by saying that the sign "creates in the mind of that person an equivalent sign, or perhaps a more developed sign. The sign that it creates" he called "the *interpretant* of the first sign. The sign stands for something, its *object*" (2.289). The phrase "or perhaps a more developed sign" ought to have been rendered, "or perhaps a more or less developed sign." Signification does not derive exclusively from the representation of the object in the sign and the mediate representation of the object in the interpretant being the *same*. Neither does signification become a reality only when the representation in the interpretant is "more developed" than the representation in the sign. The only criterion for significance to come into effect is that there be something shared between the interpretant and the sign or representamen. Having this in mind, we may rewrite the second definition of the sign already cited (2.274) with the following parenthetical modification: "A *Sign*, or *Representamen*, is a First which stands in such a genuine triadic relation to a Second, called its *Object*, as to be capable of determining a Third, called its *Interpretant*, to assume the same [or similar] triadic relation to its Object in which it stands itself to the same Object" (2.274). I stress this amendment because, as I shall show, a certain measure of nonidentity between representamen and interpretant becomes quintessential if we are to understand culture as a creative process enriched by agreement as well as disagreement, understanding as well as misunderstanding. Having this in mind, we may better appreciate the openness of the semeiotic process as presented by Peirce in the following definition: "A *Sign* is anything which is related to a Second thing, its *Object*, . . . in such a way as to bring a Third thing, its *Interpretant*, into relation with the same Object, and that in such a way as to bring a Fourth into relation with that Object in the same form, *ad infinitum*" (2.92).

In these definitions of the sign, we may see laid bare the atomic structure of the sign, wherein is embedded the very essence of the dialogic of all communication, especially that of human communication. In this irreducible structure of the sign obtains the most elementary dialogue. In this definition of the sign, we find the sign (or representamen) inviting, as it were, the interpretant to "perceive" or "understand" the object as it (the sign) "perceives" or "understands" the object. Insofar as the interpretant is incapable of "perceiving" the object in a manner identical to that in which the sign "perceives" it, a dialogue is initiated in which other interpretants are welcome to participate, every interpretant in itself being capable of acting as a sign to further interpretants, and so on. In any dialogue, if there is total agreement between two interlocutors, further dialogue becomes unnecessary, if not impossible. In fact, if two people were to be sequestered from everybody else, the probability of their dialogue ending in silence is likely to be high. It would certainly not be unfair to trace the petrifaction of many a marriage into mute numbness to the cessation of dialogue caused by a superfluity of agreement. Fortunately, men and women, as social beings, are not confined to a single dialogue but sojourn in and travel through polylogues (to steal a term from Kristeva), a process that helps maintain a certain measure of anisomorphism between sign and interpretant. There must remain some measure of such an anisomorphism for the dialogic process to breed or invite (depending on the point of view one takes) further interpretants and further signs to partake in the open and ever-expanding semeiotic process.

In this irreducible structure of the sign, we also have the most elementary unit of reasoning, an invitation to reason, to converse, to convene. I shall have more to say on *convene* and its cognates *covenant* and *convention* when we discuss the Peircean symbol below. For the present, I would like to expand on what I mean by "reasoning." To phrase it differently, dialogism may be considered to be a special kind of reasoning. Peirce's own definition of the term *dialogism* is worthy of note: "A dialogism is an argument which may be analyzed into constituent arguments; each of the constituent arguments is characterized by having only 'one premise and two alternate conclusions' " (cited in Kevelson 1982: 161). While syllogisms are characterized by a single conclusion contained in its major and minor premise, "the dialogism is a process of reasoning which attempts to account for the method by which new information is discovered, processed, and integrated into a continually evolving, open-ended system of reasoning, which parallels the actual method of creating human discourse" (Kevelson 1982: 161). Furthermore, Kevelson notes that dialogism presents

> a means of breaking up, or dividing, an argument into a number of arguments, each of which has only one premiss but two, alternative, disjunctive conclusions. Each of the conclusions can then become a premiss, or Theme, of subsequently evolving arguments. Conceivably, . . . arguments based on the structure of the Dialogism may be evolved indefinitely until one finds, for the time being, some satisfactory conclusion. (Kevelson 1982: 162)

The structure of the basic syllogism is:

> All men are animals, and all animals are mortal;
> Therefore, all men are mortal. (Kevelson 1982: 161)

The structure of Peirce's dialogism is:

> Some men are not mortal; therefore,
> Either some men are not animals, or
> Some animals are not mortal. (Kevelson 1982: 161)

The reader who is interested in pursuing Peirce's dialogism may do so by reading Kevelson's paper and being guided by it to the pertinent original papers of Peirce. I will close this discussion with a point about the openness of a dialogue that finds its elemental structure in the openness of the sign itself. Every representamen is a premise that proffers a conclusion, which conclusion, however, is not identical to the one impressed upon the interpretant. Thus, if the elemental triadic sign is arrested, as it were, at any given instance in its evolution, two disjunctive conclusions may be manifested. Herein lies the openness both of the dialogic and of the semeiotic processes, characterized by indeterminacy, dynamism, and an evolution toward a greater refinement of debate. Furthermore, this very dialogic attribute of the sign makes the creation of culture in the communicative act that is engaged in by the anthropologist and the informant both possible and interesting. I shall reserve for later discussion the role of the anthropologist in the creation of culture and move on to consider the next unit idea in our definition of culture, signs of habit.

Signs of Habit

We have said that the signs that constitute a culture are regnant and generative signs of habit. I have adopted the concept of habit from Peirce. By appreciating Peirce's concepts of belief and doubt, we can arrive at an understanding of his concept of habit. "Man is a bundle of habits" (6.228). Belief is habits become conscious (4.53). Becoming conscious of habits is a distinctively human attribute, making reflection, and even critical self-reflection, possible. Doubt is what blocks, interrupts or shocks belief. Doubt is the privation of habit (5.417 and 5.512). Whereas habit and the consciousness thereof (belief) sustain a state of calmness and satisfaction, doubt creates quite the opposite. Doubt is "an uneasy and dissatisfied state from which we struggle to free ourselves" (5.374).

Signs of habit, therefore, are largely, if not entirely, unconscious. This is not to imply that they are passive modes of behavior, however. On the contrary, they are active determinants of action. "The feeling of believing is more or less a sure indication of there being established in our nature some habit which will determine our actions" (5.371).

Peirce's "habit" is very similar to what Pierre Bourdieu calls *habitus*, "the durably installed generative principle of regulated improvisations, [which] produces practices which tend to reproduce the regularities immanent in the objective conditions of the production of their generative principle" (1972: 78). Within the dominant epistemological framework of Western thought, wherein nature and culture are seen as a set of binary opposites, "habits" may be seen as *natural*. Peirce, the monist that he was, did not subscribe to this dominant framework. For this reason, he was able to consider matter as "not completely dead, but [as] merely mind hidebound with habits" (6.158). Or, as Apel puts it, for Peirce, "laws of nature are taken to be petrified habits" (1981: 34). Habit taking, for Peirce, is not an instinctual process, if instinct is to be construed as a noninferential, "natural," process. "Intuition" is another concept attributed to human cognition as if it were the foundation or the "natural" basis of all knowledge. Peirce's opposition to the doctrine that cognitions are or can be intuitive cuts across the rationalist-empiricist divide. Neither logical principles nor sense data are foundational, in the sense of being non-inferred. Rather, all knowledge is mediated, and mediated through signs. (This is neither the place nor the time to engage in an elaborate defense of this claim, but the interested reader may refer to William Davis [1972] and Almeder [1980] for an elegant undertaking of such a task.) Therefore, the process of habit taking is an inferential process, albeit one that is tacit or even unconscious, so much so that it is equated with such "natural" immediacy as intuition and instinct.

If knowing is a *process*, then knowing is a process in time. Citing Peirce (5.284), Davis observes that "*no* experience whatever is an 'instantaneous affair, but is an event occupying time and coming to pass by a continuous process.' Instances are mathematical fictions" (1972: 10). Even something that appears to be so immediate as pain is not intuitive but is, rather, the product of a "process of comparison, since the mind judges pain, like tone, by the *frequency*, not intensity, of nerve impulses. (But time is required to judge the intensity of pure quantity too)" (1972: 10).

Nerve impulses and other perceptual judgments are almost exclusively indexical signs, that is, signs whose significance is a function of the necessary contiguity of *object* and representamen. Humans, as social beings who make their own history, by contrast, are immersed in a life-world of symbols, that species of signs that owe their significance to convention. Symbolic signs, however, are no less constitutive of habit than are indexical signs, and they are equally prone to settle into the unconscious grooves of habitual dispositions. On this point Bourdieu observes, "the 'unconscious' is never anything other than the forgetting of history which history itself produces by incorporating the objective structures it produces in the second nature of habitus" (1972: 78–79).

In our exposition of the structure of the sign, we said that the representamental First and the objective Second are meaningfully brought together in the interpretational Third. In a later chapter we will consider Peirce's phenomenological categories of Firstness, Secondness, and Thirdness in greater detail. For now, it suffices to know that whereas Firstness designates that category of pure quality or even a pure qualitative possibility considered in abstraction from everything else, and whereas Secondness represents sheer existence, brute fact, or actuality, Thirdness is that gentle force that mediates First and Second, bringing them into significant relationship. *Habit* represents Thirdness almost to perfection (5.538). Habit appeases the irritation of doubt and, conversely, makes belief possible. Commenting on this mediating function of habit, or rather, habitus, Bourdieu correctly observes that "the habitus is the universalizing mediation which causes an individual agent's practices, without either explicit reason or signifying intent, to be nonetheless 'sensible' and 'reasonable' " (1972: 79).

I must hasten to remind the reader that the "habit" of Peirce or the "habitus" of Bourdieu do not pertain to the dispositions of any one individual. As has been mentioned earlier and as will be seen below, for Peirce, what was of significance with respect to his doctrine of truth, knowledge, and inquiry, was the community. He spoke not of individual opinions but of the final opinion of the community of inquirers. He spoke not of individual interpreters but of a community of interpretants. In a similar vein, Bourdieu speaks of a "community of dispositions" (1972: 79). We may speak equally well of a "community of habits."

> One of the fundamental effects of the orchestration of habitus is the production of a commonsense world endowed with the *objectivity* secured by consensus on the meaning (*sens*) of practices and the world, in other words the harmonization of agents' experiences and continuous reinforcement that each of them receives from the expression, individual or collective (in festivals for example), improvised or programmed (commonplaces, sayings), of similar or identical experiences. The homogeneity of habitus of what—within the limits of the group of agents possessing the schemes (of production and interpretation)

> implied in their production—causes practices and works to be immediately intelligible and foreseeable, and hence taken for granted. (1972: 80)

Signs of habit that are constitutive of a culture are also regnant and generative. This means that these signs or significant constructs perfuse the cultural life of a people and are generative of other, more conscious, ideological signs as well. The anthropological method works backward, so to speak, from the consciously articulated and manifestly acted-out signs to the unconscious repository of the signs of habit.

I hold with Schneider that some signs (his "symbols"), or significant constructs, constitute a system of meaning that is generative of other signs in the culture in question. That is, these other signs bear distinct traces of the parent constructs or signs of habit, and these regnant signs of habit pervade the culture's significant texture. The systematicity of these pervasive and generative signs of habit should not, however, be exaggerated. I differ with Schneider in his assertion that the "culture is a total system; it does not have loose ends and unintegrated parts that do not articulate with other parts" (1976: 219). Here I must concur with Geertz that a "hermetical approach to things . . . seems to run the danger (and increasingly to have been overtaken by it) of locking cultural analysis away from its proper object, the informal logic of actual life" (1973: 17). The systematicity of a cultural system is relative, even weak, a point best illustrated by Geertz's own metaphor of the octopus, in which cultural organization

> is neither the spider web nor the pile of sand. It is rather more the octopus, whose tentacles are in large part separately integrated, neurally quite poorly connected with one another and what in the octopus passes for a brain, and yet who nonetheless manages to get around and to preserve himself, for a while anyway, as a viable, if somewhat ungainly entity. (1973: 407–408)

The act of postulating *signs of habit* as the distinguishing feature of a culture may lead one to conclude that to subscribe to such a view entails, as a necessary corollary, a subscription to the view that culture is a sequestered and immunized system of signs, invincibly coherent. Such an assumption is unwarranted for several reasons. First, the signs of habit that we are concerned with in the life of a community of social and historical human beings are predominantly symbols. In a symbolic sign, the representamen and object are held together by convention and not by continguity (as with indexes) or by similarity (as with icons). Therefore, regardless of how habit-fraught symbolic constructs become, the very fact of the arbitrary and convention-dependent bond that holds the three correlates of such signs makes them more vulnerable to destabilization and change than are the indexical habits in nature. Second, signs of habit are integrally linked to and find actualized expression in nonhabitual, consciously enacted and articulated signs (mainly symbols). They are not safely sequestered but are vulnerably exposed to the daily traffic of signs. Third, the conscious-unconscious divide is not to be understood as impermeable. Signs of habit do not lurk in the arcane recesses of a domain comparable to the Freudian unconscious, nor are they cryptically inscribed onto a palimpsest awaiting decoding by a structuralist. Rather, they are so much a part of the light of day that they go unnoticed and are brought into consciousness only through conscious reflection—and even then, most often only when an individual is "shocked" into doing so by a stranger, who might happen to be an anthropologist. The possibility of such a communicative encounter is a fourth point that undermines the view of a hermetically sealed set of signs. This fourth point also leads us directly into the last portion of our definition of culture, the communicative act in which the anthropologist and informant(s) engage. Before we tease out this part of the definition, however, we must return once more to the semeiotic sign and its triadic structure.

Sign Types and the Multimodality of Signification

When we temporarily departed from our discussion of the sign structure a few pages back, we had already established the triadic constitution of the sign as made up of representamen, object, and interpretant. We are now in a position to generate ten logical sign types from the fact of these three correlates.

In unpacking the structure of the sign, Peirce traces a sign from its point of logical and ontological deployment to its interpretive execution. In order to do this, he divides a sign into three subcategories, abstracting and isolating each correlate for the purpose of analysis (a method that he calls "prescinding").[12] Thus, he invites the reader to examine the representamen as if it existed independently of the other two correlates, fraught with the potentiality of signification and yet freed for the sake of analytic scrutiny from the sign relationship. He does the same for each correlate. These correlates, thus prescinded, may be represented as in table 1.

TABLE 1

	Sign, or representamen (first)	*Relationship of sign to object (second)*	*Relationship of sign to interpretant (third)*
First	Qualisign	Icon	Rheme
Second	Sinsign	Index	Dicent sign
Third	Legisign	Symbol	Argument

[12]"Precision and abstraction are two terms for the same process; and are now limited not merely to separation by the mind, but even to a particular kind of mental separation, namely, that by *attention* to one point and *neglect* of another. That which is *attended* to is said to be *prescinded*; and that which is neglected is said to be *abstracted from*" (Peirce 1982: 518). In the same section from which this quote has been taken, Peirce goes on to distinguish among Precision, Discrimination, and Dissociation.

The first column contains three modes of representamen, the second, three modes of objects, and the third, three modes of interpretants. Each column, or subcategory of a sign, can be further divided horizontally into three modes. The first row contains representamen, object, and interpretant as relative Firsts, the second row contains them as relative Seconds, and the third row as relative Thirds.

The representamenal First is called a *qualisign*. It is a sign whose representative capacity lies in its quality. Redness, for instance, in Tamil Nadu may signify fertility in some contexts. But as pure potential or possibility, it remains a qualisign. When redness becomes embodied in a *sāri*, it is a *sinsign*, a representamenal Second. But as soon as it is thus embodied, it calls forth or invokes a more general order or general possibility of representation; a bridal sāri thereby invokes a convention. This is a *legisign*. Elsewhere Peirce distinguishes these three modes of signs as tone, token, and type.

Similarly, the object, too, when examined independently of the completed sign structure, may be seen to present itself as a First, a Second, or a Third. Terrence Deacon (1978) explains it like this. If for the moment one can ignore the interpretant and examine the manner in which the object and representamen are brought together, the kind of relationship these two bring into the sign relationship, then one may see three modes of relationships. If an iconic sign is examined, it may be noted that some quality of the object is represented in the icon. The iconic sign and the object must in some way resemble each other; they must share some quality. Examples of iconic signs range from a piece of the cross to diagrams, maps, blueprints, and onomatopoeia.

An indexical sign, by contrast, is a sign in which resemblance or shared quality does not define the relationship between object and representamen, but, instead, contiguity or concurrence defines their significant link. Smoke and fire, red litmus and acidity, and deictics in language—all of these are examples of indexical signs. Indexical signs are what we call facts. They are "obvious," even more obvious than icons to their users. In regards to indexical sign functions in language and culture, the reader is referred to Michael Silverstein's seminal paper, "Shifters, Linguistic Categories, and Cultural Description" (1976), in which he not only shows the preponderance of indexical signs in language and culture but also demonstrates how an understanding of the functioning of indexical signs in culture emphasizes the indispensability of context in any significant linguistic or cultural analysis.

A symbol is not related to its object either by contiguity, by shared quality, or by resemblance. Convention alone links a symbol to its object. *Covene* and *covenant* both derive their meaning from the Latin *convenire*. In a symbol the conventional sign, object, and representamen are brought together within the sign relation by virtue of an agreement and not by virtue of any quality intrinsic to either object or representamen. Words are of the order of symbols. The object to which a word refers is of a general nature; symbols are not indicators of any particular occurrence of a thing but of a "kind of thing" (Peirce 2: 301).

This is an appropriate point to interrupt the exegesis of Peirce's theory of signs and return to examining the reasons for my insistence on the substitution of *signs* for the customary *symbols* in my definition of culture.

David Schneider, even more so than Geertz, claims to be interested in the native's point of view, in native categories. In cautioning the field-worker against going to the field with a rigidly defined frame of analysis, he says: "The more clearly the field worker has in mind what he is after the less likely it is that he will discover what the natives' cultural categories are; how the natives define them, construct them and manipulate them; or what they mean to the natives" (1968: 10–11). From the analyst's point of view, a culture may be a system of *symbols* and meanings. But from the native's point of view, his culture is constituted of indexical and iconic signs in addition to symbols. Schneider is quick to respond: "The study of culture symbols (and presumably indexes and icons as well) and the study of culture as a system of symbols and meanings are very separate and different affairs" (1976: 206). Such a study is, however, metacultural and not cultural. Making the symbolic system (I use *symbolic* intending its full semeiotic connotation) the locus classicus of one's analysis or "cultural account" is done at the expense of not appreciating what the cultural system, with its rich panoply of iconic, indexical, *and* symbolic signs, means to the natives themselves and *how* this cultural system means to them. This is what, I believe, distinguishes Geertz's cultural interpretation from Schneider's cultural account. The difference is not merely a matter of prose style; the difference lies in the fact that Geertz, though he does not systematically develop or explicate his interpretive method, appreciates the fact that signs in culture (he, too, calls them *symbols*) are not only symbolic but indexical and iconic as well, a fact that Schneider finds clearly ignorable with respect to his cultural account. Look, for instance, at Geertz's definition of religion. Even though he does not use *symbol* in the precise Peircean sense but uses it as a substitute for the Peircean *sign,* the indexical function in religious beliefs is clearly brought out: "Religion is a system of symbols which acts to establish powerful, pervasive, and long-lasting moods and motivations in men by formulating conceptions of a general order of existence and clothing these conceptions with such an aura of *factuality* that the moods and motivations seem *uniquely realistic*" (1973: 90).

A second defect or danger built into the Schneiderian symbolic analysis is in the anthropologist being called upon to flaunt his dubious privilege of what Richard Rorty critically called (with respect to epistemological philosophers) the role of cultural overseer who knows everyone's common ground, "the Platonic philosopher king who knows what everybody else is really doing whether *they* know it or not" (Rorty 1979: 317). An interpretive cultural account, by contrast, sees understanding to be "more like getting acquainted with a person than like following a demonstration. . . . We play back and forth between guesses about how to characterize particular statements or other events, and guesses about the point of the whole situation, until gradually we feel at ease with what was hitherto strange" (Rorty 1979: 319). Such an understanding can be attained only through an appreciation of the multimodal nature of signification in a culture and not by arriving at a unimodal (symbolic), privileged, metacultural account.

Back to Peirce's taxonomy and the third correlate, the interpretant, again remembering we are, for the purpose of analysis, prescinding the interpretant as interpretant qua interpretant. The interpretant is classifiable by the manner in which the sign represents itself in the interpretive context; as a sign of possibility, a sign of fact, or a sign of reason. The first is called a rheme, the second, a dicent sign (or dicisign), and the third, an argument. As a sign of possibility, morphemes in language—suffixes, prefixes, infixes—are instances of linguistic rhemes. Deacon (1978) also cites the lines or boxes of a diagram or a pointing finger as it is involved in a gesture as examples of rhemes. What distinguishes a rheme as a rheme and not a dicent sign is the attribute that one cannot determine the truth or falsity of a rheme. A rheme is pure interpretive potentiality whose very appropriateness is not determined until it is actualized in use, in a context, in an instance, at which time it becomes a dicent sign. An appreciation of rhematic signs is crucial for an understanding of grammatical process (see, for example, Sapir 1921, chap. 4) and is no less important for understanding cultural processes. In order to be sensitive to rhematic signs with all their potentiality and possibility, one has to have acquired a keen feeling as to when an allusion, a suggestion, the drift of a conversation, the tenor of a discourse, or the color of a joke are pregnant with meaning. A field-worker begins to *experience* the culture in which he studies as soon as he begins to cultivate such a sensitivity. I underscore *experience* in order to distinguish it from understanding. For instance, I consider Joyce's *Ulysses* and *Finnegans Wake* as works of literary art that come close to being truly cultural accounts. What is true of these works is also true of culture. Understanding these works is not the point; in fact, many devotees of Joyce are honest enough to confess that they don't understand him. What is important for them (and what ought to be equally true of the anthropologist with regard to the culture in which he studies) is that they experience the novel. Understanding, when and if it does come, is a bonus and worthy of commendation, if the one who does understand can also explicate.

Since a rheme signifies only a possibility, as I have said above, its truth or falsity is not even an issue. The most one can discern is its appropriateness or inappropriateness in a dicent context. As a rheme it promises to convey some further information regarding a fact or event. A dicent sign, contrastingly, can be understood as either true or false. Sentences, propositions, judgments, a diagnosis are all dicent signs. But as Deacon states it, "The truth or falsity of the dicisign cannot be ascertained without reference to the argument context to which it presents itself. Thus, although a dicisign is either true or false it can supply no reasons as to why this must be so" (1978: 158; see also Peirce 2: 309–310).

An argument is a sign of inference. It is "a Sign of the state of the universe . . . in which the premises are taken for granted" (Peirce and Welby 1977: 34). An argument is constituted of three inferential modes, the first two being the well known processes of induction and deduction, and the third, the lesser known one of abduction outlined for us by Peirce (7: 202; see also E. V. Daniel 1981). Truth as truth and the true nature of belief are established in the argument context. The argument provides us the canons upon which our view of the world in its most indubitable sense is based.

Argument, as a significant locus of truth and belief, may be illustrated by an example A. J. Ayer (1968) employs to clarify quite a different aspect of Peirce's philosophy, which nonetheless suits our purposes equally well. Ayer points out the impossibility of a person's taking two sheets of paper and writing on one of them all propositions that are true and on another all those propositions that he firmly believes, with the proviso that the two lists be mutually exclusive. It is both imaginable and probable that some of the propositions our friend firmly believes in are quite false and that many propositions he does not believe in are quite true.

> He could not say, or rather he could not judge that "Such and such propositions, which I firmly believe, are false" or "Such and such propositions are true, but I don't believe them." In each case it may well be that both components of the conjunction are true, that the man does firmly believe the proposition which he mentions and they are false, or that they are true and he does not believe them. But while we can say this about him, he cannot significantly say it about himself, or rather, he can say it only retrospectively. (Ayer 1968: 15)

The argument as an interpretant, then, is a sign that makes indubitability possible. The *argument* in fact is the non-arguable basis that makes argument possible. Schneider's regnant and generative signs belong precisely here, at least insofar as they are used by and are meaningful to those who find embedded in these signs their beliefs and their truths.

Of course we do remember that the separation of the three correlates, their prescinding, has been an artifact of our analysis. In fact, for a sign to be a sign, it must partake of all three correlates, one from each column in table 1. The result is that we have ten sign types[13] defined in accordance with the particular combination of the three aspects of the sign.

[13]These ten divisions of signs are listed below with examples that readers may work through. The brief notes that follow the sign type and example are intended to explicate the logic underlying each sign type.

a. *Rhematic iconic qualisign (e.g., a feeling of "red," a sensory quality).*

An examination of table 1 and the sign types provided in footnote 13 makes it evident that not all combinations of the three aspects of the sign are logically possible. Thus, a sign that is in itself a qualisign (and not a sinsign or a legisign) cannot be an index or a symbol, for an index already presupposes a sinsign, and a symbol presupposes a legisign.

As a qualisign, its representative power rests on its uninstantiated qualitative possibility; it is iconic because its eventual signification will depend on its having some quality in common with the object it stands for; it is rhematic because as pure possibility it would be meaningless to ask of it whether it were true or false. Even the question as to its appropriateness or inappropriateness is not relevant, since it has not occurred in a dicent context.

b. *Rhematic iconic sinsign (e.g., an individual diagram, mimicry).*

It is a sinsign because it is an existent fact and not a mere possibility. It is an icon and a rheme for the same reasons as in (a), except that the iconicity in question is a current fact rather than a future possibility.

c. *Rhematic indexical sinsign (e.g., a spontaneous cry in the forest).*

All as in (b) above, except for its being an index, which means that its link with the object for which it stands is not by virtue of the quality it shares with that object but by virtue of its contiguity or cooccurrence with the object.

d. *Dicent indexical sinsign (e.g., a fever, mercury in a thermometer).*

All as in (c) above, except that the interpretant is a dicent sign, by which is meant that its interpretation is no longer a mere possibility, a guess, but a fact; the nature of the link between representamen and object has been established by its instantiation.

e. *Rhematic iconic legisign (e.g., a typical diagram).*

As a legisign its representamenal quality belongs to a general law or type; as a legisign it also embodies a sinsign and a qualisign as well. That is to say, each instance of it embodies a definite quality that renders it fit to call up in the mind the idea of a like object. Insofar as it has not been deployed in an interpretive context, it remains a rheme.

f. *Rhematic indexical legisign (e.g., deictics in language, a pointing arrow).*

All as in (e) above, except that the occurrence of the representamenal token is connected spatiotemporally with a contiguous object that it seeks to represent.

g. *Dicent indexical legisign (e.g., a Fahrenheit thermometer, a clock, a street cry).*

All as in (f) above, except that the interpretive context is, as in (d), an established fact.

h. *Rhematic symbolic legisign (e.g., a common noun).*

The deictic *that* is a rhematic indexical legisign, since it directs one's attention to a single object rather than draws attention to a general concept. A common noun, by contrast, because it is symbolic, does precisely this; it signifies a general concept. The rheme and the legisign are as dealt with above.

i. *Dicent symbolic legisign (e.g., a proposition).*

With a common noun, as a rheme, its truth value is not an issue. A proposition, as a dicent sign, claims to be really affected by its object. "It is raining" is supposedly a proposition claiming to be representative of some real event. It is,

Neither can it be interpreted as a dicent sign or as an argument. Likewise, the highest level of interpretant that a sinsign could entail is that of a dicent sign. This scheme thus yields a maximum possibility of ten sign types.

Let me hasten to assure a reader who is unfamiliar with Peircean semeiotics (and impatient with neologisms to boot) that he or she is in no way required to recall the terminology developed here with respect to the sign types. At most, I will invoke the more general triad of signs abstracted from this scheme, which are commonly referred to by virtue of the kinds of relationships that obtain between the representamens (more familiarly identified as signs) and the objects, as icons, indexes, and symbols—working definitions of which will be provided below. It suffices to know that not all signs are, from a culture's point of view or even from a cultural point of view, symbols, characterized by and for the users of these signs as defined by their arbitrariness. Peirce's three trichotomies just begin, and only begin, to reveal the complexity of signification. Even a rudimentary appreciation of this fact is bound to enrich any interpretive cultural account attempted by an anthropologist.

Before we leave this necessary digression into the nature of the sign and continue with the rest of our definition of culture, I would like to abstract the following moral from this exercise.

By the rhetorical device of analytical alliteration, I have attempted to make the point that a sign is irreducibly triadic, and so is meaning, whose constituent elements are

---

of course, appropriate to ask whether a proposition is true or false. Truth or falsity themselves, however, are matters that can be settled only with respect to an argument context, with its entire convention about what is true and how it can be rationally established.

j. *Argument symbolic legisign (e.g., a syllogism).*

Peirce is clearest on this: "An Argument is a sign whose interpretant represents its object as being an ulterior sign through a law, namely, the law that the passage from all such premisses to such conclusions tends to the truth" (2.262).

signs. A hermetic structure of relationships, abstract and free-floating, even if it is called a grammar, is meaningless. To be meaningful a grammar must be grounded in the interpretant. The meaning of a message—any message—is not defined by its internal relationships alone. A message means something only when it means *to* someone, and this transaction often entails a *somewhere* and a *sometime* as well.

I must again hasten to reassure the assiduous reader who has taken pains to examine the examples offered in each class of signs and has understandably wondered why a particular example should not belong or also belong somewhere else. Such puzzlement is clearly justified: Most, if not all signs are mixed. Signs, including symbols (especially symbols), are polysemic. This point, which has become almost a truism, was most lucidly made for the first time, to my knowledge, by Edward Sapir (1921), and has been put to maximum and effective use by Victor Turner (1967, 1969 and 1974) and by Victor Turner and Edith Turner (1978). Turner, however, by his selective attribution of polysemy to ritual and religious symbols, implies monosemy to other symbols, especially those signs that he calls "signs." Here I believe Turner to be wrong. Any mathematician who has struggled with the problem of trying to arrive at a univocal sign will testify to the impossibility of such a task. A sign, by its very nature, is polysemous. Turner is correct, however, in that some symbols, especially ritual and religious ones, tend to display their polysemic attributes with far greater élan than do others. The aspect of the sign that I have tried to bring forth is not its polysemy or its multivocality but its polychromy or multimodality. Iconic as well as indexical aspects may be concealed within the same sign. A sign runs in a bundle of cables, so to speak, not in single strands. A sign whose significant capacity is effectively determined by the copresence of a symbolic and an indexical mode of signification has been called a "duplex sign" (Jakobson 1957) or a "shifter" (Silverstein 1976). A polychromatic or multimodal sign can be likened to a jewel, with as many as ten facets, if not more, each facet having three angles. In the experience of human interpretants, often only one facet will tilt toward the observer-interpreter, catch light, and throw it back; the other facets merely refract light. The reflecting facet, then, becomes the dominant mode. This does not, however, deny the existence of other modes of signification; modes that are sometimes expressed subjunctively and at other times remain potentialities. Different contexts help bring to light different aspects or modes of the sign.

A satisfactory cultural account must evidence a sensitivity to the multimodality of the signs in that culture, a sensitivity to the significant color that comes to be dominant to those who traffic in these signs in their daily lives, and a sensitivity to the partially or fully concealed modalities that refract the significance emitted by the dominant modal facet. I shall pay particular attention to this polychromatic attribute of the sign in chapter 4.

I wish to abstract one other point from this excursion on sign types in anticipation of a theme that I shall develop in the text and leave as a hypothesis for further examination. I will argue that some cultures choose, in general, to display one particular sign modality in preference to others. Specifically, I will argue that in Hindu India, iconicity is valued over symbolization, whereas in the modern West, the quest for indexical and symbolic signs is valorized.

The Sign in Culture and Self

Culture is the product of human beings' trafficking in signs, mainly symbols. It is public. It does not exist in peoples' heads as a structure or template to act by or live by. This much Geertz has argued quite eloquently (1973, chap. 1). The semeiotic position calls for much more. As Singer has argued in a recent paper (1980), a semeiotic perspective requires one to consider not only the signs of self but also the fact that the self is a sign or, if you prefer, a web of signification. It is easy for us to accept that the self is not an inert physical substance. Given the pervasiveness of

Cartesian thinking in our contemporary culture, however, it is very difficult for us to admit that the self is not a "permanent Cartesian mental substance with the powers of introspection, intuition, and universal doubt which is dispelled by the unity of the 'I think' " (Singer 1980: 489). In other words, our positivist regime demands of us an admission, overt or covert, that pure objectivity is possible, that universal and analytic categories are what they claim to be (Quine's seminal 1960 essay notwithstanding) and that it is feasible for or even incumbent upon the anthropologist to divest himself of all nonanalytically supported mental baggage and approach the object of his study with an open and scientifically clean mind.

Man himself is a sign. As a semeiotic sign or symbol he is not a closed, completed entity. He is ready and open to connect with, to enter into dialogical relationships with other selves and other signs; when he does so connect, he significantly reconstitutes himself. As a semeiotic sign he is never actual: he is always virtual. The following quotations from Peirce will make this point clear:

> We have already seen that every state of consciousness [is] an inference; so that life is but a sequence of inferences or a train of thought. At any instant then man is a thought, and as thought is a species of symbol, the general answer to the question what is man? is that he is a symbol. (7.583, quoted in Singer 1980: 487)

Another statement most pertinent to our investigation of the cultural concept of the self in Tamil culture is Peirce's explication of the dialogical conception of the self, a conception to which Ricoeur (1978) and Habermas (1979) return from different angles almost three-quarters of a century after Peirce.

> A person is not absolutely an individual. His thoughts are what he is "saying to himself," that is, is saying to that other self that is just coming into life in the flow of time. When one

> reasons, it is that critical self that one is trying to persuade; and all thought is whatever is a sign, and is mostly of the nature of language. The second thing to remember is that the man's circle of society (however widely or narrowly this phrase may be understood), is a sort of loosely compacted person, in some respects of higher rank than the person of an individual organism. (5.421)

Or, as in Spivak's quotation from Proust:

> It was not one man only, but the steady advance hour after hour of an army in close formation, in which there appeared, according to the moment, impassioned men, indifferent men, jealous men. . . . In a composite man, those elements may, one by one, without our noticing it, be replaced by others, which others again eliminate or reinforce, until in the end a change has been brought about which it would be impossible to conceive if we were a single person. (Derrida 1976: x)

These understandings of the self are in far greater concordance with what Marriott finds to be true with respect to the concept of the person in India than is the dominant, permanantly integrated and bound Cartesian understanding of the self. Marriott finds the term *individual* to be a highly misleading one for an adequate understanding of the concept of the person. He considers "dividual" a far more apt characterization of the Hindu person (1976*a*). We shall return to this point time and again in the main text.

The Anthropologist, the Informant, the Conversation

A sign is never at rest; its dialogic structure makes this impossible. It is dynamic. The same is true of culture—as a web of signification it is one with the process of signification itself. Thus, culture ultimately is an open-ended process. This point may be best illustrated by Peirce's view on the process of reasoning, which for him is a form of semeiosis, a trafficking in thoughts, a trafficking in signs.

> Thus every reasoning involves another reasoning, which in its turn involves another, and so on ad infinitum. Every reasoning connects something that has just been learned with knowledge already acquired so that we thereby learn what has been unknown. It is thus that the present is so welded to what is just past as to render what is just coming about inevitable. The consciousness of the present, as the boundary between past and future, involves them both. Reasoning is a new experience which involves something old and something hitherto unknown. (7.536)

Reasoning, for the field-worker, entails a conversation with informants. This conversation is also the locus of the cultural process. Lévi-Strauss went so far as to equate the craft of anthropology with this conversation: "For anthropology, which is a conversation of man with man, everything is symbol and sign, when it acts as intermediary between two subjects" (1966: 115). For Lévi-Strauss, however, this conversation is where the structure of culture, which is the structure of the mind writ large, is manifest. The preoccupation with the quest for structure is so hegemonical in Lévi-Strauss's writings that a monologue and a monologic take the place of a truly dialogical conversation, except in *Tristes Tropiques* (1974), where this quest is slightly relaxed and he finds man conversing with man. The semeiotic point, however, misses Lévi-Strauss. HIs semeiology stops short of involving the interlocutors themselves as integral parts of the sign system, as interpretant signs.

The conversation the anthropologist engages in is a special kind of conversation. To begin with, as I have already remarked, it is a conversation with informants. As Schneider made it clear over a decade ago (1968: 8–9), the anthropologist does not interact with respondents as do sociologists, or with patients as do psychologists. This much is easy for most anthropologists to accept. But many anthropologists still believe in "samples," helped along by low-level mathematical techniques in probability and statistics. Informants do not come in samples; they are largely self-selective. They may not meet the criteria of statistical significance. How many Hitlers were there? How many Gandhis? Cultural anthropology, from a statistical point of view, is partial. It is partial toward those "natives" who allow the field-worker access to their web of signification, who extend him or her the opportunity to connect with it, even though by such generosity they are subjecting their web of signification to creative transformation.

Yet the cultural anthropologist is not completely insensitive to the question of how representative an informant is of those among whom s/he lives and with whom s/he is most frequently involved in culture-making processes. Loquacity alone does not make an informant representative. For that matter, the conversation we have been referring to in this chapter need not be and is not limited to a conversation in verbal signs alone. There are ways in which a sensitive anthropologist can and does evaluate consensus.

For instance, the data in chapter 4 on sexuality are not the kind of data that can be obtained from the mouth of the average villager. As good fortune would have it, my informant was able to self-select himself to draw me into a world that remains strictly private for most villagers. There were times when our discourse on matters of sexuality involved other villagers as well, who, as soon as they understood that I was comfortable in the web of signification that my main informant was spinning, participated in it, at times at a furious pace, throwing in a comment here, a refinement there, an objection somewhere else. I on my part would not always play the uninformed interrogator but used this opportunity to deploy in their midst the Arunta theory of procreation or the Trobriand notion of the "unimportance" of intercourse. Bemused skepticism and critical objections followed. Animated debate ensued. A cultural discourse was created. Whether or not the theory of sexuality that finally emerged—the "said" that I redeemed from the "saying"—was already there in their heads is irrelevant. Of interest is the fact that a cultural discourse was created, a discourse in which more than a few interested members in the community became entangled—and entangled with ease.

The positivist question likely to follow goes something like this: Can we not go back and reconstruct a questionnaire (a culturally sensitive one, of course, now that the discourse has been figured out) that confirms consensus in a reliable manner, perhaps along the lines of componential analysis or propositional analysis (D'Andrade 1976 has provided us with a paradigmatic one)? Apart from the fact that sensitive data proffered in informal discourse are often not elicitable through formal techniques, there is a more serious reservation with respect to such formal techniques, a reservation that is dimly prefigured in an early paper by David Schneider (1965), in which he gently critiques Goodenough's componential analysis of Yankee kinship. For a fuller appreciation of the inadequacies of formal analysis of this ilk, I refer the reader to two studies. One is a short and pithy paper by Michael Silverstein (1976) in which he takes on the tradition of semantico-referential grammarizing (of which cognitive anthropological theory and techniques are a part) and points out its inadequacies; the other is a more expansive study by Pierre Bourdieu (1972), which deals with the same issue in antipositivistic terms.

In my own work the impotence of cognitive anthropological or propositional analytical techniques with respect to certain kinds of cultural data was brought to the fore with respect to the data of chapter 2. There I deal with two lexemic items that in the formal, lexicographical (or in Silverstein's terminology, the semantico-referential) mode were translated as "village." The two terms were considered equivalent, if not synonymous. Keen observation of the context of their use, however, revealed that these two terms, *ūr*, on the one hand, and *kirāmam*, on the other, concealed within them two entirely different and distinct symbolic systems. No amount of formal, cognitive anthropological techniques could have elicited this difference.

These terms were somewhat similar to Whorf's cryptotypic categories. The analytic point with respect to the positivistic penchant for fixing facts or opinions by means of formal techniques, such as propositional analysis, may be made by restating the essence of Silverstein's argument, forwarded in his 1976 paper. Silverstein refers to a semantico-referential grammar, which includes the transformational generative grammar in linguistics and the cognitive anthropology and structuralism in anthropology. In these approaches the meaning of a message or a sign, 0, is taken to be a function of a semantico-referential grammar, G. This G is formal, its structure determinate and fixed. Silverstein shows, with countless and provocative examples, that such a theory of meaning is very inadequate. He argues instead for expanding meaning so as to make it the equivalent of a pragmatic grammar, G′. From a pragmatic point of view, $\theta = f(G') = f(G,x,y,z,l,t \ldots)$, where *x* is the speaker, *y* the hearer, *z* the audience, *l* the location of discourse, *t* the time of discourse, and so on. Clues to the subliminal pervasiveness of a certain symbolic construct emerge when the researcher is willing and able to transcend a limited, semantico-referential grammatical perspective and open up to the constellation of a greater array of pragmatic variables. Such clues more often than not reside not in verbal symbols but in shifters or duplex signs (Jakobson 1957; Silverstein 1976) that are indexical, or in rhematic iconic qualisigns that may be betrayed in a gesture, a joke, or a preference for a sāri of a certain color or a shirt of a certain material. Unfortunately there are rarely systematically or sequentially formulatable questions that can lead the investigator to these clues or to the underlying significance they may potentially reveal. It is a blessing to arrive at such a formulation, as I have done in chapter 2 with respect to the distinction between ūr and kirāmam. Even then, the formulation may not have application beyond the immediate problem and context. More often than not, one's second question will be determined by the first response. Such is the nature of a conversation; such the nature of dialogue.

The conversation of the anthropologist is special in yet another way. I have said earlier that the positivist believes that the researcher can and must divest himself or herself of his or her own presuppositions of the order of things, while the semeiotician maintains that such a task is impossible. Yet the craft of anthropology at its best requires the field-worker to relax his or her own symbolic constructs, to subject them to or prepare them for a process of disarticulation. In all his writings Victor Turner has shown us time and again how within a culture itself, liminal and liminoid processes loosen and disarticulate symbolic constructs of societies. The same ought to be true of fieldwork. Of course, different field-workers succeed to different degrees in this attempt at repose, and even the same field-worker is able to slacken the hold of his existing web of signification more successfully in one context than in another, even when among the same people. The hallmark of an anthropologist in the field is the willingness to try. Roy Wagner sees the whole matter thus: "Whether he knows it or not, and whether he intends it or not, his 'safe' act of making the strange familiar always makes the familiar a little bit strange. And the more familiar the strange becomes, the more and more strange the familiar will appear" (1981: 11).

Culture making: A Creative Art

If Geertz maintains, for whatever polemical reasons, that culture is not in people's heads (1973: 10) and if Schneider feels constrained to respond by asking rhetorically, If not in people's heads, then where else? (1976: 206), a genuinely semeiotic point of view will hold that culture is both inside and outside peoples' heads, in their past as well as in their present, and has implication for the future. It is to be located in the creative act of communicating. Wagner calls it "the invention of culture." The anthropologist "invents 'a culture' for people and they invent 'culture' for him" (1981: 11).

The anthropologist's invention or creation is the result of two, or rather three, simultaneous activities. To begin with, he concedes to the distinction and difference between his own culture and their culture. He also concedes to the fact that only a miniscule part of his cultural repertoire will be employed to initiate the "conversation" with the "native." One is reminded of Sapir's analogy relating language to an utterance or sentence, "It is somewhat as though a dynamo capable of generating enough power to run an elevator were operated almost exclusively to feed an electric doorbell" (1921: 14). Perhaps another analogy, another way of looking at the same process, will help. It is as if two gaseous planets whose veritable molecules were signs were drawn together and were only capable of illuminating and being illuminated by the sides that were mutually exposed, while the other parts, the greater parts, remained eclipsed in darkness, in disuse, bracketed away. This separation of the exposed from the unexposed, the illuminated from the hidden, the proffered from the reserved marks the first "conversation"-motivated activity.

The second activity is marked by the deconstruction of the proffered, or presented, part. Given that our metaphor holds our planets to be gaseous and capable of interpenetration, we shall also assume that they are capable of substance exchanges and mutual transformations. In our semeiotic idiom we may say that there are certain webs of signification of the native into which we may sink with ease and form easy semeiotic links. Let's return to our planet metaphor, however. Insofar as the anthropologist presents a segment of *his* planet of signs, he does so (or ought to do so) with the willingness—even the wish—to see its deconstruction, a process that will be facilitated by the third activity.

This third activity entails the simultaneous presentation of the native's planet of signs. In this admixture both bodies are obviously going to undergo transformation. The trick, however (and this is where the issue of deference comes in), is to minimize the transformation of the native's planet and maximize that of one's own. The creation or invention that the native presents as culture and the anthropologist interprets as a culture is precisely this area of admixture, this area of significant intercourse, this area brought together into mutual interpenetration in the communicative act, an act that is, as I have intimated in my definition of culture, a creative one, in which both anthropologist and informant(s) are involved, but in which the creativity of the informant(s) is given preeminence.

Now imagine our interpenetrating semeiotic planets slowly rotating, so that every cubic area of each planet is at one time or another commonly shared by both planets. This, after all, is something that ought to happen in the best of all possible worlds; every possible nook and cranny of the anthropologist's world is subjected to creative deconstruction through a genuine communication and communion with that of the natives. We do not, however, live in the best of all possible worlds, even though there is no harm in trying to make our world into one.

I must hasten to disabuse the reader who sees in this scheme "the myth of the chameleon worker, perfectly self-tuned to his exotic surroundings, a walking miracle of empathy, tact, patience, and cosmopolitanism" (Geertz 1976: 222), even though I would not scoff as readily as Geertz does at those field-workers who are blessed with "more-than-normal capacities for ego effacement and fellow feeling" (p. 236), provided that they are not mere pretensions. The problem with the myth, however, is that the chameleon, for all its extraordinary mimetic achievements, emerges finally with its identity intact. This feat, from a semeiotic standpoint, is an impossibility.

In essence, what I have attempted to convey by this metaphor is the implication and import of that age-old, incomparable sine qua non of anthropological field method known as participant-observation. In these days of positivistic hyperbole, where grant applications provide special sections for listing techniques and even apparatus, the import of this apparently weatherworn hyphenated concept recedes to arcane recesses of a plan of study. My intention in this book is to restore the concept to its rightful place.

I intend as well to show that the hyphen that divides participation from observation is a stubborn one, an unrelentingly vigilant sentry forever keeping the two apart. The best an anthropologist can hope for is that with every participatory experience s/he will have enhanced his or her observational understanding.

I am not yet done with the metaphor, nor with the chameleon. Beyond experiencing and understanding, the anthropologist is called upon to tell his or her story to folks back home, to intellectuals and to academics and to those who simply enjoy reading anthropology. The story s/he tells them is a cultural account. This cultural account (I agree with Geertz) is an interpretive one. Now, the problem with going all native does not lie so much in this activity's pretensions to "more-than-normal capacities for ego effacement" or in claims to being a "walking miracle of empathy" but rather in that the more native one becomes, the less of a story one has to tell—or for that matter, the less need one will have to tell a story.

Let me illustrate this point semeiotically. Interpretation is not unlike metaphor. Stated differently, interpretive possibility may be said to inhere in its metaphoric structure. I am fully aware—even painfully aware—of the unsettled and unsettling debate on what a metaphor is. I am going to have to pretend (and have the reader pretend with me) that all the controversy and refinement is mere impertinence (in every sense of that term) for our purpose at hand and that the following basic view of metaphor will suffice. (For the reader who insists on my taking a stand, let me say that I am broadly on the side of such metaphoricists as Ricoeur [1977], Max Black [1962], and Beardsley [1972] and am aware of the excellent alternatives that stand in opposition to these studies, those by John Searle [1979] and Donald Davidson [1978].)

Basic both to the structure and to the event of metaphor is the fact that in a metaphor two signs are involved. To begin with, in their premetaphoric representation they are disparate and belong to distinct significant contexts. In metaphor the two signs are brought together because of some quality they share. That is, the two signs are partial icons of each other. When they are brought together in a metaphor, such as the line from T. S. Eliot's "Love Song of J. Alfred Prufrock" "Streets that follow like a tedious argument" or the phrase "Love is a red rose," they are icons of each other in that qualities are common to my love and a rose or to a particular kind of street and an argument. Complete isomorphism, however, does not exist between the pairs of icons, for if that were the case, they would not be metaphors. As in a Venn diagram, there is a shared semantic and sensory area and an area that is not shared. While the isomorphic attempts to create semantic and sensory homogeneity, the anisomorphic reminds one of the referential heterogeneity. Furthermore, this anisomorphism reminds one of the icons' symbolic content. This ambiguating mixture of sense and representation (in Ricoeur [1978], Ferge's opposition between *Sinn* and *Vorstellung*), however, directs one's attention to it—a mechanism that gives it metaphoric force. This attention-directing function is predominantly indexical.

If we move back to our metaphor of the interpenetrating planets, there likewise we find iconicity as well as aniconicity; and it is this duality that makes an anthropological account possible, and this anthropological account or interpretive product is structurally, as well as in terms of Sinn and Vorstellung, metaphoric.

Nor am I done with the chameleon: Metaphors are iconic Thirds in that the convention or symbolic function inherent in the metaphor is quite evident. An image or a statue, in contrast, is an iconic Second. Its iconicity is more dominant than in the case of the metaphor. Its separation from its object, however—ergo its contiguity with it (in reality or in the mind)—remains apparent, and hence its indexical function is conspicuous. Enter our chameleon, a splendid example of an iconic First. In the case of protective coloration in nature, the representation (the color of the animal or plant) blends in so perfectly with the background, its iconicity reaching a hue of such perfection, that it masks all rather than conveys any information (Deacon 1978). The case of the field-worker gone all native is no different. A cultural account is by definition an interpretive account, and as an interpretive account it must be capable of conveying information even as a metaphor does.

Interpretation entails a movement, a movement that brings the interpretive subject and the interpretive object together into partial coalescence. The movement, however, as I have indicated elsewhere (Daniel 1983*a*), can take place in two ways. On the one hand, the anthropologist can draw the interpretive subject to himself with barely a movement on his part. The proverbial armchair anthropologist belongs to this kind, and so, I am afraid, do the structuralists, among others.[14] In some instances, we may say with retrospective wisdom, arrogation of native categories has been so extreme and complete that situations of iconic Firstness were created with hardly anything left worth calling interpretation. On the other hand, the anthropologist can consciously move toward the interpretive subject, divesting himself or herself, in the move, of his or her own native symbolic constructs. The latter is clearly the preferred, nonethnocentric movement. However, noninformative iconic Firstness achieved in this direction is not desirable either. I believe this is where ethnosociology and interpretive anthropology part ways.

[14]Notable exceptions are to be found in applications of structuralism by those studying aspects of their own culture. In such instances we see a de facto incorporation of a *cultural* interpretant into the analysis. I think here of Roland Barthes's *Mythologies* (1972) and Veena Das's paradigmatic study of the *Dharmāraṇya Purāṇa* and the *Grihyasutra* in their pragmatic contexts (1977).

There have been several criticisms of ethnosociology since it was first formulated in several working papers in the early seventies and found its first attempted application in Ronald Inden's Ph.D. dissertation (1972, revised and published in 1976). The first programmatic statement on ethnosociology was presented in 1973 at the Ninth International Congress of the Anthropological and Ethnological Sciences by McKim Marriott, revised and published in the same year in which Ronald Inden's dissertation was published (1976). The unsurpassed essay on the caste system by the same authors appeared in print in the 1974 edition of the Encyclopaedia Britannica, intended, I presume, to be yet another application of the ethnosociological method. In 1976, in a response to a critical letter in the *Journal of Asian Studies*, Marriott, after defending his ethnosociology, recommended, "[It] would not be a bad objective for [Western social scientists] to make themselves—the knowers—somewhat like those South Asian objects that they would make known" (1976*b*: 195). Marriott, admirably and with gallantry, has attempted to turn things around. Enough of Weberizing and Durkheimizing Indian ethnological data. How about Manuizing and Paninizing Western culture, including the culture of science, for a change?

There have been several critical evaluations of ethnosociology, Trautman's (1980) and Good's (1982) being the latest. Even though their criticisms make sobering and constructive contributions, Trautman, implicitly, and Good, explicitly, miss the crucial, critical point. The issue is not whether one is able to locate the distinctive features of a culture via componential analysis or some such formal technique, or whether the application of generalized social systems theory conforms to the rigors of analyticity, or whether ethnosociological theory, by being no less culturally constituted than the classical Hindu lawbook *Manudharmaśāstra,* falls short of the exacting standards of a universal model. The issue is rather that anthropology and sociology are part of Western man's concerns and are constituted of Western cultural symbols. Regardless of how much we may ethnocize anthropological theory, anthropology will be part of the Western or westernized intellectual's symbolic system. When I was a schoolboy, the school was very "British," even though it was in Sri Lanka (then Ceylon). As good former British subjects, we were supposed to have a thing called a hobby. It was supposed to help one find a job later in life. We collected butterflies, stamps, and labels of jam tins imported from South Africa. A boy in my neighborhood who went to a Hindu school collected empty bottles and newspapers. That was his hobby, but he did not know it. He sold them and shared the money with his mother. He is now the owner of the local soda company. As for hobby qua hobby—this has yet to take root in Sri Lankan culture; the neighborhood boy's activities failed to connect with the web of significations we were part of. The same goes for anthropology and sociology; and I dare say that nuclear physics is far more at home in South Asia than is social science. The desire and need to study other peoples and to invent other cultures with them remains a preoccupation of Western man. Ethnosociology, in the full sense intended by Marriott, is an anachronism.

This leads me to yet another point, that of understanding a culture in its own terms. This is a noble goal and must be pursued by what I have already characterized as a concerted move toward the interpretive subject and by deference to the creative input of the native. This goal, however, cannot be pursued to its limit. It must stop short of iconic Firstness if the integrity of anthropology is to be retained; or if it does reach that stage, there must be a way to retreat a bit so as to restore metaphoric potentiality and interpretive possibility. Thus, to be meaningful, an ethnosociology must define itself paradoxically: as hoping to reach a goal it hopes never to reach.

I, for one, doubt that the ideal state of iconic Firstness can be reached. Traces of one's own symbolic constructs will remain. In chapter 7 I have recorded my experience of a pilgrimage that I undertook with seven fellow villagers. The experience was so intense, physically and emotionally trying, that I found it increasingly difficult to get out of the participating side of the hyphenated concept participant-observation, onto the observational side. At times I thought my merger was going to be complete. Even during moments of greatest emotional and physical consummation, however, traces of my past remained, so that I was only afforded traces of what I was after.[15]

There is one more term in my definition of culture which I have yet to deal with. It is the "misspelled" word also borrowed from Jacques Derrida, *différance*. I shall defer its analysis until the end of this study, the more appropriate context for such an undertaking.

In dedicating this introduction to those who read introductions, I have attempted to pass on to the reader the burden of deciding whether this should be first or afterword. (Not a very responsible thing to do, I grant you.) In fact, I ought to have dedicated this to the two groups of readers of the text in its introduction-free, prepublished, manuscript version: one group commending me for not spoiling the reading experience with an introduction and instead plunging the reader headfirst into ethnographic thickness, the other group urging me, for clarity's sake and for the sake of those twice removed from the Chicago jāti of anthropology, to write such an introduction. Furthermore, this section, not unlike most introductions, is a fiction insofar as it pretends to have been written prior to the writing of the text—when in fact it was written after the

[15] I use the term *trace* in the sense that Jacques Derrida has used it. "Derrida . . . gives the name 'trace' to the part played by the radically other within the structure of difference that is the sign. (I stick to 'trace' . . . because it 'looks the same' as Derrida's word; the reader must remind himself of at least the track, even the spoor, contained within the French word.) Derrida's trace is the mark of the absence of a presence, an always already-absent present, of the lack at the origin that is a condition of thought and experience" (from the translator's preface to *Of Grammatology* by Jacques Derrida, 1976: xvii).

reading of it (see G. C. Spivak in Derrida 1976: x). Bearing this in mind, for the conscientious reader who has read this as an introduction, I leave these words paraphrased from Hegel: Don't take me seriously in an introduction. The real anthropological work is what I have just written, *Fluid Signs: Being a Person the Tamil Way*. And if I speak to you outside of what I have written, these marginal comments cannot have the value of the work itself. Don't take introductions seriously. The introduction announces a project, and a project is nothing unless it is realized (from Derrida 1976: x). For those who have read this after reading the text, I would like to leave you with the following: Having read the text and then the introduction, you realize that I have written *sous rature*, which Spivak has translated from Derrida's original as writing "under erasure": "This is to write a word, cross it out, and then print both word and deletion. (Since the word is inaccurate, it is crossed out. Since it is necessary, it remains legible.) To [adapt] an example from Derrida . . .: '. . . the sign ~~is~~ that ill-named ~~thing~~ . . . which escapes the instituting question of [anthropology] . . .' " (Derrida 1976: xiv).

Such is the nature of culture. Such is the nature of interpretation.

About This Research

The field data on which this study is based was gathered between March 1975 and September 1976, when my wife and I carried out anthropological field research in the village of Kalappūr (a pseudonym). *Kalappūr* means "place of mixed substances." This village with a population of over two thousand persons is located in the South Indian state of Tamil Nadu, twenty-three miles northeast of Tiruchirappalli. Supplementary data were gathered from significant informants in Sri Lanka during the three months preceding our stay in India and the two months after we left India.

Following customary ethnographic practice, the names of informants provided in this book are, in all instances, not the actual names. Pseudonyms have been attached to informants whose identity I have found it discreet to conceal.

Since what follows is an interpretive account, it is only fair to offer the reader some significant biographical data. I am a native Tamil speaker, born in the Sinhalese-speaking south of Sri Lanka to a South Indian Tamil father who changed his name from something divine to something daring in order to marry my mother, a Sri Lankan Anglican whose mother tongue was English. My father's English was poor, his Sinhalese ineffective; my mother's Tamil was excruciating, her Sinhalese reserved for the servants. (They have been married for almost half a century.) For me, at least, anthropologizing began early.

PART I
Toward Compatibility

2
An Ūr Known

On a Sunday morning two weeks after my wife and I had settled in the village of Kalappūr, the humdrum pace of village life was startled by the arrival of a chauffeur-driven Mercedes-Benz. From the brilliantly polished limousine emerged a conspicuously wealthy and cosmopolitan-looking gentleman. Villagers hastened to inform me that this gentleman was an Āru Nāṭṭu Veḷḷāḷa (henceforth ANV) businessman from Malaysia who prided himself on having had the distinction of being the first ANV to go to college. I was also told that when this gentleman's father first arrived in Malaysia at the turn of the century, he did so as a laborer looking for work on one of the many rubber plantations of that country. A series of successes propelled him from poverty to plenty within a decade.

I was later to learn from the distinguished "visitor" himself the purpose of his visit. He did come to see his ancestral lands. More important, however, he came to make arrangements with one of his kinsmen, a distant "cousin" and caretaker of his property in Kalappūr, for the proposed arrival and six-month stay of his son in the village. I asked the gentleman why he felt so strongly that his son must not merely visit the village but live in it for a number of months. In response to my question, he recalled his own life.

He grew up in a traditional family in Kuala Lumpur. His father, even though wealthy, never gave up his *vēṣṭi* for trousers nor did the family eat at a table but sat on a mat and ate from banana leaves.[1] "Rich and poor ANVs were in and out of our house, reminding me in so many ways that I was one of them, an ANV," he recalled. By the time he was ready to go to college to England, he had no doubt about what it was to be an ANV—or so he thought. However, prior to leaving for England, his father insisted that he go to his ancestral village (*conta* ūr) and live on its soil for four months. At that time he despised the very idea and had heard enough stories about the village to despise it as well. Yet he had no choice but to comply with his father's wishes. With that air characteristic of men wisened by experience and age, the gentleman from Kuala Lumpur told me, "Now I know that it was only during those four months in Kalappūr that I came to know who I am and what it is really to be an ANV." When I questioned him as to how exactly he acquired this knowledge, he told me that he had done so "by bathing at the village well, drinking its water, and eating the rice that grows in the fields of Kalappūr." Then he emphasized, ". . . to know who I am, I had to get to know the soil of this village (ūr) which is, after all, a part of me."

He also maintained that his business acumen became suddenly sharpened after he had spent this period in the village (ūr).[2] He concluded his narrative by saying: "If this was so important for me, you can imagine how much more important it is for my son. He wears trousers and thinks

[1]A vēṣṭi is a lower garment worn by Tamil men. Trousers are a mark of westernization.

[2]ANVs as a jāti are believed to excel in business acumen, which is strengthened when they reside in the ancestral villages of their jāti. This point will be discussed in greater detail later.

that he is Chinese or some such thing.[3] All that he knows of India is Bombay, if you can call that India. He will be a miserable failure in life if he does not return to his village [ūr]."

After a meal of rice harvested from the fields of Kalappūr and a drink of water from the village well, the gentleman sped away in his limousine. Even before the dust settled on the tracks, I realized that I needed to know much more than I already knew about this entity known as the ūr. The task was not easy, because of the obstacles placed in the way of arriving at its essential, pragmatic meaning (Silverstein 1976: 11–15), which also happened to be cryptotypic (Whorf 1956: 105); a task continually frustrated by the obfuscation created by the more readily proffered semantico-referential meaning (Silverstein 1976). What follows is essentially a report of my attempt to understand the meaning of ūr in all its vicissitudes.

One of the most important relationships to a Tamil is that which exists between a person and the soil of his ūr. To understand this relationship, we must begin with an analysis of the meaning of this spatio/territorial concept in both its lexical context as well as in its use. At the outset, it must be said that the term *ūr* can by no means be easily defined, but perhaps the closest approximate definition would be, a named territory that is (1) inhabited by human beings who are believed to share in the substance of the soil of that territory, and (2) a territory to which a Tamil cognitively orients himself at any given time.

Let me take up part two of this working definition first. It implies a shifting and contextual use of the word ūr. For example, in the common question, "Are you going to the ūr?" the ūr in question could be the neighboring village, town, district, state, or country. It is *the* place immediately

[3]An allusion to the fact that his son keeps the company of westernized Chinese and Sri Lankan friends in Malaysia and does not interact extensively with members of his own caste or even fellow Indian Tamils.

relevant to the person in terms of his current travel plans. To clarify the context of this usage of ūr, let me elaborate with an example.

In Tamil Nadu, to ask someone the directly phrased question, "Where are you going?" is not only rude but also casts a pall of inauspiciousness over the proposed journey. The question would be especially ominious as well as rude if it were to be asked of an elder, or one "full of *mariyātai*."[4] The sense or meaning of the question itself is not rude and inauspicious. Rather, the syntax is malefic. It has something more than "illocutionary force" (Austin 1962: 145); it is the negative counterpart of a good mantra; it is efficacious black magic. Since the syntax is critical, the same question may be asked quite inoffensively if rephrased. A common alternate and acceptable formulation of the question is, "Are you going to the ūr?"

The residents of Kalappūr know where a given fellow villager or group of fellow villagers is likely to go when setting out. Ramasamy makes his weekly visits to the taluk headquarters every Wednesday; Kandia goes to the market in the district capital every Friday to buy provisions for his village shop; the *pūcāri*,[5] when dressed in a bleached vēṣṭi and shirt with a shawl across his shoulder, goes to the taluk courthouse because he is invariably involved in one litigation or another; Palanisamy and his friends, when dressed up in their colored Terri-Cotton shirts and white vēṣṭis, are on their way for an evening at the movies in the neighboring town of Maraiyūr. So the question "Are you going to the ūr?" addressed to any one or more villagers whose habits are known is quite often a way of confirming what one

[4]*Mariyātai* means respect or honor. Not only do human persons as well as divine persons possess mariyātai, but in any hierarchical encounter, the lower-ranked person must "give" or "do" mariyātai to the higher-ranking one. Highly detailed and pragmatically rich studies of this concept are to be found in Appadurai and Breckenridge 1976 and Dirks (forthcoming).

[5]A non-Brahmin temple priest. In Kalappūr the pūcāri was a wealthy ANV landlord and leader of one of the two main village factions.

already suspects. A simple yes as a response helps confirm the hunch and satisfy curiosity. In such instances the question may even be only another way of a person's saying hello to another or a way of making a courteous comment or inviting participation in small talk.

There are times, however, when the questioner, X, will not have a clue where the other, Y, is going because the time at which Y happens to be leaving the village is not in keeping with his habits (for example, if Palanisamy and his friends were to wait for the bus in the morning rather than in the evening) or Y is dressed in a special way or is carrying a suitcase that he ordinarily does not carry or, like the resident anthropologist, Y has erratic travel habits—he could be going to Tiruchy Town, the state capital in Madras, to the neighboring state of Kerala, or merely to the adjacent village to attend the twenty-sixth wedding of the season. In instances such as these, the "ūr" contained in the question remains unknown and hence the query "Are you going to the ūr?" calls for more than a yes response. It becomes only polite for Y to specify his destination, thereby answering the underlying question, "Where are you going?"

The following dialogue illustrates the difficulty in trying indirectly to pinpoint the particular referent of the term *ūr*; it also highlights the idiocentric or the person-centered definition of *ūr*. Ūr can and does vary according to any given person's changing spatial orientation.

On this particular occasion I was walking down the street toward the bus stand with my red shoulder bag containing my tape recorder. I was startled by the question that came from behind a shady tree, "Are you going to the ūr?" It was Sadaya Kavuṇṭan (henceforth S), a man whose smile I would describe as cherublike if it weren't for the red betel-leaf stain on his teeth.

Anthropologist (henceforth A): Yes. [Now ūr, given the unpredictable travel habits of the anthropologist, could conceivably refer here to the center of the village, another village, the town, or to any other place.]

S: Seems like you are off to Tiruchy?

A: No.

S: I don't see the lady [the anthropologist's wife] with you.

A: She is at home.

S: So you couldn't be gone for too long. You'll be back tonight, won't you?

A: I think so.

S: I hear that there is a wedding in Veḷḷalūr [a neighboring village].

A: Is that so?

S: Are you going to it?

A: No.

S: Then it must be some other wedding.

A: No, I am not going to a wedding. I am just going [*cumma pōrēn*, a common Tamil expression that is semantically vacuous because of its over inflated polysemy].

S: Seems like Sir doesn't want to tell me where you are going. You can trust me.

A: I trust you. What is so bad about telling you where I am going?

S: Then tell me, won't you?

A: What?

S: [Laughing] Alright. Go and come.

A: Goodbye.

S: Alright. Goodbye. [after I had walked a few feet further down the road, shouting from behind me:] The buses don't run today. So wherever you are going it will have to be within the ūr [i.e., within the village of Kalappūr]. Of course, if you tell me where you wish to go, I could take you on my bicycle to the bus stand in Varattūr [another village closer to the main road, three miles from Kalappūr].

A: No, I am just going to the center of the village.

S: That's what I thought. Go and come. They say that the bus might come after all.

In some contexts, the meaning of ūr overlaps with the English word *home*. Thus, when a Tamil asks the question of a stranger, "What is your ūr?" he is really asking, "Where is your home?" As in the case of the English word *home*, the contextually determined speech event will determine the response. Thus, if a Tamil is asked this question when he is in Sri Lanka, he will reply that his ūr is India. If he is in Kerala, he will reply, "Tamil Nadu," and if in some part of Tamil Nadu itself, he will refer to the district, neighboring town, or to his particular village.

Tamils also distinguish between the ūr that is merely one's current residence or home and the ūr that is one's real home (conta ūr), that is, the place whose soil is most compatible with oneself and with one's ancestors. Thus, even to second-generation Sri Lankan Tamils, the Indian village of Kalappūr is still their conta ūr, since it is the ūr most suited to their bodily substance.

One invariably encounters one or more castes in any given ūr which have lived in that ūr for many generations. Yet members of those castes maintain that this ūr of their domicile has soil incompatible with their caste and that is only compatible with certain other castes, the dominant caste in particular. The ūr whose soil is compatible with their own caste, that is, their conta ūr, they claim to be in some other place sometimes so distant in space and time as to be more ideal than real; an ūr with which no contact whatsoever has been made in a great many years and an ūr in which none of their fellow caste members remain. Such is the case with the Brahmins of Kalappūr, who view Kalappūr as the ūr of their kinsmen for a number of generations but not as their conta ūr, which could only be a land with "sweet" soil, land preferably given to them by a king or wealthy benefactor.

In the same caste (jāti) there may be further generic subdivisions, such as *kōttiram, vakaiyarā* (variously defined lineages or clans), that may claim different territories for their conta ūr.

While any named territory whose soil proves to be most compatible with a given genus of human beings becomes their conta ūr, the fact that any territory whatsoever that may be more or less compatible with one or more human generic units qualifies for the status of ūr makes the referential possibilities of ūr almost limitless. The only limiting factor that sufficiently narrows the word's referential focus to facilitate its meaningful use in speech is the fact that ūr, an external space, is defined person-centrically, in terms of its relevance to a given ego rather than in terms of a purely semantic category that refers to a bounded territory common to all Tamils at all times and in all places.

This proclivity to define space person-centrically is also evident in the contextual usage of the term *nāṭu*, which is ordinarily glossed as "country." When a Tamil speaks of his nāṭu, he may, according to the context, be referring to the whole of India, to the state of Tamil Nadu, to the territory of the ancient Tamil dynasties (e.g., Cōḷa Nāṭu, Cēra Nāṭu, etc.), to the area that is his immediate locale (e.g., Konku Nāṭu—Beck 1972: 19), or even to a handful of ancestral villages such as the Āru Nāṭus (six villages), which constitute the homeland or "country" of the Āru Nāṭṭu Veḷḷāḷars (ANVs). In order to determine the referent of nātu it is necessary, as in the case of ūr, to figure out what "country" the speaker is referring to in that context. His spatial as well as cognitive orientation—what he at that moment chooses to call his country—determines the contextual meaning of nāṭu.

Not all Tamil spatial terms are, however, of this person-centric type. In marked contrast to the terms *nāṭu* and *ūr* are the terms *tēcam* and *kirāmam*, which are of Sanskrit origin and which refer to nation/country and village, respectively. Both terms refer to bounded, standard, universally accepted, and constant spatial units. The government determines what is a tēcam and a kirāmam, and it is the same for everyone. There is no contextual variation in the use of these terms.

A Tamil's first encounter with the term *tēcam* (from Skt. *dēsh*) most probably is during his first school lesson in geography, in which context tēcam refers to country or nation. This primary geographico-political meaning of tēcam remains uppermost in his mind throughout life. Many of the older villagers I spoke to, in particular the older women who had never attended school, never used the word tēcam, and several of them did not know what the word meant.

The national anthem of India is referred to as the *tēcīkap-pāṭal*, and maps are called *tēcīkappaṭam*. South Indians who used to listen to the Tamil channel of Radio Ceylon (now the Sri Lanka Broadcasting Corporation) have heard the station identify itself as "ilankai vānoli tēcika [from *tēcam*] oli-parappu." Those who read the newspapers and listen to All India Radio encounter the word *tēcam* in connection with many of the national programs and plays.

The word *tēcam* is by and large a political concept, and for those who are not interested in national politics (as is the case with most villagers in Tamil Nadu), tēcam remains abstract and affectively distant. As one informant phrased it, "tēcam belongs to the government, and the government is in Delhi" ("tēcam aracānkatti cērntatu, aracānkam ṭilliyai cērntatu").

The word kirāmam is similarly abstract and distant. It refers to the revenue village and thus to a political unit created for the purpose of taxation and the organization of local government (*panchāyat*). A kirāmam is under the jurisdiction of the *taluk* ("county"), which is governed by the district, then by the state, and ultimately by the national government.

The differing concepts underlying the Sanskrit terms *tēcam* and *kirāmam* and the Tamil terms *nāṭu* and *ūr* can best be clarified by the simple process of asking a Tamil, "What is your x?"; where *x* stands for either tēcam or kirāmam, only one answer is possible for a Tamil. In the case of tēcam, the answer will be India, and in the case of kirāmam, the respondent will give you the name of his revenue village. When, however, the question is, "What is your nāṭu?" the respondent can specify any place that to him at that moment strikes him as his country, whether it be India as a whole or the cluster of villages to one side or the other of the river in his village locale. (For example, for ANVs the villages east of the Ayyār River are called Kīṛa Nāṭu [Eastern Nāṭu], and those to the west of the river are called Mēla Nāṭu [Western Nāṭu]. This classification is relevant to and known only by ANVs.) If *x* stands for ūr, the answer could range from a foreign country to the person's own natal village.

In short, *tēcam* and *kirāmam* are terms whose meaning is relatively context free, universal, and fixed, whereas *nāṭu* and *ūr* are person-centric terms that derive their meaning from the contextually shifting spatial orientation of the person.

This person-centric definition of space is in keeping with the person-centric orientation of Hindu culture. For instance, there is no *dharma* (code for conduct), no unit of time, no food or soil that is moral or good for all persons. Even as moral laws are not universal and vary according to jāti, stage of life, individual life circumstances, and so on, so there is no universal rule for what kinds of foods are most compatible with all people. Minimally transacting castes[6]

[6]This terminology derives from Marriott's (1976) fourfold classification of transactional strategies typical of different jātis as well as from persons as observed in South Asian culture:

a. Minimal transactors are those who prefer whenever possible to refrain from giving as well as receiving. To the extent that they do transact, they limit such transactions to relatively highly integrated substances—money, precious metal, raw food—as opposed to highly particulating substances, such as cooked food or water. Vaiśyas, goldsmiths, are minimal transactors, for example.

find "cooling" foods more compatible, whereas maximally transacting castes favor "heating" foods. Even within a caste, however, there is variation. Thus, a particular Ācāri (minimally transacting caste) may find the traditionally cooling diet of his caste incompatible with his particular bodily substance. He may, therefore, have to resort to more heating foods. Even in the classification of foods as either hot or cold there is individual variation. For example, Sunther, the son of one of the wealthier ANV landlords of Kalappūr, has been unable to drink milk from the age of four, probably due to the absence of lactase in his system. Consequently, his mother has decided that cow's milk is too hot for him, although ordinarily milk is considered to be a cold food.

This person-specific view of reality is, of course, in keeping with the Hindu's underlying understanding of substance and the rules for its proper mixing. Because each person has a uniquely proportioned composite substance, in his search for equilibrium he must observe unique codes for determining what substance is compatible with his bodily substance. Considerable effort is expended by the person in determining just what external combinations will suit him best—what time (according to astrology) will be most auspicious, for example. The Hindu is, in short, well accustomed to a very idiosyncratic definition of what is moral, what is compatible, what is relevant, and so on. This is not to suggest that there are no universal cultural premises underlying his search for compatible actions and relationships but that as a uniquely constituted, internally composite entity, he is vulnerable, as is any other composite

---

b. Maximal transactors are those who both give and receive relatively freely. Examples are Kṣatriyas, ANVs.

c. Optimal transactors (Brahmins, for example) give but shy away from receiving.

d. Pessimal transactors, willingly or otherwise, end up receiving far more than they give. What they do give, if anyone would receive, is limited to substances of high integrity that do not easily particulate. Untouchables are pessimal transactors.

substance, to the unique conditions of place, time, and other equally vulnerable substances with which he comes in contact. For this reason he must find what is suited to him and his unique essence at any given moment in time and position in space. It is, therefore, not at all odd for the Tamil to readily accept a very person-centric, idiosyncratic, and shifting definition of space. Space, like time and dharma, is meaningful only in its relationship to particular places and at particular times. (See also the person-centric use of the term *ātmīya-svajana* "one's own people," Inden and Nicholas 1977.)

Another and equally illumining aspect of Tamil spatial concepts can be learned from examining the Tamil's perception of boundaries. Freed from context and forced into a semantic slot or a lexicographic gloss, ūr and kirāmam may be misleadingly represented by native informants as semantically isomorphic and mutually substitutable in use. However, the fact that this isomorphism is apparent but not real becomes evident when one turns to the task of discovering boundaries for ūrs and kirāmams. I was to strike upon this significant distinguishing marker by accident at first. Subsequently, however, I was able to devise a mini-experiment of sorts in order to systematically tease out the differences between ūr and kirāmam in terms of the boundary concept. To begin, let us consider the following example.

If you were to show a villager a map of Kalappūr and ask him to point to the *kirāma ellai* ("boundary"), he would describe with his finger the village boundary line as indicated on the map. He would be able to tell you that this "line" divides the territory that bears the name Kalappūr from the territory that does not. If you were to ask the same villager at the same time, displaying the same map, to show you the *ūr ellai*, he would most likely be somewhat annoyed at your naivete—if not stupidity—and tell you, "Why, the kirāma ellai and the ūr ellai are the same!"

Even with no map before us, when I have asked informants whether ūr ellai and kirāma ellai are the same, they have assured me that the answer is obviously yes. Yet I was to strike upon the difference between the terms, quite by chance, in a conversation with Ponnambalam, an ANV landowner of Kalappūr. The previous evening we had discussed various subjects related to the ūr ellai of Kalappūr. Our discussion had centered mainly on the guardian deity whose *pativu* ("stone representation") was located on the southern edge of the village. Ponnambalam described to me in detail the nightly rounds the deity made; the festival and sacrifices performed for this deity once in every five or six years; the danger of crossing the ūr ellai at midnight for fear of being attacked by this guardian deity; and so on. That night Ponnambalam left my house after I had obtained a promise from him to accompany me to the ūr ellai some time that week. The next morning I met him in the center of the village and asked him if he had the time to take me to the village boundary. The critical twist to my question was that I asked him to show me the kirāma ellai and not the ūr ellai (at that time I had assumed the semantic equivalence of the two terms). To my surprise, Ponnambalam begged ignorance and told me that I would be wiser to contact the village accountant or the government surveyor, who visits the village quite often, if I wished to see the kirāma ellai. I hastened to remind him that only the previous night he had told me that he could and would show me the kirāma ellai. Recall beamed on his face, and he said, "Oh, you mean you wish to see the ūr ellai. Why didn't you say so? Come, let us go right away." Thus saying, he led me to the southern edge of the village to see the pativu of Karuppu Sami, the guardian deity.

The distinction between ūr and kirāmam may be arrived at in yet another way. During my fieldwork, I often asked villagers to draw me the map of the village. Three types of maps resulted from the experiment. When asked to draw a kirāmam map, informants frequently responded with hesitation and would tell me, "Why, you can get that [i.e., a *kirāmappaṭam*] from the village accountant or the *munsif* [village policeman]." Those who did agree to draw one invariably began by drawing a linear boundary in the shape of a square, rectangle, circle, or other less regularly shaped enclosing form. They then proceeded to fill in the main roads, houses, temples, and so on in the interior of the village. They would also occasionally label the villages that surround Kalappūr. These maps I labeled type-one maps.

When villagers were asked to draw ūr maps, they were considerably less hesitant to do so, already hinting at a conceptual distinction between the terms *ūr* and *kirāmam,* which are prima facie equivalents. There were no suggestions that such a map could be obtained from more reliable sources, such as the surveyor or the munsif. The maps drawn in response to this request were of two types. In both cases the drawing began not with the periphery of the village but at its center, with the noting of the important places, such as the temple, the priest's house, the crossroads, and so on. Only then did attention shift to the periphery. All the respondents took great care to mark the shrines of the sentinel deities, the points at which roads or the village stream enters the village, and the haunted tamarind trees that dot the edge of the village. The only variation in the maps was that some informants drew a linear boundary line around the ūr, whereas others did not. I labeled the ūr maps with boundary lines type two, and the ūr maps without boundary lines type three.

In order to (1) tease out the underlying conceptual differences between kirāmam and ūr through examining the way in which contextual reference to the terms affected their use, and (2) to discover whether the boundary line is essential to an ūr map, and more significant, whether a boundary is essential for an ūr, I conducted the following experiment.

I gave map drawers of all three types one of the following two instructions. Instruction (1) was "show the kirāma ellai first, and then the ūr ellai." Instruction (2) was, show me the ūr ellai first, and then the kirāma ellai. The following results were obtained.

Type One (Kirāmam Maps)

Those informants who were given instruction number one reacted with surprise or irritation when I asked them to show me the kirāma ellai. A frequent response was, "Why, there it is. I've already drawn it." Or they would simply try to emphasize the sharply delineated boundary line by marking the names of the villages whose territory begins on the other side of the line. When asked to show me the ūr ellai, however, they evidenced no irritation, indicating that the question was not, as in the case of the kirāmam ellai, redundant. Further, instead of pointing to the linear boundary or the villages bordering Kalappūr, they began to mark the important shrines along the border. Most began with the shrine to the sentinel deity, Karuppu, who guards the southernmost border of the village where the cremation and burial grounds are located. They would also draw in the points of entry of major roads, the stream, and so on. In short, their concern with the boundary of an ūr was with the vulnerable points along its border and not with the boundary line as such and how it legally separated the land belonging to Kalappūr from the land belonging to the neighboring villages.

When another group of type-one map drawers was presented with instruction number two, which asked first for the ūr ellai instead of the kirāmam ellai, the same difference in emphasis was noted. Yet because the boundary line was already drawn on these kirāmam maps, it was not possible to determine whether the shrines and intersecting roads were just given as additional information about an ūr ellai or whether the line itself as a boundary was irrelevant for an ūr.

Type Two (Ūr Maps with Boundary Lines)

When these map drawers were given instruction number one, which called first for a delineation of the kirāmam ellai, they did not react with irritation, as had type-one informants. Rather, they would simply run their fingers along the boundary line and say, "This is it." When asked to show me the ūr ellai, they hastened to point to the shrine of Karuppu if it happened to be on the map already, or if it had not been marked, they hurried to rectify the omission, as if it was inexcusable of them to have forgotten such an important landmark. They would then point to the intersecting roads, other shrines, and so on. When instruction number two was given to a separate sample of map drawers the emphasis in their responses was again the same, indicating that whatever the order in which the terms were introduced in a discussion, the terms had distinct separate meanings. As in the responses of type-one informants, however, it was impossible to determine unequivocally whether the boundary line was really essential to the ūr map. To get at this point more directly, I provided the same instructions to type-three informants.

Type Three (Ūr Maps Without Boundary Lines)

When given instruction number one, type-three informants would respond as did type-one and type-two informants. When given instruction number two, though (that is, to indicate the ūr boundary when no linear boundary then existed on the map), only one of the twelve informants drew a circumscribing line. All the others pointed to the shrines (and so on) along the periphery of the village. The person who did draw a boundary line did so, I believe, because he had already marked all the relevant points along the ūr ellai and had discussed them at great length; he therefore had no reason to believe that I would ask him a question for which he had already given an answer. Hence, he must have assumed that what I wanted him to show me was what he had left out, that is, the kirāmam ellai, which—again understandably from his point of view—I had merely called an ūr ellai because of its apparent identity to the semantico-referential meaning of the term *kirāmam ellai*.

It is clear from this experiment that *kirāmam* and *ūr* have different cultural meanings despite the fact that they can both refer to the same territorial unit, the village. Kirāmams are legally defined spatial units with boundary lines of an exact and clearly demarcated nature. The ūr, as a village, is a spatial unit with the focus on the center of the village and with a vulnerable "frontier" (Embree 1977) or a periphery through which foreign substances from beyond the village enter (in the form of ghosts from the cremation grounds, visitors and intruders via the roads, and deities via the stream).[7] The sentinel deities, of which Karuppu is the most important, are stationed along this frontier at these vulnerable points in order to protect villagers from harmful invaders. Karuppu is said to make an extra-long pause during his nightly rounds along the frontier of the village at the points where roads enter the village in order to see whether strangers are entering the village. Some villagers tell me that even Kalappūrans crossing these points after midnight are open to attack by Karuppu.

The ūr has a boundary, which was depicted by a line by some villagers, but this boundary is not the legislated boundary of the kirāmam. The boundary line as such was not central even to those who drew it (i.e., they never pointed to the line but rather to the shrines and so forth along the border). The majority of ūr map drawers were of type three, who drew no boundary line, and the type-two map drawers were predominantly high school boys who evidenced considerable confusion over how to go about

[7]Māriamman from Palghaṭ in Kerala is believed to enter the village annually via the stream in the form of a floating lime.

drawing an ūr map. My guess is that their familiarity with maps in atlases through their study of geography tended to predispose them to favor beginning with an outline or boundary line. Quite frequently I found students relabeling my use of the expressions *ūr paṭam* and kirāmappaṭam as "maps" in such statements as "I don't draw good maps, sir." Or if the one to whom the original request was made seemed to hesitate with incomprehension, a second boy would translate my request with a clarifying statement, such as, "He wants you to draw a map of Kalappūr." In short, they already had preconceived the notion that what I really wanted them to do was to draw a map, such as the ones they had encountered in geography class, which were, of course, of tēcams and kirāmams, and not of nāṭus and ūrs.

Given the contextual confusions introduced by the experiment itself, I would suggest that an ūr does not have, in Tamil cultural terms, a clearly delineated boundary line, as does the kirāmam, and that in the correct drawing of an ūr map, the ūr ellai is depicted most accurately by the shrines and intersecting roads that mark the vulnerable points along the village frontier.

I believe the discovery that an ūr, the culturally more significant and indigenous concept of territory, does not have a boundary sheds a new beam of light on the continuing explorations into the issue of regionalism in India. Over a decade ago Bernard S. Cohn (1966) cogently suggested that a region may find its defining feature in a "symbol pool." His suggestion and insight merit commendation in that the notion of a symbol pool with metaphoric persuasion as well as empirical promise urged scholars on regionalism to turn away from the notion of boundaries to that of the centers of regions. A decade later the search for boundaries as one of the defining features of regions continues against all signs indicating the futility of such a search. Subbarayalu (1973), David Sopher (1977), and Ainslee Embree (1977) in their own ways have shown that the boundary concept is not an indigenous concept, even if it is a modern one. Embree's choice of *frontier* to describe a region's edges or periphery over the fixed boundary is closer to the indigenous territorial concepts, but he does not take up Cohn's suggestion either to direct his search inward, away from the boundary—even if it is but a fuzzy one and called by another name, that is, frontier. In directing one's quest inward, as I shall do in the case of my study of ūr, one discovers entities that go even beyond Cohn's "symbols." What is discovered is the very "substance" of a territory, that is, the soil substance of an ūr, and further, how this substance mixes with the bodily substance of the human inhabitants of the ūr.[8]

Ūr-Person Relationship

The villager's concern is not only with what substances enter the ūr and affect its inhabitants but with the effect of these alien substances on the substance of the ūr itself. Concern with the effect on the quality of the soil substance of the ūr is understandable given Tamil beliefs that the soil substance is ultimately mixed with the bodily substance of the ūr's inhabitants. Such ūr-person substance exchanges are frequently referred to by villagers in informal conversations, such as the one I had one afternoon with Rangasamy Piḷḷai.

Rangasamy Piḷḷai (henceforth R) had just read in the newspapers that there had been a military coup in Bangladesh and that Mujibu Rahman and most of his kinsmen had been murdered by members of the new regime.

R (to anthropologist): Have you seen this meaninglessness [aṭṭakācam]? Wouldn't it have been enough to have

[8]See Ronald Inden (1976: 59–61) for another account of the influence of territory on personal substance.

murdered one or two persons? He has wiped out the whole lot, family, wife, children—all.

R's wife: It is the food they eat. What do you expect will happen to the brain [mūḷai] if all one eats is beef and beef fat?

R: Oh, come off it. After all, the white man, too, eats beef. Will he ever commit such a meaningless crime? Tell me?

Then R went on to relate an incident during the British raj in India in which freedom fighters had caused the derailment of a passenger train. The saboteurs were caught. All the survivors and many of the villagers who were at the site of the accident were ready to beat the culprits right then and there. But the British authorities arrested and imprisoned the offenders until they had a fair trial. This, R thought, was the fairness (*nērmaiyum niyāyamum*) that the British had and the Indians lacked, in spite of the fact that the British ate beef. He continued.

R: All this talk about one getting the *putti* of an elephant gone mad by eating beef is so much lies. If you ask me why these people commit such meaningless crimes, I blame this soil. This nāṭu. This ūr. That is, the soil of India, Burma, Sri Lanka, Bangladesh, and Pakistan is soaked [saturated] with the putti of meaningless tragedy and injustice. *Not just its putti, its very kuṇam is such.* [my emphasis]

Inta māṭṭeracci tinratāla matiyāna putti varumnu colluratellām poi. Ivan yēn inta mātiri aṭṭakāsam paṇṇurānnu kēṭṭīnkanna inta maṇṇu tān kāraṇam. Inta nāṭu, atāvatu, intiyā, barmā, cilōn, vankāḷatēsam, pākistān maṇla aṭṭakāsamum aniyāya puttiyum ūrippōi keṭakkutu. Putti ennanka, kuṇamē appaṭinka.

On another occasion I was to encounter a similar reference to an ūr affecting its inhabitants; in this case, it was my wife and myself.

It was a humid evening in March when we came to know that our servant girl had struck up an affair with a young man who ran one of the local shops. Not wishing to complicate our already complicated fieldwork, we packed the girl off to her own village and home two hundred miles away.

The following day our neighbor, whose nosiness was surpassed only by that of the two anthropologists, wished to know from me why I had fired the girl. I told him that she was fired because she performed her duties quite unsatisfactorily. He probed for specifics. I gave him a few: "She leaves food stuck on the dishes"; "she doesn't sweep the house well"; "she burned my wife's blouses while ironing them and said that bats had chewed on them"; and so forth. He asked for more. "She doesn't get along with the cook."

"Specifics, please." I listed a few more. It didn't make sense. A few more questions. Anthropologist skirts them. Unsatisfied and unimpressed, he finally exclaimed, "in only six months the putti of this soil has infected you. . . . There is yet a vestige of stammering. Give it six months more and untruth will flow like water" ("Ennanka āru mācattila inta maṇṇu putti tottiricci, . . . innum konccam tikkal irukku. Innum āru mācam pōkaṭṭum poi taṇṇi pōla ōṭunka").

Such a transformative relationship between ūr and person is certainly worthy of closer analysis.

When a person thinks of traveling to a new ūr (whether a new village or a new country), his first thought is to try to discover if one of his people (which could mean one of his countrymen, his fellow villager, or preferably a fellow caste member or kinsman) has successfully settled there. This attempt to locate one's own people in a new ūr is not motivated by any desire to establish ties of friendship or even acquaintance with the people. Rather, it is based on the assumption that if the new ūr is compatible with one of one's own, there is a good chance that it will also be compatible with oneself. Of course, the more similar the bodily substance of the person in the new ūr is to one's own substance, the surer the indication of ūr compatibility. Therefore, it is best to locate at least a fellow caste member if not a close kinsman in the new ūr. To illustrate the seriousness of this search for compatibility, let me relate a discussion I had with a young ANV by the name of Devadas.

Devadas was a young man of about thirty when I met him. He was born in Sri Lanka and had returned to India with his family when he was twenty-four years old. On their return his father embarked upon a business venture with his "Indian" parallel cousin[9] and invested all his savings in this enterprise. The business ended in disaster. The cousin, however, emerged from the ruins richer than he had been before. Devadas's father lost everything. The experience was so traumatic for the father that he speedily slid into premature senility, leaving the responsibility of overseeing the family and its affairs to Devadas. The father's financial fiasco and his uncle's schemes that precipitated the fiasco made such an impression on Devadas, however, that he vowed never to have any dealings with his fellow ANVs. He went so far as to attend services at a Seventh Day Adventist Church and threatened to marry off his sister to a friend of his of the Naiḍu jāti.

During the early part of our stay in Kalappūr, an opportunity opened up for Devadas to go to Pondicherry to learn the operation of a coconut-fiber factory. The friend who had arranged for this program was a non-ANV of Tiruchy who introduced Devadas to several of his good non-ANV friends in Pondicherry and told him that he could board with any one of these friends, and that he should certainly go to them for support, help, and friendship whenever the need arose.

After Devadas gave me a rundown on all the details, including the nature of his friend's friends and the available hospitality, he said, "I wonder if there are any of our people (meaning ANVs) in Pondicherry." I asked him whether he

[9]Classificatory brother.

wanted to know this in order to avoid his fellow ANVs. He told me that, indeed, such knowledge would serve such a purpose, but beyond that, he wanted to know whether an ANV could get along in that ūr; or more exactly, whether that ūr would be compatible with an ANV ("Veḷḷāḷanukku anda ūr ottuvarumānkra kēḷvi tān irukku").

Two days later I met him, and he seemed pleased. I asked him if he was going to Pondicherry. He answered in the affirmative and immediately proceeded to tell me with almost a sigh of relief that he had located a fellow ANV in the outskirts of Pondicherry; what was more, he told me that this ANV was a kinsman—his father's brother's (the same "uncle" who swindled Devadas's father) wife's sister's husband. At first I thought that Devadas's pleasure at locating this kinsman resulted from his discovery that by the complex dynamics of interfamilial rivalry Devadas's father's brother happened to be the common enemy of both this newfound kinsman and himself, even though this kinsman was more proximally related to his father's brother than to his father. Further inquiry established that this was not the case and that, on the contrary, there was considerable intercourse betwen the Pondicherry kinsman and Devadas's father's brother. Finally I asked Devadas if he intended to visit this kinsman when he got to Pondicherry. Devadas bristled with indignation at the very idea. "That son of a harlot is not worthy of my stepping on his porch . . . , and if he sets foot at my door, I shall shoot him!" I asked him what reason he had to be pleased in knowing that another ANV lived in Pondicherry. He said, "One of us is making a living there, what is there to keep me from making it there, too?" ("Nammalla oruttan anta ūrla poḷaikkirāntānē nammalum poḷaikkiratukkenna?").

Before we can discover just what it is in the mixing of ūr and person substances that makes for compatibility, we must first learn something about how the exchange itself occurs. Let us for the sake of clarity deal with a particular kind of ūr, namely the ūr as a village.

According to Mayilraj (an ANV), a person absorbs the nature of the soil (i.e., the soil's putti—defined later) by eating the food grown in village fields and by drinking the water that springs from the soil into village wells. According to Devaraj, another ANV, residence in the village alone is sufficient. I asked him whether he meant that by associating with the people of this ūr, I will gradually acquire their ways. He replied:

> That is also true, but what I am saying is different. Assume that there isn't a soul in this ūr. And assume that each night, every night, you place your bed in the center of the ūr and sleep in it. Assume that all you do is sleep in this bed but neither drink any water nor eat any food that is of the ūr. Will you not contract the ūr putti? You certainly will. Give it six months. Lies, deceit, theft, . . . all these ūr kuṇams will join with [in] you. Your putti will go bad.
>
> atuvum vāstavantān. ānā nān colratu appaṭiyillenka. inta ūrla oru ācāmiyumillōnnu vaccikenka. nīnka ovvoru rātriyum ūrla iruntu vantu ūrkāṭṭila kāṭ [cot] pōṭṭu paṭuttu tūnkurīnkannu vaccikkenka. inta ūr taṇṇiyāvatu inta ūr cāppāṭāvatu toṭāma cummā tūnkiṭṭu kāleiyila eṛuntu pōrīnkannu vaccikkenka. ūr putti tottāma irukkumā? Irukkavē irukkātu. āru mācam pōkaṭṭum. ūr poi, pittalāṭṭam, kaḷavu, ūr kuṇam attanaiyum cēntukkum. onka putti keṭṭupōkum.

An ācāri (smith) who was present during the discussion tried to clarify the point by saying (in English) that the ūr has an "effect" on its inhabitants. In his other uses of this English word, he employed it to describe the way in which the planets affected persons, as in "Saturn has a bad effect on the third child born on a Friday" or in referring to *darśan* as only having an "effect" when the deity returns your gaze ("the diety must look at you in such a way that it has an effect on you").

Thus, the ūr can have an effect on its inhabitants, just as the planets have an effect on humans and deities have an effect on their devotees. For this effect to be accomplished, there need be no ingestion of food or water.

Persons affect the substance of the ūr simply through their residence in the ūr and also through the combination of their food and water leavings, their bodily wastes, cremated and buried bodies, and so forth, all of which mingle directly with the soil of the ūr.

A few months after we had moved to Kalappūr, a drought of several years was broken, and the fields began to yield more abundantly than before. Villagers would often attribute this improvement in the crops' yield to our good effect on the soil of the ūr. They also attributed the rains to us and noted that a neighboring village had received very little rain despite its proximity to Kalappūr.

Let us turn now to an examination of the dynamics of ūr-person exchanges, particularly in light of the villager's search for compatibility.

One variable in ūr-person compatibility is the flavor (*cuvai*) of the soil (*maṇ*). According to Sivaraman, a Brahmin villager, soils can come in six different cuvais ("taste/smell" or "flavor"), namely, sour, sweet, bitter, astringent, pungent, or salty. Certain jātis can thrive only on soil of a certain cuvai. Thus, Brahmins should live on sweet soil, Kṣatriyas on astringent soil, Vaiśyas on sour soil, Śūdras on bitter soil, the gods on pungent soil, and demons on salty soil.

Since Sivaraman is a Brahmin, he claimed to know little or nothing about astringent, sour, bitter, pungent, and salty soils. But he was able to elaborate on sweet soil. According to him, sweet soil is to be found under one of two conditions: (1) the land should either be deltaic or on top of a mountain that is holy, and (2) the land must be either a boon from a deity or the gift (*inām*) of a true Kṣatriya king. Sivaraman claims that Sri Rangam, the little temple town north of Tiruchy, satisfies both these conditions. It is located in the river delta of the Kaveri and is a gift of a Cōḷa king, according to some, or the gift of Viṣṇu, according to others.

The soil that is on top of a mountain is watered by sweet rain and hence is also sweet. The soil that is in the river delta is watered by the river's sacred waters and hence is sweet. Soil that is irrigated by water from deep wells, tanks, and canals is either bitter, sour, or astringent.

Kalappūr is not deltaic, nor is it on top of a mountain. When the monsoons come, drains and ravines flow and overflow with muddy water that carries one village's waste products and dirt into the next; before the overflow can be purified by a sacred river, it seeps into the soil. Sivaraman thinks that Kalappūr's soil is bitter, Śūdra soil, and therefore unsuited to a Brahmin. "How can a Brahmin prosper eating food grown in bitter soil?" ("Prāmiṇan kacakkura maṇṇila viḷayira cātatta uṇṇā eppaṭi munnēruvā?"). This soil is seen as generous to the Śūdra, however. An ANV, according to Sivaraman, will not be a successful cultivator if he were to attempt to live off the earth in the sweet-soil town of Sri Rangam.

Another variable is the type of ūr itself. According to Periyasamy, the blacksmith, jātis that don the sacred thread (Brahmins, Ācāris, and so on) will not prosper if they live in a village with a name that ends in the suffix *-ūr,* as in Kalapp*ūr,* Mett*ūr,* and Maray*ūr.* This is so because the soil in the villages thus named belongs to or is "a part of" some other jāti ("vēra jātiyai cēnta pūmi"). Such soil, according to Periyasamy, will never be benevolent to anyone except those to whom that soil belongs or of whom the soil is a part. Thus, the soil of Kalappūr belongs to the ANVs, and therefore only they can thrive on it. Kavuṇṭās and other jātis that do not wear the sacred thread may reap some benefit from the soil, but not much. Of course, Kavuṇṭās have villages whose names end in -ūr and whose soil belongs to the Kavuṇṭās. In these villages the Kavuṇṭā jātı will thrive on the soil, whereas the ANVs and other jātis will not thrive as well. However, the relationship between the soil of such an ūr and the jātis that wear the sacred thread is one of complete incompatibility. In Periyasamy's words,

> For us [sacred thread-wearing jātis], no good can come of that soil. Our jātis are clean jātis. We do not like to eat food cooked by them. My grandfather used to tell me that to eat food cooked in the house of another jāti is like eating their leavings [*eccil*], even if it is first served to us. It is the same with the soil. It is their soil. When we eat something grown in this soil, their stomachs begin to burn with envy. "Look," they say, "he is eating from our soil." They don't even have to say it. The mere thought might occur to them. They have a right to think like that. It is their soil. But when they think such a thought, the food grown in the soil becomes their leavings. It is alright for the other jātis to eat such leavings. It will do them no harm. Such is their kuṇam. For us who wear the sacred thread, it disagrees with [or is incompatible with] our bodies [or constitution] [*namma uṭambukku ottuvarātu*]. For our jātis, the code [*kaṭṭuppātu*] is to eat with care.[10] We are incompatible with this soil. Such is our kuṇam.

Note that Periyasamy has made two different points, namely, that the soil of the ūr itself will not be benevolent to others and also that the jāti to whom the soil belongs will also not be benevolent. Their anger or envy will transform the food grown in the soil to leavings (eccil).

Periyasamy noted, however, that this is not the case in villages whose names end in suffixes other than -ūr. Examples are Olappalayam, Sirukudi, Navalpatti, and Kallukkuri. According to Periyasamy, the earth in these villages does not belong[11] to anyone in particular. The sacred thread-wearing jātis, along with all other jātis, have a right (*urimai*) to this land. "We can all use it and it will give [fruits] to each fairly in accordance to his labor." ("Namma ellāru-

[10]The word *pakkuvam*, translated here as "care," also means to keep safely, protect by concealment, make suitable by certain special operations, etc. It is, in Marriott's transactional scheme, an optimal, if not a minimally transacting strategy (Marriott 1976*a*; also see n. 6 this chap.).

[11]It must be noted that "belonging" here has nothing to do with the holding of the legal title to a plot of land. Rather, it implies a deeper, inalienable, and substantial relationship between certain persons and certain soils.

manta maṇṇa payanpaṭuttalam. Anta maṇṇu avanavan oṛaippukkētrapati palan koṭukkum.")

At this point I can only hypothesize a principle underlying the different value Periyasamy as an Ācāri ascribes to villages whose names end in an -ūr suffix, as opposed to those that end in other suffixes.

To begin, two factors need to be taken into account. First, Periyasamy is an Ācāri whose jāti is, like most of the sacred thread-wearing jātis with which he is familiar (such as the Brahmins and Paṇṭārams of Kalappūr), a transient caste that lacks attachment to a particular place or a particular soil. Second, if we return to our attempted definition of ūr, we see that we have attributed to ūr two characteristics: (1) it is person centered, and (2) it is a named territory with whose soil humans share substance and establish varying degrees of compatibility. The second part of the ūr definition thus implies that with any given ūr, different human genuses establish different degrees of substantial compatibility. Extending this, we may say that for any given person or human genus, some ūrs are more of an ūr than are other ūrs. Stated differently, we may say that a given ūr has greater "ūrness"—defined in terms of compatibility of shared substance—with respect to one jāti than it has with respect to other jātis.

Now, any ūr whose ūrness is accentuated by the addition of the suffix *-ūr* to its name seems to me to syntactically as well as semantically emphasize its ūrness vis-à-vis a given person or jāti that is known to have established a special relationship of substantial compatibility with that ūr. A relationship of compatibility thus emphasized also implies that a literally greater, more intense, and more exclusive relationship of substantial compatibility inheres between such an ūr and its indigenous or "favored" jāti than obtains in the case of an ūr where such an emphasis is absent. Because of the intensity of this special relationship, jātis that are excluded from this relationship experience the exclusion more intensely. The inherent "inhospitality" that is generated by the exclusivity of such an ūr is more sensitively felt by those jātis whose transient habits require them to continually readjust and reestablish compatible relationships of substance with new soils. Given such a style of life, it is natural for these jātis to prefer ūrs that are less exclusive, whose preexisting soil-person compatibility is not heightened by a name that emphasizes its exclusivity.

Perhaps the most important variable in ūr-person compatibility is the type of kuṇam and putti substances of both the ūr and the person. Although it may seem odd to think of soil as possessing kuṇams, one has only to refer to the creation myth cited in the Introduction to find that every kind of substance is composed of kuṇams. Kuṇam, which can roughly be glossed as "quality," is a substance that fuses the particular qualities of mind and body. For example, when villagers speak of a person as being of a stingy (*eccil tanam*) kuṇam, they mean that this kuṇam substance characterizes his mental and physical substance as a whole. Although the quality of being stingy might appear to be psychological in nature and not meaningfully applied to a person's body, to the Tamil, to whom mind and body are simply different manifestations of one substance, it is sensible to speak of a person as being composed of and suffused by a stingy kuṇam substance. The psychological ring to "stingy kuṇam" still haunts us, however, when this term is used to describe not a person (who can be stingy) but the soil of an ūr. When Tamils say that Marayur has a stingy kuṇam, they may mean three different things.

1. This is a way of saying that the residents of Marayur are stingy, but much more than this is implied.
2. They also mean that the soil of Marayur itself is of a stingy kuṇam. In this meaning of the term, the soil itself is not thought of as a person and hence cannot manifest its stingy kuṇam in the way humans do (i.e., in consciously willed acts of stinginess). The soil can, however, cause its human residents to exhibit stingy

behavior. (I will explain the mechanics of this effect below.)

3. Finally, in a context in which the soil of an ūr is spoken of as a form of the goddess Pūmātēvi, it is a "person." Therefore, when people say that Marayur is a stingy ūr, they mean quite literally that this particular form of Pūmātēvi is stingy and will be niggardly in dispensing the blessings of bountiful crops.

The above example illustrates two ways in which Tamils think of and refer to the soil of an ūr. In some contexts, an ūr is not thought of as a person. It is simply a type of substance that is less differentiated than the substance of human beings. In other contexts, however, the soil is treated as a person who interacts with villagers on a person-to-person basis (i.e., the soil as Pūmātēvi).

This dual perception of the ūr creates problems when villagers refer to the putti of the ūr. *Putti* is usually translated as "intellect" or else as dispositions manifest through the process of intellection. Insofar as putti does have considerable semantic overlap with kuṇam in that both are translatable as kinds of dispositions, the subtle difference between the two requires elaboration. This difference is to be found in the use of putti as disposition to refer to that kind of disposition that is expressed through active, decisive consciousness. Kuṇam, in contrast, is a passive quality, an inherent disposition regardless of consciousness and prior to decisive expressions of such a quality. According to most villagers, putti has its seat in the brain (mūḷai).[12] When speaking of the putti of the soil in contexts when the soil is treated as a nonperson, it seemed odd to me to talk of the intellect of a brainless form of substance. When I asked villagers whether they really meant that the soil had puṭti,

[12]A few villagers who were familiar with body-sheath theory, which holds that putti is located in the *manōmayakośam*, a formless body sheath, did not associate putti with the brain.

many answered that it is merely a figure of speech. According to this view, the kuṇam of the soil effects changes in the putti of persons. Through a conflation of cause and effect, the effect is seen as an attribute of the cause. Ponnambalam Piḷḷai attempted to illustrate this point of view by the following analogy: "We call a madman– 'one whose mind is afflicted by bile,' that is, *pittan* [from *pittam*, "bile"]. But is it correct to say that bile is mad? Madness [*pittu*] is a disposition. Because it is caused by bile, we call it pittu. But because of this we cannot say that bile is madness. All we can say is that bile has the quality of causing madness."

In the context of referring to the soil as Pūmātēvi, however, informants would reply, "Can you say that Pūmātēvi (Mother Earth) does not have putti? This soil is part of Pūmātēvi. Therefore, this soil must have putti." ("Pūmātēvikku putti illaiinu collalāmā? Inta maṇṇu Pūmātēviyaiccentatu tānē. Atanāla inta maṇṇukku puttiyuṇṭu.")

Perhaps an underlying resolution of the problem of whether or not soil has putti is that putti, like kuṇam, can exist in a nascent or primitive form in less differentiated substances, such as the soil, and express itself fully as consciously directed "intellect" only in entities differentiated enough to qualify as "persons." (To the Tamil, the archetype of person (*āḷ*) is the human being.) The issue of whether or not the soil is a person would then be separate from the issue of whether or not the soil substance has putti.

In common parlance, one can speak of an ūr or a person as having a stingy putti as well as a stingy kuṇam. At first I was confused by the apparent overlap of the two terms. However, in time I was to discover that putti refers to surface-level traits, which may change, whereas kuṇam refers to deep-level traits, which, except in extreme circumstances, remain unchanged.

This difference becomes important when we return to consider the way in which the kuṇam and putti of the ūr and the person affect one another.

The kuṇam of an ūr (i.e., of its soil) can change the putti of an inhabitant, but not his kuṇam. To illustrate this point let me relate the homely proverb given to me by Sivaraman.

> A calf that spends its time with a pig will, even as a pig does, eat feces. Here it can be said that the calf has gotten the feces-eating putti. If the calf is returned to pasture it will certainly go back to eating what is natural to it—grass. The pig, however, eats feces not only because it is its putti to do so but because of its kuṇam. You can't change that.

Another example of how the kuṇam of the soil can change a person's putti is that of the ANVs who migrated two or three generations ago to the tea plantations of Sri Lanka. According to ANVs who did not migrate, the Sri Lankan soil, or the *Cinkaḷa Nāṭu* (i.e., the Singhalese South) is believed to nourish *kēnapputti* because *kēnam* ("gullibility") is part of the soil's kuṇam. (A *kēnan*, or more commonly, a *kēnappayal* [*payal* is a derogatory term of address] is a "sucker," a gullible person who trusts anybody and everybody. A kēnan, to an ANV, is a far more despicable human being than one who swindles his own mother.) This opinion of Sri Lankan soil is based on at least three observations. First, the degree of trust with which Sri Lankans (ANVs included) interact among themselves, particularly in the informal lending of money, is seen as kēnam. Second, it is known that returnees, or repatriates who come "home" with considerable savings can be (and often are) swindled into penury by their relatives. Third, many ANVs of mediocre business acumen are observed as having made fortunes in Sri Lanka. Such an observation was best represented by Karuppiah Piḷḷai, who presented the matter like this:

> If 100 Veḷḷāḷās were to go with Rs 1,000 each to Madras or to Bombay to start a business, only one would become famous. The rest would sell oil, camphor, and areca nuts. Only one in 10,000 Veḷḷāḷās would be a success in any of the

six nāṭus [ANV country]. The remaining 9,999 would be cutting one another's throats while the successful one tells the dead men's widows to hand over their *tālis*[13] for safe-keeping in his pawnshop. If 100 Veḷḷāḷās go to Sri Lanka, 99 of them will gain wealth and fame. This is possible only because three-fourths of the Sinhalese have kēnapputti.

From these attitudes toward the effect of Sinhala soil on ANVs, several points can be gleaned.

1. ANVs are of a crafty, scheming, enterprising kuṇam (*cāmarttiyamuḷḷakkuṇam* or *tantirakkuṇam*). This kuṇam makes ANVs good businessmen. Yet in India, among their fellow ANVs, an ANV must be exceptionally scheming to be financially successful.
2. The kuṇam of the Sinhalese and of the Sinhala soil is *kēnakkuṇam* (also *kēnapputti*). ANVs who settle in Sri Lanka and interact with Sinhala soil are affected by both the kuṇam and putti of this soil. As a result, their putti changes from scheming and crafty (*tantirapputti*) to gullible (kēnapputti). The soil cannot change their kuṇam, however, although it can obscure the expression of their inner kuṇam quality. Thus, although the Sri Lankan ANVs had developed a kēnapputti, their crafty kuṇam still found some expression in their business acumen, which, while muted by their putti, was still sharper than that of the Sinhalese who are of kēnapputti and kēnakkuṇam. When, however, the Sri Lankan ANVs returned to India, their muted tantirakkuṇam was insufficient to save them from the swindling schemes of their Indian kinsmen.

Indian ANVs said they had observed that the only repatriates who managed to retain their fortunes were those who returned gradually—those who had made frequent

[13]The tāli is the gold marriage emblem tied by the husband around the wife's neck at the time of marriage.

trips to India before ultimately leaving Sri Lanka. They had spent varying periods of time in their ancestral villages not only learning the ways of their Indian kinsmen but becoming reattuned to their conṭa ūr. The effect of such trips was to change their putti of gullibility (kēnapputti) into a putti of enterprise (*cāmartiyapputti*) if not of craft (tantirapputi), thereby making putti concordant with their kuṇam of enterprise or craft (tantirakkuṇam or *cāmartiyakkuṇam*). The only other repatriates who fared well were those who settled outside ANV territory and therefore did not have to compete with the scheming *-cum-*enterprising putti of the Indian ANVs.

Yet another example of the kuṇam of the soil affecting the putti of persons is that of the non-ANV jātis that reside in Kalappūr. Their putti, like that of the ANVs who went to Sri Lanka, was changed by the soil of Kalappūr. Thus, by their own admission, Periyasamy and Sivaraman say they have acquired the tantirapputti of Kalappūr, although they say their kuṇam has not been changed. "And for this reason," Periyasamy was to tell me, "we know all the tricks of the ANVs, but we cannot beat them. This putti is part of their kuṇam. It is not so with us." ("Itanāla veḷḷāḷanuṭaya 'trix' attanayum terinccunkūṭa nammalāla avana munta muṭiyātunka. Avanukku atu kuṇattōṭa cēnta putti. Namakkō appaṭiyilla.")

Thus far I have given examples of the way in which the soil of an ūr changes the putti of its residents. The putti and kuṇam of the residents, however, can also change the substance of the soil.

Villagers rarely spoke of residents altering the putti of the soil, but temporary and surface-level changes in an ūr were discussed, as in the case of our favorable impact on Kalappūr. The kuṇam of the soil, like the kuṇam of a person, is relatively fixed and unchanging. Yet in rare instances, the kuṇam of the soil can be changed. What follows is a brief and often-related history of the ANVs, which focuses in particular on their migration to Kalappūr and on the ritual sleight of hand that they employed to oust the resident Toṭṭiyans and to simultaneously change the kuṇam of the soil so that it would be compatible with the kuṇam of their own jāti.

How Kalappūr and the Six Nāṭus Became the Ūr of the ANVs

The ANVs are not natives of Kalappūr in any strict sense. Four hundred years ago they lived neither on the east nor the west banks of the river Ayyar. In those days the ANVs were in Sidhambaram. They were not even called Veḷḷāḷās. They were known as Kavuṇṭās. In those northern parts of Tamil Nadu, the highest farming jātis are still called Kavuṇṭās, as in Konku Nāṭu (Beck 1972). The name Āru Naṭṭu Veḷḷāḷar was assumed only after these Kavuṇṭās from Sidhambaram had settled in the six (Āru) Nāṭus on either side of the Ayyar River in the present-day districts of Tiruchy and Nāmakkal. They called themselves Veḷḷāḷars to distinguish themselves from the local goat-herding Kavuṇṭās.

In the latter days of their stay in Sidhambaram, this kingdom was ruled by a king who was a Moslem. (Some say he was a Nāyak, other say he was a Mysorian—"in any event," according to one informant, "his jāti was so different from that of the ANVs that he might as well have been a Moslem.") One day the king of that ūr spotted a beautiful girl of the ANV community and desired to marry her. The king being a Moslem, the proposition was not only unacceptable but unthinkable for the ANVs.

Drastic measures had to be taken. The king's chief minister, who was an ANV, feigned compliance with the king's wishes and spent all the daylight hours conspicuously tending to every detail of the elaborate preparations that are called for in a royal wedding. In the nighttime hours, however, he organized his people and planned their escape. At the midnight hour preceding the day of the wedding, the ANVs left Sidhambaram. The stealth and silence of their escape is beautifully captured in the following description handed down in the legend.

> The only living creature to see us leave was a cow at the city's southern edge. And the only sound to be heard was that of her calf nuzzling her udder for milk. [By the time the king awoke to the morning's reality, the] green vines and tendrils that had been dislodged and disturbed by the escaping pilgrims regained their grasp on the bark of forest trees and continued their ascent, and the grass that had been trodden upon by ten thousand escaping ANVs had regained its posture and sap and concealed the footprints of an anxious night.

By sundown that day the ANVs were seeking a refuge in an alien kingdom in an ūr that belonged to the Toṭṭiyans.

Now it so happened that the time when the ANVs reached the six nāṭus of the Toṭṭiyans was one of great famine. At first the Toṭṭiyans offered the fleeing ANVs one night's shelter and one meal. The following day, however, rain clouds were seen in the western skies. The Toṭṭiyans considered this a good omen brought about by the arrival of the ANVs and their own kindness and hospitality to these destitute strangers. As a result, the hospitality of a second night's shelter and a second meal was extended to the ANVs by the Toṭṭiyans.

The next day brought yet another sign. There had been a stellar configuration observed by the astrologer which foretold the death of the Toṭṭiyan Zamindār's son. This ominous constellation reversed itself on this day in what amounted to a celestial miracle. There was little doubt in the minds of the Toṭṭiyans that this, too, had something to do with the presence of the strangers. The hospitality to the ANVs was extended once again.

On the third day, moments before the departure of the ANVs, a messenger brought word that the workmen who had been digging a well for several months had finally encountered a moist rock bed. Another good omen!

An emergency meeting of Toṭṭiyan elders was called, and it was unanimously decided that three good omens in a row could mean nothing else than that the visitors could stay.

The Toṭṭiyans told the ANVs that they were free to remain in the six nāṭus and earn their upkeep by serving the Toṭṭiyans both inside the homes as well as in the fields. As a prerequisite to the incorporation of the ANVs into the six nāṭus, however, the ANVs were called upon to shave their heads, because they had such a superabundance of lice that shaving was the only recourse left to the Toṭṭiyans if living together was going to be possible. Because their heads were once thus shaven and because the ANV males continue to shave all facial hair regularly to this day, they were and still are (only as a nickname) called Moṭṭa Veḷḷāḷar, or the Bald Veḷḷāḷar.

The rain clouds that were spotted in the western skies never did bring rain. The celestial miracle seen by the astrologer turned out to be no miracle at all; or if there was a miracle, it was not in the stars but in the "miraculous" discovery on the part of an incompetent Toṭṭiyan astrologer of the method of carrying out, for the first time, the correct computation, which reversed the error of his previous faulty computation. As for the well, the moist rocks never turned into the hoped-for living spring.

However, none of these disappointments embittered the Toṭṭiyans toward the ANVs. In fact, the nonfulfillment of the omens went by unnoticed. The rains did eventually come, of course, but no sooner or later than they would have come in any event. The Zamindār's son lived to be a Zamindār himself, even though it was certainly not because the stars had changed their minds. Old wells dried up and new ones were dug. Some yielded water, others yielded none. The Toṭṭiyans, however, became dependent on the ANVs for different reasons. They had many things to learn from the ANVs. The art of agriculture was principal among these. They were also fascinated by the ANVs' ability to plan their budget and save during years of plenty for lean years. Weights and measures were introduced to the six nāṭus, as was the science of arithmetic.

Through much ingenuity and skill[14] the ANVs gradually acquired the right to own land. Within a few decades' time after their arrival in the six nāṭus, the ANVs earned the privilege of receiving *pracātam* (the god's leavings) first on every alternate year. Hardly a generation had passed before the question of to whom the six nāṭus belonged arose. The ANVs presented what seemed to be a patently ludicrous claim that the six nāṭus had been theirs since the inception of their jāti on earth. The Toṭṭiyans, quite understandably, took offense and challenged the claim. The Toṭṭiyans, however, had lost much of their political power and wealth to the ANVs by this time and so were unable to forcefully reestablish their ancestral rights to land, labor, and political support.

The only option left for the Toṭṭiyans was to take their case before the goddess Kāmācci, whose temple was located in the main ūr (now Kalappūr) of the six nāṭus. The Toṭṭiyans challenged the ANVs to light camphor on a handful of earth and to swear before the goddess that this earth was theirs. If this challenge was not met, the Toṭṭiyans warned the ANVs that they would have to pack up their belongings and leave the six nāṭus. The Toṭṭiyans were sure that they had the ANVs outwitted this time and that the

[14]Anecdotes abound that illustrate the ingenious means by which the ANVs acquired wealth, power, and prestige. Most of these may be reduced to the motif of bartering. The ignorant Toṭṭiyan is in trouble—usually of a financial nature. The ANV possesses the knowledge that will enable the ensnared Toṭṭiyan to get out of his troubles. This knowledge he will only impart at a price, however, usually in terms of one right or another. By a series of such clever bargains, the ANVs are eventually freed from all obligations of service to the Toṭṭiyāns and become their equals in every way.

ANVs would have no choice but to fail to take up the challenge rather than to swear falsely before the goddess and be instantaneously destroyed by her wrath.

The challenge was broadcast across all the six nāṭus by the town crier (Veṭṭiyan) from each of the ūrs. The ANV elders withdrew to contemplate a course of action. Much to the surprise of the Toṭṭiyans, they emerged from their meeting to announce acceptance of the challenge, saying that on the following Friday at noon, when the temple bells sounded, they would swear to their rights over the six nāṭus in the presence of the goddess while the camphor flame burned. Once the initial surprise of the Toṭṭiyans had passed, they interpreted the proclamation of the ANVs as merely a face-saving gesture, and they expected the ANVs to be gone by the time the cock crowed on that Friday morning.

The ANVs' plan was quite different. They sent a runner by night to go back to Sidhambaram and bring from there a potful of soil.

The cock crowed and the Friday dawned, but the ANVs had not left the six nāṭus. At midday, when all shadows had shrunk to the fullest, the temple bells sounded, and the elders of both Toṭṭiyan and ANV communities gathered in the temple to do *pūjā* to the goddess Kāmācci. After the pūjā was done, even though it was the turn of the ANVs to receive pracātam first, they charitably allowed the Toṭṭiyans to go first, "like any good host ought to do for a worthy guest."[15] After every villager had received pracātam, one of the ANV elders stepped into the courtyard before the goddess, lit camphor on a pot of earth, and holding the pot before Kāmācci said:

Mother of grace, mother of darkness
Mother of comforting light
I place before you and swear before you

[15]Note the ironic reversal of host-guest relationship between Toṭṭiyan and ANV expressed by this statement of the storyteller.

> that the soil in this vessel is the soil
> of your people, the soil of the ANVs ancestral home. [*jenma ūr maṇ*]

The Toṭṭiyans waited in silence to witness the goddess in her wrath smite the ANVs—if not with death, then with some terrible and shamefully visible (*veṭkakkēṭāna*) scourge; but they were disappointed and shocked to see the goddess retreat into the sanctuary with a smile on her face. Angered, ashamed, and dejected, the Toṭṭiyans packed up their belongings, gathered their cattle, women, and children, and left the land of the six nāṭus that very night, never to return to or reclaim any of it ever again.

When the last Toṭṭiyan had left, the ANVs from all six nāṭus and the sixty-three ūrs gathered to celebrate in front of the Kāmācci temple. This day of celebration fell before Sivarātri. The goddess was visibly pleased with all the festivities. The village was filled with activity. Merchants came from far and near, hawkers set up stalls by the side of the roads, sweet stalls sprang up like so many colored mini-*kōpurams* ("temple towers") at the entrance to the temple, and Ferris wheels competed with merry-go-rounds for the young and the daring. In the words of a modern-day millionaire industrialist of Madras who is an ANV himself, this historic day was described as "the day on which free enterprise was born and the ANV forefathers set down the rules for good business."

The day following Sivarātri, the pot of earth on which the "false oath" (*poi cātcci*) was made was brought before the ANV elders, and it was divided among the twenty ANV *kōttirams* and the sixty-three ūrs in which the kōttirams were scattered.

This soil was then ploughed into the fields of the ANVs and has since become a permanent constituent element of these ūrs. The amount of this soil that was ploughed into the fields of Kalappūr, however, was proportionately greater than that ploughed into any of the other villages of the ANVs. This was so because Kāmācci, who smiled on the pot of soil when the false oath was taken, lives in Kalappūr. For this reason, the ANVs of Kalappūr are believed to have a special aptitude for business as well as an above-average talent for cheating. "Therefore, you see," concluded the ANV bard who told me the story, "our ancestors changed the kuṇam of this soil. This is no ordinary feat. It only happened because Kāmācci herself smiled so strongly on the soil. Otherwise, soils don't easily change their kuṇam. The soil is like a woman. Have you ever seen a woman change her kuṇam?"

In the end, we return to the underlying concern of the Tamil for establishing a relationship of identifying compatibility with an ūr, whether by *ūr* he means a country, a state, a district, or a village. This concern with compatibility results from the belief that an ūr is an entity composed of substance that can be exchanged and mixed with the substance of human persons. Such concerns with compatibility were noticeably absent in the case of tēcam and kirāmam, which are purely political and legal definitions of territory and which, therefore, do not summon forth in the Tamil the associations and concerns relative to substance exchange.

It is the ideal of every Tamil to reside in his conta ūr—that ūr the soil substance of which is most compatible with his own bodily substance. Such compatibility can only be achieved when the kuṇam of the soil is the same as the kuṇam of one's own jāti. This ideal is not often achieved. People such as Sivaraman, the Brahmin accountant, and Periyasamy, the blacksmith, must go where they can find employment, even if this means living in an ūr that is not congenial to the substance of their jāti. Thus, Sivaraman would have prospered best on sweet soil, and both of them, according to Periyasamy, should have lived in ūrs that did not end in the suffix -ūr, since such places are unsuited to the sacred-thread-wearing jātis. Yet both Sivaraman and Periyasamy have managed to adjust themselves to their ūr, in part because the kuṇam of the soil has transformed their puttis, rendering them crafty like the ANVs, although not as accomplished. This craftiness, although adaptive, is a mixed blessing. To most non-ANVs, cheating is still considered a sin that will result in bad karmam and eventually in punishment. Thus, the Brahmin who has become a wily schemer will pay for it in karmic retribution. Such adaptive transformations of putti may have other, more immediate dysfunctional consequences relating to other areas of a villager's life, consequences that take him beyond the limits of Kalappūr and its soil.

For instance, it is widely held that non-ANVs who live in ANV villages are able to come out ahead in most transactions that they make with their kinsmen who live in non-ANV villages. There are certain Kavuṇṭā villages, for example, northeast of ANV country, that have sworn off all manner of transactions (marriage and material) with the Kavuṇṭās of Kalappūr, ever since these northeastern Kavuṇṭās were made victims of a scandalous and humiliating deception with regards to a marriage alliance seventy-five years ago. The Kalappūr Kavuṇṭās are regarded by their northeastern kinsmen as having become ruthlessly underhanded, like the ANVs, by having acquired the ANV putti. Thus, the Kalappūr Kavuṇṭās' acquisition of ANV putti was considered to have so tainted their bodily substance that the two groups of Kavuṇṭās were no longer compatible enough to permit intermarriage.

The substantial relationship that a person establishes with a certain ūr is, therefore, not at all trivial. The consequences of such a relationship can be far-reaching, affecting the very nature of social obligations and ties. When the apparently innocent and polite question "What is your ūr?" was asked of me by the villagers of Kalappūr, I had no idea that in my response there lay potentially a store of information. Moreover, when I was asked to give my conta ūr, I was being asked not merely to betray my intellectual disposition (putti) but to divulge an essential part of my nature, my kuṇam.

As I have indicated in my prefatory remarks, compatibility itself is a special though degenerate (as opposed to genuine) form or order of ultimate equilibrium, or equipoise. The principle that determines when equilibrium in its limited context of "making compatible" is attained is *cukam*. Cukam is the state of being healthy, blissful, satisfied, stable, and calm. When two entities are united or brought into close association with each other and result in cukam, these entities are said to be compatible.

There are two dimensions to cukam, one temporal, the other spatial. The questions that determine the extent of cukam are: Cukam for how long? Cukam for how many or how much? A dish of sweets may cause in a diabetic a state of salivary unrest that yearns to be appeased. Six *gulāb jāmans* (super-sweet North Indian dessert) may well appease this salivary activity. But for how long? (And, needless to say, with what further restless consequences?) Are sugar and the diabetic compatible? Not quite. An ANV who has migrated to Malaysia or Sri Lanka and finds that the relatively easy acquisition of wealth satiates the uniquely ANV need for success in business enterprises may indicate that Sri Lanka or Malaysia is compatible for him with regards to his penchant for making money. This may bring cukam to him and to his immediate family. But what of the ancestral gods he has left behind in village India? What of their cukam? And what ultimate consequences for his cukam will result from the ancestral gods' *cukaminmai* ("lack of cukam")? This is the question of compatibility to how many or to how much. In terms of an alcoholic's "individual" habits and needs, palmyra toddy may find in him an immediately compatible partner. A person is not, however, an "individual." A person includes his wife, his children, his kinsmen, his jāti fellows, and even extends to include his ancestors and ancestral deities. Herein lies the spatial extension of cukam and its derivative, compatibility.

In this chapter we have seen that ūrs have some of the same qualities and attributes that humans do and that these are substantial qualities. The corollary of this is that a qualityless substance is an impossibility in the Tamil world view. We have also encountered that enigma of Indian anthropological fieldwork: What are the limits of metaphor? When does something begin to be literal? I shall begin the following chapter by attempting to throw further light on this problem and then move on to consider the dynamics of the intersubstantial compatibility that inheres between a person and a house.

In the Introduction, I indicated that the themes and subjects in each one of the ethnographic chapters present themselves as a series of concentric enclosures. Such an organization in itself is, as has been mentioned, no more than an artifactual imposition of architectural coherence. Of greater importance in this opening ethnographic chapter, however, has been the fortuitous encounter with the way in which Tamils conceptualize the ūr as distinct from kirāmam. The ūr is not so much a discrete entity with fixed coordinates as a fluid sign with fluid thresholds. This same conceptualization will be seen to recur, like a rhyme, in each of the following chapters' subjects. And as Charles Tomlinson wrote,

> The chances of rhyme
> are like chances of meeting—
> in the finding of fortuitous, but once found, binding.
> (from "The Chances of Rhyme").

3
A House Conceived

> Our three Red Champak trees
> had done it again,
>
> had burst into flower and given Mother
> her first blinding migraine
> of the season
>
> with their street-long heavy-hung
> yellow pollen fog of a fragrance
> no wind could sift,
>
> no door could shut out from our black-
> pillared house whose walls had ears
> and eyes,
>
> scales, smells, bone-creaks, nightly
> visiting voices, and were porous
> like us.
>
> —A. K. Ramanujan (From his poem,
> "Ecology," *Poetry*, November 1981)

In the preceding chapter we noted the various ways in which persons conceive of and seek for relationships of identity or compatibility with their ūr. The same concern for compatibility is evidenced in the person-house relationship. Before we explore in greater depth the cultural dynamics of this relationship I would like to anticipate the objection that I could be overliteralizing or particularizing (in the sense of nineteenth-century particular physics) a set of concepts that were intended to be merely metaphoric.

The corollary to this objection may imply that I am denying Tamils the capacity for figurative speech and thought.

Yet I am doing neither. Metaphor and metonym, simile and irony, and conceivably all the tropes listed by Aristotle, and a few more, abound in the speech of Tamil villagers. However, what remains incontrovertibly true, as would be attested to by any researcher fluent in Tamil or Sinhala (and which I presume to be true of other South Asian languages as well), is that the line that divides the figurative from the literal is a thin and fragile one. Better yet, this dividing line may be likened to the ūr ellai encountered in the last chapter. The matter is even more basic: It comes right down to the power of words. The awareness of the illocutionary and perlocutionary forces of words is commonplace among Tamil-speaking villagers; an awareness that, for occidental linguistics, had not made its entry until 1955, when J. L. Austin delivered nine startling lectures, published seven years later in a little book entitled *How to Do Things with Words* (1962). For the Tamil, some words and some people's words *do* more things than other words and some other people's words, in the sense of having actual effects on other things and persons.

Within figurative speech itself, Tamil favors metonym over metaphor and synecdoche over metonym. Following Hayden White's (1973) rendition of the classical tropes, I understand metaphor to be a figure of speech in which one sign is related to another by virture of their mutual resemblance, a resemblance, however, that is predominantly determined by arbitrary convention. As I indicated in the Introduction, a metaphor is an iconic Third in which symbolic signification dominates. In metonym, a part stands for the whole by a process of reduction. When the crown is taken to stand for the kingdom, the whole is metonymically reduced to one of its most significant or symbolically condensed parts. A. K. Ramanujan, in his superb translation of fifth-century Tamil love poems, shows how the various features of the five landscapes are metonymically related to the "interior landscapes," or emotional dispositions, of the hero or heroine in a given poem. To mention a sea gull or a *kurinci* flower is to bring to mind not only the exterior landscape in which these live or grow—the seashore or the mountains—but also to describe the internal state of the hero or heroine as forlorn with separation or invigorated with the fullness of union (1967). One set of poetic images by their indexical apposition or metonymic contiguity brings to mind others by a process similar to what Gaston Bachelard called *retentissement*, or reverberation (1964). While it is clear that as in classical Tamil poetry and in contemporary village Tamil speech as well, metonymy is far more prevalent than metaphor, the bias of figurative language even tends away from metonymy and swells toward synecdoche. In metonym the signs involved in the figurative event still retain their individuality, so to speak. In synecdoche, however, as Hayden White points out, it is not merely a case where the part stands for the whole in which the whole is reduced to one of its parts, but the part selected to represent the whole suffuses the entire being of the whole that it represents. Thus, in the example "He is all heart," the person is not metonymically reduced to the organ of the heart; rather, certain conventionally attributed qualities, such as gentleness, kindness, generosity, and the like, are believed to suffuse the person's entire being.

Words in the Tamil context take a further step away from pure metaphor. In this step metonym and synecdoche are brought together, except that the former is relieved of its indexical boundedness and the latter of its symbolic conventionality. At this new crest, ridge, or apex of significance, then, an unbounded metonym and a nonsymbolic synecdoche coalesce; at this point tropology ends and literality begins. An appreciation of the prevalence in Tamil culture of this "figurative reality" vastly enhances the fieldworker's appreciation of Tamil culture as a whole, as I personally discovered. This means that at this level of apical significance, to admit literalness is not to deny figurativeness, and vice versa. And given the nature of a ridge or crest, one's judgment can as easily be tipped in the one direction as in the other. With this proviso, let me consider the main subject of this chapter, houses, which, like ūrs, are persons, and yet are also nonpersons.[1]

The word *vīṭu*, like the terms *ūr* and *nāṭu*, is defined person-centrically. What a given person refers to as his vīṭu changes according to what structure is contextually relevant to him at any given time. Thus, to a speaker, a vīṭu can mean the external structure of a house, the particular residential unit of his nuclear family in a house inhabited by a joint family, a particular room in the house inhabited by a joint family, or a particular room in the house (nāṭu vīṭu). For example, let us consider the case of the brothers Sababathy Piḷḷai and Arunasalam Piḷḷai. These two brothers and their families share the same ancestral house. Because of deep-seated enmity going back almost a decade and a half, however, they live in two separate halves of the house and avoid entering the half of the house that belongs to the other. During the early days of my acquaintance with Sababathy Piḷḷai, whenever one of the brothers' wives had occasion to refer to their vīṭu, the entire house, that is, "house number fifteen," was the referent. During this early period they either assumed that I was ignorant of their fraternal rivalry or that such knowledge on my part had little or no significance to them inasmuch as I was an outsider. In time, however, as I became a part of the village life, I noticed that the brothers and their wives referred to "our vīṭu" (*namma* vīṭu) with the unmistakable implication that the object referred to was their half of the house only, not the house as a whole. Often I was brusquely corrected for failing to make this distinction. Thus, the very meaning of the term *vīṭu* shifted according to the changing orientation of the speakers as, in time, they came to treat me as a fellow

[1]Carter, in an otherwise excellent essay on the person concept in western India, tends to indicate that Maharashtrians (unlike the Tamils) conceive of "the person" as a bounded entity with no figurative-literal extensions and intentions. Such a view, I submit, is partial and inadequate (Carter 1982).

villager who ought to pick up clues for the changing contextual usage of the term.

An extreme spatial reduction of the referential meaning of vīṭu is evidenced when the term becomes coextensive with the human body. One such reduction is encountered in a regional version of the *Cilappatikāram*. In this variant of the epic, the virtuous Kannaki, having realized that her husband has been unjustly put to death by the king of Madurai, sets forth from her house in the direction of the royal city to demand justice. The poet portrays the heroine departing from her own house, walking down the road, and turning back to look upon the abode she has just left behind. She wails:

> Oh life that has left that house
> won't you leave *this* house too?
>
> Ammanai [anta vīṭṭai] viṭṭu ēkeina uyirē
> Immanai [inta vīṭṭai] viṭṭu ēkāyō.

In the first line of the above couplet, "life" is synecdochically subsumed or conjoined with her departed lord, and "that house" refers to the physical structure of their home. In the second line she laments that life has not left "*this* house," referring to her body.

This poem not only illustrates the range and flexibility of the term *vīṭu* but it anticipates house-body analogies that will become important in our later discussion.

There is much more to understanding what a vīṭu is to a Tamil than merely noting the range of structures to which the term itself can refer. A house, to a Tamil, is more than just a structure built to the specifications of the owner. It is, like all other forms of substance, in constant flux, mixing with and changing according to the substances that come in contact with it. Even as persons are concerned with controlling the substances that combine with their bodily substance, so are they concerned with what substances cross the vulnerable thresholds of their houses and combine not only with their bodily substance but with the substance of their houses. To illustrate these concerns, I will introduce you to a piece of relevant ethnography.

In interpersonal relations, Tamils feel cozy and comfortable when in crowds. Among ANVs, the tendency to cluster is even more marked than among other jātis. In ANV villages, young boys, young men, and even older men would rather sleep in a row on mats outside their houses or on some neighbor's veranda in a group than retire to the privacy of their houses. Even women, who are confined to sleeping indoors, invite neighbors and kinswomen to come sleep with them—slumber parties being nightly events. Among ANVs solitude is not sought after, not even in times of sickness. A sick person—especially a sick person—must not be left alone to suffer loneliness in addition to illness. One of the fears most often expressed by both men and women is that of being alone. The ultimate fear and humiliation is having to die alone. In the words of one informant, "We like to live together. We try to be together when we are alive. For what if the worst of karmams was to happen to us, and what if we were to die alone. Then at least we can say, let it go [*pōnā pōkutu*]; at least when I was alive I lived closely [*nerunki*] with people."

A similar preference seems to prevail with regard to houses. They are built very close to one another, contiguously, if possible. In Kalappūr, as in all ANV villages, houses tend to be clustered in the "center" of the village in an area known as the *ūrkāṭu*, which is distinguished from the fields and forests, called *kāṭu*. ANVs who have traveled with me to several Konku Veḷḷāla and Konku Kavuṇṭār villages of the Namakkal and Salem districts express a mixture of surprise and disapproval at finding houses in the middle of rice fields, removed from the clustered center of the village where the bazaar is located.

The interpersonal and interhouse organization of space is not merely mutual structural replication. Rather, the ANVs' fear of solitude is believed to be shared by their houses. I was to discover this very interesting fact from my landlord, Poraviyar Piḷḷai (hereafter PP).

PP represents by ANV standards a pioneer, a "rugged individualist" of sorts. One might even call him an eccentric who ventured into new and unknown territory quite alone. This is how it happened.

Before 1959 PP was a poor man who lived in a house with a thatched roof thrown over mud walls, which enclosed three rooms with cow-dung floors and a floor area of four hundred square feet. In this house he lived with his wife, their six children, and his insane sister. Between 1959 and 1960, with the help of his sons, he acquired considerable wealth. It became clear to PP that he had become too wealthy for four hundred square feet of floor space. However, he was crowded in by neighbors who would neither sell nor move to allow him to realize his desire for lateral expansion.

It so happened that during this constrained period of his monetarily burgeoning existence, plans to build a hospital north of the village's center were being made. PP made the decision to move out of his territorial trap to become a neighbor of the proposed hospital. His fellow ANV villagers clearly considered his behavior to be eccentric, as did his wife. But PP had other plans; he was not going to move out alone. He would build a new village around himself, perhaps a hamlet to start with and ultimately a village, of which he would be the founder. Therefore, in addition to building himself a concrete house southeast of the hospital, he built several mud huts and extracted the promises of some poor families of Mutturājā, Ācāri, and Cakkiḷian jātis that they would move with him. He also succeeded in convincing his wealthy Malaysian cousin (MBS) to build himself a "status symbol"[2] in his natal village next to PP's new house. (This house was to subsequently become the anthropologists' residence.)

[2]ANV villages, especially Kalappūr, are liberally dotted with large houses built by absentee or expatriate landlords as "status symbols"—the term being one of the English expressions completely incorporated into ANV vocabulary—by which they would be remembered. Thus they would be assured that their success stories would become a part of village life, gossip, and even lore.

Initially, however, PP's Ācāri and Mutturājā clients reneged on their promises to move into their new houses. For several months, according to PP's own rendition, he spent sleepless nights, inviting every passerby to come in and chat with him. When PP ran out of visitors, he would circumambulate the exterior of his house, and with his walking stick, he would beat on empty oil drums, which he had placed solely for such a purpose at various points around the house, shouting—according to his wife, "in a very threatening, seemingly menacing but really frightened voice"—saying, "Hey who is that? Hey, you! Who is that?" ("Yārṭā atu? Yēnṭa nī! Yārṭā atu?")

When I asked him what exactly he feared, he listed in the same breath, "ghosts, snakes, and thieves" ("pēi picācu, pāmpu kīmpu, tiruṭan kiruṭan"). The grouping of ghosts, snakes, and thieves into the same entity, that is, the object of his fears, revealed something significant. What he did indeed fear was the damage that might be caused to his house and to his family by the invasion of unknown substances. This point was revealed to me most clearly when one day my Brahmin research assistant expressed a curiously different point of view.

My assistant had said that if he had the choice, he would build himself a house far removed from the crowded center of the village and that he would not invite Cakkiḷians, Parayans, and other low jātis to live in huts around his house, since a house thus located would be visited by every passerby, be he a member of a low jāti or a menstruating woman. PP immediately responded by saying that such an attitude was typical of Brahmin mentality, or *pāppāra putti*.[3] PP continued,

> There is nothing to be feared from a Parayan or a Cakkiḷian. If he touches a dead cow and touches my porch, I can easily wash it and recite a few *mantras*, and it will be alright.

[3] *Pāppān* is another name for a Brahmin, or *prāmiṇan*. In ANV country, *prāmiṇan* is the only term used when respect is intended. *Pāppān*, however, is a derogatory term.

> This kind of thing my wife does every Friday in any event. But into a lonely house [*tannicca vīṭu*], things we do not know creep in [*pukuntiṭum*]. When difficult times set in, you have to spend much money and property to hire diviners and specialists to find out whether what crept in was ghost, snake, or thief.

When I later asked my assistant if he really would prefer to live in an isolated house, he had changed his mind after PP's admonition and said that the best alternative would be to live in an *agrahāram* (Brahmin neighborhood), where he would not have to contend with low castes or intruders, such as ghosts or thieves.

Transactionally expressed, the contrast between PP, the Veḷḷāḷā, and my research assistant, the Brahmin, is an interesting one. PP, being a maximal transactor, did not fear any transaction whatsoever, provided he was sure of the result of the transaction. However, such control over the outcome of a transaction was possible only with known substances. The unknown substances over which his control was in doubt were what he feared. My Brahmin assistant, in contrast, preferred to shy away from all transactions that obviously did not contribute to the enhancement of his own substance or the substance of his house.

To return to our main story of PP, his new house, and his dream hamlet, the Ācāris and the other jātis did eventually move into their new houses, a fact that did console PP to a certain extent. The new settlement, however, proved not to have even a pale resemblance to his dream hamlet, let alone village.

During our stay in the village, PP would ramble on many a night about his loneliness in being so isolated. I had initially understood his loneliness in reference to himself, his family members, and other persons who were somewhat removed from the buzz of the village's center. One day, however, he spoke of how his house would fare after his death. He was seventy-four years old, and his wife was not much younger. He was worried that his house still did not and probably never would have *ottācai*, or "companionship." I asked him specifically if he intended it to be occupied by one of his children's families, and whether it was their isolation that concerned him. He assured me that this was not the case, since all his sons had businesses outside the village and had homes of their own, and they would never find living in Kalappūr convenient or attractive. The house, he was sure, would be inhabited by strangers. I asked him why he should worry about these strangers being alone and feeling isolated. "It is not who lives in it that I speak of, but of the house itself" ("Nān colratu vīṭṭila kuṭiyirukkiravanka patti illa inta vīttayē patti tān enakku kavalai"), he replied pensively. He continued,

> Your house and my house are alone here with no other house for company and comfort. And that is not good. Those huts [pointing to the dwellings of the Ācāris and Mutturājās] will fall during one of these monsoons, and those cowards will scurry like scared ants back to the ūrkāṭu. These houses will remain . . . alone.
>
> Onka vīṭu ottacaikku vēra vīṭukaḷillāma taniccirukku. Atu nallāyillinka pārunka. Anta kuṭicaika ētō oru maṛa kalam vantatum maṭincu viṛunturunka appa anta pōkkirip-payaluka veruṇṭu erumpuka pōla peranṭaṭiccikkittu ūr kāṭṭukku ōṭuvānuka. Inta vītuka ippatiyē irukkunka . . . tanicci.

This curious statement adds another dimension to the cultural meaning of *house*. Not only are houses, as are ūrs and persons, of substance that can be contaminated and changed by mixing with other substances (hence the concern with what kind of substance crosses the vulnerable thresholds—windows and doors—of the house and affects its own substance and that of its inhabitants) but houses are also "aware" of their vulnerability. They have personlike needs for companionship, and experience loneliness and fear when isolated.

The personlike attributes of houses complicate the search for person-house compatibility. When a villager seeks to build a house that will be compatible with his own substance, he cannot simply specify the structure of the house and thereby ensure the quality of its substance and hence its compatibility with his own substance. Rather, the house, like a child, is conceived, develops, is born, changes during a formative period, and may eventually die. In the creation of a child, no matter how much care is taken to unite partners of only compatible substance at an auspicious time and with the necessary ritual precautions, once born, the child establishes its own, unique kuṇam and develops according to its own fate ("head writing"—talai eṛuttu). The child may be unlucky for itself or for its parents, maternal uncle, and so on. Similarly, its kuṇam type may clash with that of one of its parents, and their resulting interaction may have adverse effects on parent and child. Likewise, a house, although built with the utmost care, may develop into an incompatible offspring of its owner, with a horoscope that can cause the owner's financial ruin or death and with an incompatible kuṇam substance that can, when mixed with that of the owner (through his residence in the house), harm both house and owner. Thus, when a villager begins to build a house, he does so with considerable trepidation, fully aware that what he is creating is not an inert structure over which he has absolute control but a being whose horoscope, kuṇam, and even "feelings" (houses can have evil eye, feel lonely, and so on) will intimately affect him and his family.

I turn now to a consideration of the rules and rituals that villagers utilize to try to determine, to the extent possible, the substance of a nascent house.

Selection of a Site

Before a house is begun, the site on which it is to stand ought to meet the following criteria if possible.

First of all, the site must not be occupied by any other house, be it the ruins of a former house (indexed by pieces of firewood and roof tiles) or the inhabited house of any of certain animals, such as snakes, mice, rats, and ants. These animals are believed to have permanent dwellings of their own, which are *their* houses. Therefore, building a house where these animals live is like building a house where a house already exists.

Second, the site should not contain the remains of any dead thing, be they human remains (if the spot was formerly a cremation ground) or the remains of a house that has "died" (i.e., been abandoned) and fallen into ruin. If any wood, teeth, bones, charcoal, ash, firewood, or roof tiles are seen on the site or even if scorpions or centipedes are present (they indicate the presence of wood), the site is considered unsuitable for a new house.

Third, there should not be any creatures destructive to building material and which, therefore, could cause a house to fall into ruin. Chief among these are white ants (*karaiyān*) and wood beetles (*vaṇṭu*).

Finally, there should not be any inauspicious creature that could harm the new house or its inhabitants. Thus, if a chameleon (*ōnān*) is found in the vicinity, the site is abandoned, since a chameleon is believed to be the incarnation of a cursed Brahmin; and for a Veḷḷāḷā, few things are as inauspicious as a Brahmin thus cursed.

The favorable signs of a good site are as follows:

1. The presence of an *araṇai* (a kind of garden lizard), a tree frog, or a crab is believed to establish that the soil is virgin soil (*kanni pūmi*), since these creatures are considered to be true representations if not of the wild, then of the extradomestic world. Therefore, the presence of these creatures is taken to index the absence of previous houses on the site in question.
2. The presence of earthworms is auspicious because it indexes the presence of water and most probably that of a water table, which could be tapped by a well.
3. The presence of coins, precious stones, gold, silver, shells, or grain is considered to be evidence of the existence of some buried treasure. When these objects

are seen, the question of whether or not there had been a house on the site does not even arise. The prospect of finding a buried treasure is sufficient in itself for the proposed house to be declared auspicious. Shells hold out hope for the possible presence of pearls. Grain is also treated as treasure.

4. Toads, gecko lizards, and spiders present an interesting variation. When these creatures are present, they are not taken to index the presence of a previous habitation but instead are believed to arrive ahead of humans and to wait in expectation of an auspicious house to be built. They constitute the "advance party" of the animal kingdom. In the words of one informant, this advance party arrives early, "so that it may welcome the new owners and builders." They foreshadow human life and activity.

Vāstu Puruṣa Pūjā

Once the building site has been inspected and declared auspicious on all counts, the ācāri may either proceed directly to place the corner post or cornerstone, or else he may perform the Vāstu Puruṣa *pūjā*. Kalappūrans were quite ignorant about who Vāstu Puruṣa is. For some it is a deity; for others it is merely a name of what is essentially a rite of divination, and an optional one at that. What is divined by the ritual is how the future house will affect the health and productivity of its owners, specifically, their fertility and their financial fortunes.

In order to perform the Vāstu Puruṣa pūjā, the ācāri digs a square hole one and one half feet on a side. Part of the fresh earth is returned to the hole, and with it a conical mound is formed in the center of the hole. Three copper vessels of water are poured into the hole by a *sumankali* (a woman who is married, has children, and whose husband is alive). When the water has been thus poured, and as it flows around the conical mound of earth that represents

Vāstu Puruṣa, a flower is dropped into the hole by the ācāri.[4] The ācāri waits for the flower to circle the mound clockwise three times. Or rather, the flower must keep the Vāstu Puruṣa to its right as it makes its rounds (see Das 1974). If the current of water stops before the third round is made, the ācāri may help it to move along by creating a current with his right hand. After the flower has made its third round and becomes stationary, its position in relation to the eight cardinal directions is noted.

Five of the eight cardinal points are called *puṣpa mankala ticaikaḷ* (*puṣpam*—"flower"; *mankalam*—"auspicious") and are auspicious for the flower. For example, if the flower stops in the corner of Kupēran (north) or Varuṇan (west), wealth and an abundance of healthy offspring are forecast. If, however, the flower stops in the three directions that are inauspicious (*puṣpa amankala ticaikaḷ*), which are the corners of Yaman (south), Agni (southeast), and Vāyu (northwest), loss of wealth, illness, and infertility are predicted.

The ritual's concern with fertility and productivity is borne out not only in the interpretation of the flower's position but in the sexual symbolism of the conical mound in a base of water (similar to the *lingam/yōni* symbolism in Śaivite temples), and more particularly, in the sexual associations connected with the flowers themselves. Tamil literature, old and new, is replete with the use of flowers in themes relating to love, sex, and marriage—more often than not in the trite symbolism of a honeybee hovering over a flower or lighting on it. The metaphor of blooming or flowering is also directly linked to a maiden's attaining of puberty, which is called *pūttal*, or "flowering," from the root *pū*, which means flower. It is noteworthy that when a girl attains puberty, the time and her location vis-à-vis the eight cardinal directions at that moment are believed to predict her future potential for bearing healthy children. Significantly, the five cardinal directions that are auspicious

[4]In some instances, several flowers are dropped, and a more complex formula is employed.

for the Vāstu Puruṣa flower are also auspicious for the fertility of the "flowering" girl.

Following the logic of the associations of fertility with certain cardinal directions, one would think that these directions would also be auspicious for sexual intercourse. Of the five directions, the western and northern quarters are the recommended ones. The eastern and northeastern quarters may be used for sexual intercourse, provided that they do not happen to be the ones in which the shrine room is located. The fifth, that is, the southwest, corner is, however, inauspicious and calls for a special explanation. Its inauspiciousness for human conception cannot be explained by the possible presence of a pūja room, for a pūja room is never located in the southwest corner of a house. Furthermore, since this corner is auspicious for the Vāstu Puruṣa flower and for the girl attaining puberty, it should by implication be auspicious for all activities metaphorically represented by the flower, particularly love and conception. Why, then, is this corner in fact deemed inauspicious for conception, and why should knowledgeable elders advise the young to avoid this corner whenever the desire for sexual intercourse is experienced? I asked this question of Subramania Ācāri. He was not sure of the answer but promised to present the question to his *guru*. Subsequently he returned with the answer the guru had given him. It was contained in this couplet.

> To conceive a child where a house is conceived
> is to invite evil.
>
> il tarikkum tikkil
> karu tarittal tītu.

Conception

It is clear from the above couplet that to a Tamil, houses are conceived and that this conception is likened to the conception of a human being. I turn then to a more detailed examination of the beliefs and rituals relevant to the proper conception of a house.

A house is conceived when the corner post or cornerstone is placed into a hole dug in the southwest corner of the site. The sexual analogies of this union become apparent in a ritual of divination that immediately precedes the moment of conception. This ritual begins with the digging of the hole. When the hole has been dug to the required depth and its walls and floor cleaned and smoothed, the soil that was dug out of the hole is returned to it. If the soil returned in this manner results in a mound rather than in a level platform or a depression, the structure to be built is believed to bring health, wealth, and progeny. When I asked my informants for the rationale underlying this particular interpretation, one informant said that "this mound of earth must be like a pregnant woman's stomach" ("inta maṇkuvial karpamuḷḷa peṇṇin vayiru pōla irrukkanum"). It must be noted, however, that when I asked him whether this implied, as I thought it naturally did, that the hole was like the womb, my informant vehemently denied such a possibility.

If the earth forms a mound auspicious for the future of the house's inhabitants and is perhaps also symbolic of the favorable development of the house itself, the ritual for the planting of the corner post or cornerstone is begun. The earth is dug out, and grains of paddy are thrown in, followed by a cup of milk. The post is placed in the hole by the ācāri, who adjusts it so that it fits in snugly. The owner-to-be or a distinguished guest or friend throws the first shovel of wet cement or mud into the hole. The ācāri proceeds to complete the filling of the hole, and the owner concludes the ritual by pouring more milk over the filled hole.

As has been mentioned, the ritual of planting the corner post is no longer the planting of a corner post as such but is, more commonly, the laying of a cornerstone. Thus, it must be remembered that all that I have described as taking place during the planting of the corner post may be translated as taking place during the laying of the cornerstone. While the sexual imagery generated by the laying of the cornerstone in a hole in the earth may not be obvious to some, including the villager who described the earth-filled hole as shaped like the stomach of a pregnant woman, I have yet to see a spherical, rhomboid, or a haphazardly jagged stone used for this purpose. Stated differently, I found it difficult not to note a distinct resemblance between the shape of the cornerstone and the phallus.

When one considers the planting of the *mūlaikkāl* ("corner post") and the textual rules that govern this act, the homology between human conception in the act of intercourse and the conception of a house becomes even more explicit than in the laying of the foundation stone.

The tree from which the mūlaikkāl is made must be a male tree (*āṇ maram*). There are thirteen recommended trees. These are areca nut (*kamuku maram*), mango (*mā maram*), palmyra (*panai*), kino (*vēnkai*), bamboo (*mūngil*), tamarind (*puli*), ebony (*karunkāli*), coconut (*tennai*), sandalwood (*cantanam*), teak (*tẹkku*), gray ebony (*acca*), Michelia champac (*canbakam*), and Indian coral tree (*palācu*). To this list, iron is added. Of these thirteen trees, bamboo and tamarind (and iron) are for the Brahmin, teak for merchants, and kino for Śūdras. The remaining seven trees may be used by anyone.

There is, however, a complication to the above prescription. In order that a given tree may be planted as a mūlaikkāl, the soil in which it is to be planted must be suited (have *poruttam*, or "compatibility") to that tree. Hence, soils, too are classified, in this case, according to the scheme of six flavors[5] (see chapter 1).

The art of choosing the type of soil suited for a given kind of tree is called *maṇ poruttam pārttal*. It is widely known that in India the earth is thought of as female (Pūmātēvi—see also de Bary 1958: 8–9), and also that the agricultural act of

[5]The flavors of the soil may be detected indirectly by the flavor of the crop that grows in the soil. For example, sweet crops will grow well in sweet soil, even as chili peppers will thrive in pungent soil.

sowing the seed is analogized to sexual intercourse (Ramanujan 1967: 59). If in maṇ poruttam pārttal, the male post is matched with the female soil for compatibility, this is clearly analogous to the matching of bride and groom in the similarly named poruttam pārttal in marriage. A further resemblance is seen in the concern shown over the dimension of the hole for the corner post: it must be suited to the size and kind (the species of tree) of the post. One of the eight mandatory poruttams taken into account when horoscopes are compared before marriage is that of yōni poruttam. This poruttam determines whether a given male's penis is suited to penetrate the vagina (yōni) of the female in question. Thus, the marriage between a man who has a rat penis with a girl who has an elephant vagina is hardly considered ideal. However, size is not the only factor implied here. It may not even be the main variable. As will be shown in the next chapter, the exchange of sexual fluids in intercourse also calls for qualitative compatibility or appropriateness. Some puritanical neo-Hindus deny that the matching of yōni and lingam has anything whatsoever to do with either the size of the sexual organs or sexual fluids. More important, they say that the variously classified yōnis and lingams are only metaphors for the kuṇam types of the partners in general. Most informants agree, however, that kuṇam is to be narrowly understood as pertaining to dispositions, proclivities, and so on, as they relate to sexual appetities in particular.

Much that has been said here of the textual prescriptions for how trees, soils, and hole dimensions should be matched has no practical value for Subramania Ācāri or the other residents of Kalappūr. Almost any tree, if it is sufficiently strong, is used as the *mūlaikkāl* on any soil, regardless of its flavor. The only tree that is exempt from this liberalization of textual prescription is the margosa, which is the female tree par excellence.

I asked Subramania Ācāri and his son why all these specific and elaborate textual rules are disregarded. At first came the expected reply: "This is *kali yuga*." I pressed my informants for further elaboration. Subramania's response was something like this.

> When God first made the soil, He clearly differentiated it according to the six flavors. Then He produced vegetables, fruit trees, and the various grain crops which He planted in whichever soil was most suited to a given plant's kuṇam. Do you think God would have planted chili peppers in sweet soil or mangos in sour soil? Then God divided man into five or six jātis and he instructed each jāti to live on a particular plot of land in which the soil's flavor was suited to the kuṇam of each jāti. But man, then as now, started having intercourse with the wife of the man across the stream, behind this hill, or on the other side of the road, regardless of her jāti. The children were mixed [*kalappu*]. Man also started transplanting vegetables and fruit trees and crops in soils that were not suited to their kuṇams. And you know what happens when you plant a sweet plant in sour soil. The sweet fruit will become slightly sour, and the sour soil will become slightly sweet. That is why today there is no soil which is *cutta inippu* ["purely sweet"], *cutta kacappu* ["purely bitter"], or *cutta uraippu* ["purely pungent"]. Likewise, there is no mango that is free of sourness or chili pepper that is not slightly bitter. Of course, you already know that there is no such thing as a pure Brahmin, a pure Vel̤l̤āl̤ā or a pure Parayan. All are mixed—expecially these Vel̤l̤āl̤ās!

To return to the ritual, the ācāri and the house owner are the main participants in the conception of the house. Although no informant specifically said that the ācāri, in planting the post, plays the role of the male, and the owner, in throwing in the earth to hold the pole snugly, plays the role of the female, both men feel that they are responsible for the conception of the house and that they thereafter stand in a special relationship to it. For this reason, they are extremely careful to prepare adequately for their part in the generation of the house. The relationship that the ācāri and house owner have to the process of conceiving the house finds its parallel in the relationship that holds between the Maharastrian god Khandoba as the conjoined god of the sun and the moon. In the case of Khandoba, as cited in Stanley's accounts (1977: 42–43), elaborate preparatory rituals precede his act of uniting the sun and moon in marriage. He is the one who joins the substance of the sun and moon and who controls the fluid-power that is released when these substances combine. Similarly, the ācāri and house owner prepare themselves to aid in the union of pole and earth by storing up *śakti* and in making themselves pure (*cuttam*) so that they can bear (*tānkalām*) the power released in the conjunction-*cum*-conception. It is implied that some of this power may be absorbed or received by the ācāri. Failure to prepare oneself adequately will adversely affect the ācāri and owner, as well as the house, which is intimately tied to the owner and which is blighted at conception itself. The two men prepare themselves by following the rules of their particular jātis for building up *śakti* and purifying bodily substance. For example, the ācāri, a member of a minimally transacting jāti, prepares by reducing even further his normal minimal transactions. When one looks at the rules the ācāri is expected to observe alongside a list of the consequences that result from violating these rules, his minimally transacting strategy becomes clear (table 2).

TABLE 2

Rule	*Consequence if violated*
Observe a strict vegetarian diet.	The house will be vulnerable to the entry of ghosts and evil spirits.
Avoid eating in others' houses and in public places.	The hearth of the house will burn its cinder to dead ash and cause the inhabitants of the house to go begging for food.
Avoid bodily contact with members of lower jātis.	Goods in the house will gradually disappear.
Abstain from sexual intercourse.	The house will be eaten by white ants.
Favor Ganapathy in daily pūjas.	The women of the house will find no respite from menstruation [m̃atakkaṛippinintru ōivu perā].

All five items in the code for conduct prescribe a "cooling" deportment.[6] The proscribed meat diet is a "hot" one and contrasts with the prescribed "cool" vegetarian diet. Eating in others' houses and public places involves one in the receiving of food, a maximal (if not a pessimal) transaction.[7] (Maximal transactions are usually associated by the villager with heat, since the combination of substances of a widely different type, such as the bodily substances of different castes, requires and produces heat.) Furthermore, in public places, one is exposed to strangers and dogs—underfed and starving beggars included—whose gaze or evil eye is capable of causing the food being ingested to spoil (*keṭṭupōkum*) and result in a "burning stomach" and illness. Spoilage results from the heat of the evil eye.

The avoidance of body contact with lower castes has as its aim, once again, avoidance of receiving unwanted substances of which these castes may be the carriers. For example, the Cakkiḷian may be a carrier of some residue of the leather and feces he handles; the Parayan may transmit some residue of leather and dead cows with which he comes in contact; the washerman is a carrier of the impurities of soiled clothes; and the barber can transmit the undesirable substances of hair and nail parings. These impure (*acuttamāna*) substances are considered to be hot in nature.

Sexual intercourse is a heating transaction from which the ācāri is urged to abstain. One of the causes ascribed to congenital deformities, the birth of weaklings and impotent sons, is the careless expenditure of valuable semen by the father prior to the moment of conception, so that when he joined his wife in order to conceive, he was in short supply of the potent substance. The case most often cited by Kalappūrans in order to illustrate this point is that of Kandasamy, a Mutturājā, whose impotence and ill health are common

[6]Chapter 4 gives a detailed account of the cultural categories of hot and cold. According to these categories, cold, the nontransacting, and stasis are related phenomena, whereas hot, the highly transacting, and the changing-moving constitute a cluster of similar cultural ideas that often imply one another.

[7]For a review of the four transactional strategies, see chapter 2, note 6.

knowledge. Kandasamy's infirmities are attributed to his father's prolific promiscuity. Villagers describe the father as the kind of man who would raise his vēṣṭi (lower garment) even if he were to see only a woman's damp sāri on the washerman's stone.

It is not clear whether the ācāri's own powerful semen is believed to be necessary, in some way, for the conception of a healthy house.

The favored worship of Ganapathy, the elephant-headed god, is not unrelated. In marriage rituals, before the bridegroom ties the symbolic tāli ("marriage emblem") around his bride's neck, he must be taken in procession to a Vināyakar (another name for Ganapathy) temple. The pūjā to Vināyakar is one of the most important rites of the bridegroom in the marriage ritual. Vināyakar is both the god of chastity par excellence in the Śaivite pantheon as well as the god of fertility. By doing pūjā to Vināyakar, the bridegroom does, according to village accounts, three things:

1. He thanks Vināyakar for helping him preserve his chastity to the extent that it was preserved.
2. He asks and receives some of the sexual potency (śakti) of this bachelor god, which he then may use toward fruitful ends in his own marriage. (The blessing of the groom by Vināyakar is considered by Tamils to be essential to the fertility of the marriage.)
3. He prays for the removal of all obstacles in the way of a successful marriage, since Vināyakar, or Ganapathy, is also believed to be the remover of obstacles and the opener of doors.

Ganapathy, by symbolizing both fertility and celibacy, recommends to the mind not indefinite celibacy but controlled sexual transactions so that potential fertility may be enhanced rather than threatened.[8]

[8]See Leach (1962: 80–102) for an alternative interpretation of Ganapathy—seen as an impotent god.

The list of consequences of violating the prescribed code emphasizes infirmities and disorders that involve maximal or pessimal heating types of transactions—the types that Ācāris abhor.

A meat diet (particularly the consumption of pork) results in the invasion of the house by the heating substance of ghosts and evil spirits. Eating in others' houses and in public places results in poverty for the inhabitants and the forced pessimal transaction of begging—a fate that minimally transacting Ācāris dread. Contact with lower castes, which in itself is a type of maximal transaction, results in uncontrolled maximal transaction of yet another kind, where one's own belongings disappear from the house and are combined indiscriminately with the substance of others. Sexual indulgence is punished by the destruction of the house by white ants. White ants eat away the beams and woodwork of a house, not only weakening the structure but also leaving behind a leprous appearance. Here, too, the punishment may be seen as befitting the crime. *Karaiyāṉ* ("white ants") is etymologically derived from *karai* ("stain, blemish, defect, impurity, rust"). A piece of wood wasted by white ants has the blemished appearance of a man's skin wasted by leprosy (*kuṣṭam*). Furthermore, leprosy is a wasting disease thought to be caused by indiscriminate and promiscuous sexual liaisons, which are exactly what the Ācāri has been warned against. For in the context of planting the mūlaikkāl, any sexual relationship, even with one's own wife, is indiscriminate, if not promiscuous.

Finally, failure to favor Vināyakar, the god of fertility, in one's daily pūjās results in infertility for the women of the house. For the Ācāris, the absence of "respite from menstruation" is another way of describing infertility. Moreover, it is a phrase that emphasizes the undesirable prolongation of a heat-producing flow of maximally combinable bodily substance (menstrual blood). Once again, the Ācāri's bias against heating transactions, which are also often maximal transactions, is reflected in the consequence of violating the prescribed code.

To illustrate the variation in preparation rules, let me give the example of an ANV house owner. ANVs, as a maximally transacting jāti, favor preparations that maximize their already maximally transacting strategy. Hence, they are enjoined to celebrate, to throw a feast, to feed the poor, and give gifts, if possible. A celebration maximizes the opportunities for transactions of various sorts. Not only are hot mutton and liquor consumed and food generously given as charity to members of untouchable and lower castes (the giver thereby opening himself to possible exchanges of substance) but the feast is also used as an occasion for the negotiation of various other transactions with visiting fellow ANVs and friends. These transactions range from buying and selling houses, land, and goods to proposing marriage alliances.

The consequence for the ANV of violating this code for preparation for the conception of the house is described in the following saying:

> The shortcomings of an unblest house are: an absence of gold and land, a cow with no milk, milk with no calf to drink it, no boons to receive or gifts to give, no issue and no joy.
>
> Ayōkkiya vīṭṭin kuraikal: ponninmai, pūmiyinmai, pacukkuppālinmai, pālukku kantrinmai, varaminmai, tarmaminmai, cicuvinmai, ānantaminmai.

These consequences emphasize the ANV fear of being unable to transact maximally, both in terms of being able to give (*tarmaminmai*) and to receive (*varaminmai*). They fear that they, as owners of the house, will be afflicted by poverty, particularly by a lack of land and gold. Land is especially important to the ANVs since they are a farming caste, and gold has traditionally been their currency in bartering. The importance of gold to ANVs is illustrated in the folk history that recounts the exploits of Theveraya Piḷḷai, a caste hero who acquired his considerable wealth by gambling with Naika chieftains using pure gold chips and by bartering with local peasants in villages all along the Kaveri River with gold ingots for wet land. He conspicuously displayed his riches by paying his servants and giving alms in the form of gold nuggets.[9]

ANVs also fear being unable to receive, as for example, in being unable to benefit from the milk of a healthy cow which is also fertile and can give them calves. On the whole, then, what ANVs fear is not so much that their homes will be afflicted by hot undesirable states (the Ācāri fear) but that they will be afflicted by cold undesirable states; be they cold poverty, cold milkless and calfless cows, cold infertility, and even the coldness resulting from an absence of sexual pleasure. In Kalappūr there are several houses that are said to be without *ānantam* ("pleasure," particularly sexual pleasure). In these houses, the men and women are known to go outside the house in search of sexual pleasure and to become involved in shameful extramarital and premarital affairs.

Building of the House

Once the ācāri and house owner have "conceived" the house, the building begins. From this point onward, from all outward appearances, a building is seen to rise with very

[9]The Ācāris' cultural disposition toward gold is markedly different. Granted, they too, like the ANVs and everybody else, realize the economic value of gold, but the tales and legends that tell of the rise and fall, the triumphs and trials, and blessings and curses of many a famous Ācāri of the distant past are invariably related not to the market value of gold but to gold as an element whose purity (unadulterated state) and impurity (alloyed state) have destroyed as many heroes as they have created. Not only does the ability to tell pure from impure gold hold thematic popularity in Ācāri folklore but the knowledge of alchemy is the mark of a true hero. Alchemy enables the Ācāri hero, through repeated processes of distillation and separation, to obtain the purest gold. Thus, while gold provides the ANV a means for engaging in maximal transactions, for the Ācāri, gold presents another medium to which he relates with minimally transacting concerns, that is, with an interest in the internal transformations of pure essences, or unalloyed states.

little fanfare, its rate of growth apparently determined by such practical and mundane factors as the size of the structure, the availability of funds, material, labor, and so on. If the development of the structure is supervised by an informed ācāri, however, several rules are carefully followed. The more skilled the ācāri and the more orthodox the owner, the greater are the number of rules of house building observed. Minimally, though, even under the guidance of the least-informed ācāri, or even in the absence of an ācāri, at least four rules of construction are followed.

First, steps are taken to ward off the evil eye. Least elaborately, this involves the planting of four scarecrows in the four cardinal directions. Some ācāris and owners will insist on eight. A Moslem gentleman, while building himself a house in one of the suburbs of Tiruchy, posted but one scarecrow over the front door of his house. He explained this action of his to me by saying that he did not believe in "all this superstitious stuff" and therefore, "simply planted only one of those chaps." It is worthy of note that the solitary scarecrow was placed in the direction of the front door (*vācal*) of the house. Even when either four or eight scarecrows are used, the one that is planted in front of the house tends to be bigger and more elaborately decorated than its fellows. This is so because the front door is considered to be the most vulnerable orifice of the house, through which evil influences, including the evil eye of passersby, might enter. It is of no mean significance that the word for door, *vācal*, is related to *vāyil* ("gate, door, opening") and *vāi* ("mouth"). In the human body, the mouth is certainly the most vulnerable orifice, through which not only food substances enter but also evil spirits and the spirits of dead persons. Conversely, when an evil spirit is exorcised, it is believed to leave the body through the mouth, usually accompanied by a huge yawn of the possessed.

Second, windows, like doors, are vulnerable, even as eyes and ears, like the mouth, are vulnerable to the entry of extraneous elements, such as the spirits of the dead. For this reason, care is taken to locate the front door and front windows of a house so that they do not face the south or the southwest, unless there are other houses across the street to "break the vision." The south and southwest are considered to be the cardinal directions in which the dead are either cremated or buried, where unliberated and restless spirits of the dead sojourn, and where Yaman, the god of death, resides. A door or a window that opens in that direction is nothing short of an open invitation to enter.

Third, during the construction of the house, care is taken not to violate the rule of incompletion. This rule is based on a division of the construction into three major states.

1. *Stāna cutti ceital*: Literally, this means to clean the building site. In smaller houses where concrete foundations are omitted, the mere cleaning, that is, sweeping and leveling of the floor, is called stāna cutti ceital. When a foundation is laid, then the laying of the foundation is considered to be the stāna cutti ceital.
2. *Manaikkōlutal* or *cuvar ētrutal*: These translate as, "encircling of the house" or "raising of the wall," respectively.
3. *Kūrai ētral*: The laying of the roof.

According to the "rule of incompletion," no stage should be completed before the next stage begins. Thus, when the foundation is laid, at least one little stone in some corner should be allowed to remain loose or improperly placed until the construction of the wall begins, after which the builder may return to make snug and cement the loose stone and perfect the foundation. The same goes for the wall. A portion of the wall must remain incomplete until work on the roof begins. Finally, when the roof is constructed, it is made of an odd number of beams, odd numbers being considered incomplete. Thus, the house as a whole remains an "incomplete" structure.

Failure to observe the rule of incompletion may result in either the stunted development of the house or in its untimely destruction. For example, when Periyasamy, an ācāri, accompanied me on my visits to various villages and towns in the Tiruchy district, he would always have an eye open for those building sites where a concrete or stone foundation had been laid at one time but now remained only as a relic of a failed attempt at house building with an overgrowth of weeds beginning to conceal the failure. He would anxiously lead me to the spot to diagnose the cause and invariably concluded that the rule of incompletion had been violated by some uneducated or unscrupulous ācāri[10] who completed the laying of the foundation before starting to work on the wall.

What is the significance of this rule of incompletion? There are two possible explanations—the first more apparent, the second less so, but both equally valid.

Let us first consider the more apparent one. According to this explanation, incompleteness is like a blemish or fault. A blemished or defective object does not invite the evil eye to itself as readily as an unblemished one would. Or stated differently, a blemish or defect draws the eye (and the evil eye also) to itself and thereby spares the unblemished part of that object from being affected by the evil eye. For this reason, informants say, infants wear a huge black spot (*poṭṭu*) on their foreheads as a blemish that acts as a magnet to evil eyes. For the same reason, even after a house is constructed, a black smear of paint or a scarecrow is allowed to remain over the front door or on the roof.

Citizens of Kalappūr generally prefer structures with facades that are neither conspicuous or flamboyant. For this reason, the house in which the anthropologist lived, built grandly and painted garishly by its rich Malaysian owner,

[10]Failure of an ācāri to fulfill his dharma by following the proper codes of house construction harms the ācāri as well as the house owner.

was considered to be highly vulnerable to the evil eye. As has been mentioned, this house, like many others built by wealthy absentee landlords, is what the villagers call a "status symbol." If one chooses to live in one of these showy structures, one must be very powerful and authoritative, like a deity or a king (teivam pōlāvatu aracan pōlāvatu tiraṇum atikāramum nerancirukkanum), and also be very geṇerous, like a good and noble monarch. Only then can one ward off the evil eye of ogling visitors and passersby. The fact that the first informant who let me in on this cultural tidbit capped it by asking me for a loan of Rs 500 does in no way diminish its value or its veracity. I did reconfirm the existence of this belief with several of my rich ANV friends, with whom I had no reason to fear or expect a request for a loan.

Sounderam Piḷḷai, Kalappūr's most renowned skinflint, who also happens to live in a status symbol that he built for himself fifteen years ago while he was in Sri Lanka, has not bothered to remove the hideous scarecrow that he had planted in front of his house at the time of its construction to ward off evil spirits. Periodically, he prunes, preens, and meticulously redecorates his scarecrow in an attempt to preserve its youth. I asked him once why he nurtured this goblin (*pūtam*) with such great care rather than replacing it, as is customary, with a less imposing object, such as a piece of iron or a blotch of paint. He proceeded to tell me in some detail of how Kalappūr is filled with cursed beggars (nācankeṭṭa piccakkārappayaluka neranca ūr) who come several times a day to his doorstep for one thing or another, and that if he were to give in one day to compassion and offer something to one of these mendicants, within an hour the rate of beggars visiting him would increase tenfold and within a week he would be wiped out of all his possessions. Therefore, "on principle," he gives to none, "except on festive occasions when it is but proper to give." He believes that because of his principles (*koḷkai*), he is highly susceptible to the evil eye of these "bottomless tubs" or "insatiable cisterns" (*aṭankā aṇṭākkaḷ*). For this reason he must keep his goblin, as he phrases it in English, "in tip-top shape."

The rule of incompletion has another, quite different aspect to it. In addition to rendering the house "blemished" and therefore less subject to the evil eye, the very fact that the house is incomplete holds out the hope for future structural additions. The house as a structure is thus not static and complete; rather, it is forever in a state of becoming, developing, and expanding.

Perhaps it would help clarify this point, if we consider the rule of incompletion at work in the principles underlying the giving of gifts. Among Tamils, as among most South Asians, a gift of cash is generally given in an odd-numbered sum. The odd number is both a blemish (in the same way that an odd number of beams in a roof marks a blemished and incomplete house), and an auspicious promise of an attempt on the part of the giver to complete the gift at some later time. Thus, the message behind the gift is: "This is but a faulty gift, an incomplete one; kindly accept it." In acknowledging its blemish and incompleteness, the giver, rather than saying, "this is it," says, "there is more to come"—the gift itself is a promise of a future gift to rectify the imperfect gift. Just as a "completed" cash gift (that is, an even-numbered sum) is smug in its declaration that it cannot and need not be bettered, so a completed house declares itself to have no reason for improvement.

The rule of incompletion implies process, movement, change, transformation, and the perennial potential for continuity. Above all, it marks the flux of life. It is antistasis, antiterminal, anticonclusive, and antideath. The rule of incompletion, I believe, helps Hindu culture to be the transactional culture that it is (Marriott 1976*a*: 109), because transactions, whether enacted or only potentially prefigured by the rule of incompletion, stress the inevitability of continuing interpersonal and intrapersonal exchange as functions of a world view that holds that things must move and be transformed, since such is the nature—if not the meaning—of existence.

The fourth common rule associated with the construction of a house has to do with its relationship to the temple. There are two components to this relationship. The first involves the house's orientation vis-à-vis the main temple of the ūr. The second is related to the height of the house with respect to the height of the *kōpuram* ("gateway tower") of the temple. Let us look at these two components in that order.

During the performance of a pūjā, devotees do not stand directly in front of the sanctum sanctorum (*cannitānam*) facing the deity squarely. Instead, the devotees stand in rows on either side, leaving an empty aisle directly ahead of the deity, and they look at the deity by turning sideways over their shoulders. This mode of receiving *darśan*[11] from the deity is usually explained as the most convenient arrangement for enabling the greatest number of people to obtain darśan with the least amount of visual obstruction. In practical terms, however, one can think of other ways of standing before the deity in order to achieve the same purpose with less inconvenience. An alternative and more persuasive explanation is also offered. According to this explanation, the power (śakti) of the deity taken directly from a frontal view would be too much for a devotee to bear.

This point was driven home with dramatic clarity on a Friday afternoon during the weekly pūjā at the Kāmācci temple in Kalappūr. The pūcāri had finished the pūjā to Kāmācci and had gone to the shrine of Periaṇṇā Swāmi, which is a separate structure in the same temple compound. Most worshippers, as usual, shuffled away behind the pūcāri. However Andiya Piḷḷai stayed behind with his gaze fixed on Kāmācci. Suddenly he moved directly in front of the goddess and began to half rant and half plead with her.

[11]This concept is complex. A rough gloss would be "vision," implying that the devotee receives a blessing from the deity through seeing and being seen by the deity.

> Look at me. I am not like the others. I neither stand to one side and peek at you intermittently over my shoulders and do *tōppukkaraṇams,*[12] nor do I cringe to a side, receive my holy ash and run. I look at you straight in the eye and ask you directly. Tell me. Have you done justice by me by what you did? If you wish to kill me right here and now, go ahead. I am not afraid of that. But do tell me this. If you wish to destroy me because I stand directly in front of you like this, go ahead and do so. That does not matter at all. But only tell me this. Would you say that you have treated me justly? If it is just then kill me. If not, destroy that scoundrel at the root. If you will not destroy him, then may I destroy him? Tell me. Look me straight in the eye and answer.[13]

In this incident, Andiya Piḷḷai's grievance was of such a grave nature that he was willing to risk his life by defiantly standing directly in front of the deity in order to plead for justice.

Houses, like human worshippers, must also not stand directly in front of the temple's cannitānam. The deity radiates śakti, most of which travels in a straight line in the direction of the deity's vision. This explains the characteristic layout of South Indian cities and towns, where a bare street is seen to extend, at times for several furlongs, with no buildings to obstruct the path of the deity's śakti. The deity's śakti can be beneficial, but one must not only be in the proper bodily state to receive this śakti but also may safely receive it only in controlled measures. People's homes are not always in a state that is conducive to the receiving of this śakti. Birth, death, menstruation, intercourse, and other biophysiological processes make a home unworthy and unprepared to receive a full and continuous

[12]A form of penance one does by sitting and standing alternately; holding one's ears with crossed hands.

[13]My apologies to the reader whose curiosity, like my own, must remain unsatiated. When I pursued Andiya Piḷḷai to find out the nature of his grievance, he told me to pack off to America.

supply of the deity's śakti. Some gods, especially the principal ones in the major temples of an ūr, radiate śakti that travels further than that of the minor deities, such as the *kula teivams* ("family deities") found within the home or in the garden. Also, some deities are more tolerant of unsuitable and impure states in their devotees than are others. In Kalappūr, Kāmācci is far more intolerant than Māriyamman, the reigning deity of another village temple.

In all major and in most minor temples, the power of the mai deity is partially intercepted and obstructed by the vehicle of the deity that faces the inner shrine. Thus, Nandi, the bull, by facing Śiva in his shrine, is said to absorb the śakti that radiates from the lingam and thereby make it safe for mortals who must cross the path of this radiant power.

The reader might wonder why I have not discussed the subject of the orientation of the house vis-à-vis the temple in the previous section under the general question of choosing the site for building a house. It is true that at the time of selecting a plot of land for a house, care is taken to choose one that is not directly in front of the temple deity. It is possible, however, for a temple to be built after a house has already been built or after the construction of the house has begun.

This, in fact, is the case with a row of houses in Kalappūr that happens to be directly in the path of the cannitānam of the Kāmācci temple, even though the row begins a quarter of a mile away from the cannitānam. This row of houses is believed to be the oldest settlement of the village, predating the three-hundred-year-old Kāmācci temple by another century. Ten out of twelve of these houses are noted for having a disproportionately high number of widows. The remaining two households are deeply in debt and strife ridden. It is quite obvious to all the villagers why this is so, and these houses have not changed ownership in over one hundred years, since no one will buy them. Even the local moneylenders will not accept any of these houses as collateral for the loans they give. These houses are inauspicious and will be inauspicious as long as the same orientation vis-à-vis the temple prevails.

The second relationship that obtains between a house and a temple and which is of paramount importance to the house, is height. A house must never be higher than the kōpuram of the main temple. In Kalappūr none of the houses is taller than the kōpuram. However, villagers do relate instances known to them where in some village, somewhere, someone built a house that superseded the kōpuram of the main temple in height and was consequently stricken with one form of misfortune or another. The anthropologist himself recalls a three-story house of his high school days' acquaintance in the North Sri Lankan village of Sithankeni, which, as a result of a slip in the stonemason's computation, turned out to be taller than the kōpuram of the Śiva temple. The man who owned this house had three sons, all of whom excelled in sports and studies and were quite popular in school and college. After the family moved into their new, three-story house, the eldest son died in a drowning accident, the second went insane and had to be institutionalized, and the third, a good friend of mine, suffered from a severe case of chronic eczematous dermatitis, which neither Western nor Ayurvedic medicine was able to cure. The villagers quite easily made the connection between the "arrogant" height of the house and its inhabitants' sorrows.

In summary then, when a house is built, at least four rules are followed:

1. Steps are taken to ward off evil spirits and the evil eye. This is done by erecting one or more scarecrows around the house during the construction.
2. The main door and front windows of the house are located so that they do not face an open (i.e., an uninterrupted) south or southwest direction.

3. During the construction of the house, care is taken not to violate the rule of incompletion.
4. The house should not be located directly in the path of the main cannitānam of the temple, nor should the height of the house exceed that of the kōpuram of the main temple.

Grahapravēsam—Birth of the House

Life (*uyir*) is also called breath (*mūccu*). Life, in the form of breath, enters the infant at the time of its exit from its mother's birth canal. The planetary configurations at this moment determine the child's horoscope, which provides an approximate blueprint of his or her fate. When a house is born, life enters through the life breath of the owner and his wife (or other married couple—*pankāḷis*[14] of the owner). Similarly, when the last living person abandons a house, it is said to die, even as a body dies when breath has left it.

In the case of a house, as in the case of the birth of a child, the planetary configuration at the moment of the first breath determines the horoscope of the house. Like persons (Kemper 1979) and temples (Beck 1976:216, n. 6), houses have their good and bad times and their unlucky and lucky periods. For example, Tiruvellarai is a Vaiṣṇava temple located on the trunk road that runs between Tiruchy and Turaiyur. This temple was built in the Pallava period and enjoyed much fame several hundred years ago. As one informant told me, "Tiruvellarai was as famous as Tiruppati is today." Several hundred years ago, however, the temple's horoscope entered a bad phase. This is why, although architecturally still quite majestic, there are portions of the temple that are overgrown with weeds and vines. When-

[14]Pankāḷis are kinsmen related by blood who cannot intermarry.

ever I visited Tiruvellarai with my friends from Kalappūr, I was reminded of this fact: "What a great temple, but the planetary influence [*kirakappalan*] is such that it has fallen on bad times."

Similar observations are made of houses, especially those that were once handsome and that have now fallen into disrepair or, worse still, have been abandoned. Such a house is said to have had an unfavorable horoscope (*rāci*).

It is said that there are very few reliable specialists who are able not only to cast but also to interpret the horoscope of a house. It is believed that the science of interpreting the horoscope of a house is quite different from the science of interpreting the horoscope of a person and that, for this reason, two identical horoscopes, one belonging to a house and the other to a person, will elicit very different interpretations.

The horoscope of a house, unlike that of a child, is not routinely cast. However, when a household falls on hard times, it is not unusual among the wealthier ANVs to track down a specialist and have him draw up or merely divine a horoscope for the house, either explaining the misfortune through it or else showing them how and when the house could be or will be able to transcend its miseries.

Formative Years

Houses, like ūṛs, persons, animals, and all other kinds of substances, have kuṇams that determine their nature (*tanmai*) and how they will respond to persons and things of differing kuṇam types. While some informants preferred to speak of a house's nature (tanmai or *mātiri*) or its *yōkam* ("luck") rather than to use the term *kuṇam*, most would refer to the kuṇam of a house in certain contexts. For instance, when people made statements such as, "This is good for the house" or, "Such and such is bad for the house," I would ask, for instance, "Good for the house in what way?" They would respond that "the house will have a bad [or good] effect on those who live in it." I would ask, "What exactly is it in the house that has such a good or bad effect?" They would reply by saying that it was the tanmai or kuṇam of the house. Other villagers, however, quite readily spoke of the kuṇam of the house and how it develops and is affected by the kuṇam of the house's owner.

The citizens of Kalappūr and most Tamils I have spoken to agree on two points with regard to a person's kuṇam. First, they say that a person's kuṇam attains its mature and relatively permanent state between the ages of three and twelve. Second, most (not all) informants maintain that after the age of twelve, a person's kuṇam cannot be altered. Even those who after a certain amount of contemplation do allow for the possibility of transforming a person's kuṇam in later years, do so by stressing that this may happen only under unusual circumstances. The often-cited examples are those of spiritual conversions, the paradigmatic case being that of the saint Appar (Yogi S. Bharathi 1970: 76–82). Villagers believe that women's kuṇams are even less likely to change than are men's. In this regard, it has been noted that women are not known to undergo such "drastic" conversion experiences. The women saints in Tamil literature and lore were saints because it had always been in their nature to be saints.[15] A person's kuṇam may also change under the stress of extreme and sudden crises or as a result of expensive, elaborate, and esoteric rituals. The fact that kuṇams can and do change is allowed for as an exception rather than as a rule.

A house, too, has its own period following the *graha-pravēsam*, which may be characterized as the formative period, when its kuṇam is in the process of assuming its

[15]See A. K. Ramanujan's essay, "On Woman Saints" (1982), for a well-documented defense of this thesis.

relatively permanent state. As to how long this time extends, no one is sure. Guesses range from several months to several years.

At the time of "conception," when the mūlaikkāl is planted, the influence of the planets on the kuṇam of the house is recognized. However, the planetary configuration at the time of the planting of the mūlaikkāl does not have as pervasive or as permanent an effect on the house as the position of the planets at the time of the grahapravēsam, or the "birth" of the house.

Apart from the nine planets, the single other factor that has as much or even more influence on the kuṇam formation of the house is its first inhabitant.[16] Now, the time of the planting of the mūlaikkāl in most well-planned houses is auspicious, and so is the time of the grahapravēsam, thereby giving the new house every possible chance of having an auspicious horoscope. The horoscope in itself, however, is not a final indicator of a house's kuṇam. The horoscope of the first inhabitant of the house and, most important, his kuṇam are brought into conjunction with that of the still-immature kuṇam of the new house. This conjunction, or, more exactly, this interaction, results in the kuṇam of the house changing to accommodate that of the owner. In turn, the kuṇam of the house affects the inhabitant. Given that most Tamils believe that kuṇams are fixed by twelve years of age, what does change in the inhabitant is not his kuṇam but his putti. This mutually accommodative and adjusting process continues until the house and the inhabitant have achieved a certain equilibrium, by which

[16]The first inhabitant is usually the owner. Tamils do not usually rent out a house that they plan to eventually occupy, since they desire to live in it first and establish a relationship of compatibility with the house. When the first inhabitants are a husband and wife, the assumption is that the husband and wife are of compatible horoscopes and kuṇams (that is, that they have *sakuṇam*—have similar kuṇams). Hence, when trouble arises, and the horoscope of the house is to be matched with that of the inhabitant, either the horoscope of the husband or the wife may be used.

time the kuṇam of the house is established, and the putti of the owner becomes predictably settled.

This accommodative process does not always proceed harmoniously, however. The incompatibility of inhabitant and house may be such that the inhabitant's putti may be adversely affected, and the kuṇam of the house may also be indelibly marked so that the house becomes inauspicious for almost anybody who chooses to live therein.

In Siruvur, a village south of Kalappūr, an ANV by the name of Aravandi Piḷḷai built himself a handsome (*maccu vīṭu*) house ideally located in the southern side of the village on elevated ground facing the north and the east. The cornerstone had been placed in the proper manner by a punctilious ācāri at the perfect moment decided upon by several Brahmin astrologers. The grahapravēsam was similarly carried out according to all the rules of tradition, with nine learned Brahmins, one for each of the nine planets, seated around the sacred fire (*hōma kuṇṭam*) chanting mantras.

Yet from the very first day that Aravandi and his family moved into their new house, strange things started happening to both Aravandi and the house. In the first week, the unusually calm and docile wife of Aravandi was seized by an evil spirit (*picācu*). As a result, she started beating up one of the servant girls and dashing copper vessels on the grinding stone. In the second week, a cow calved and died. The calf also died within two days' time. For no apparent reason, the southern window fell from its hinges. The well water became increasingly brackish. Human hair began to appear with great frequency in the food, and the food was seen to spoil faster than usual. Within a month, Aravandi lost huge sums of money in several projects in which he had invested. In a few more months, Aravandi himself had a stroke that made him an invalid. From this point onward, mysterious noises were heard in several of the rooms at night. One year after his stroke, Aravandi died, thirty years before the date given as the date of his death in his horoscope. The day following the sixteenth-day death ceremony (*karumāntam*), Aravandi's children and his widow left the house and moved to Sri Lanka, where they now live. Aravandi's wife was cured of her violent attacks and died many years later of old age, but the Siruvur house remains uninhabited.

For many years, during Aravandi's lifetime and even after his death, his eldest son, Selvadurai, with the help of specialists and diviners from Kalappūr, Sri Rangam, and even Kasi, attempted to uncover the cause for all the misfortune that had befallen them and their family. As the son recalls the entire episode, it appears that at first, several local diviners hastily concluded that some enemy, with the intent to harm, had planted an evil charm, or *cūniam*, under the house during the construction. All attempts to unearth such a charm proved futile. A couple of diviners did claim to have dug up the evil charm, but these claims proved to be hoaxes. In any event, some of the more reliable and renowned specialists clearly rejected the possibility of any charm having been buried under the house and advised Selvadurai to obtain a horoscope for the house.

After having obtained such a horoscope, Selvadurai claims to have gone about the problem just as a scientist would have done. He took the horoscopes of the members of his family as well as that of the house to astrologers who were perfectly ignorant of the problem regarding the house. When examined independently, the horoscopes of the family members and that of the house showed not a trace of ill luck, "except for minor trials that even the best of horoscopes is likely to have." Selvadurai returned to reexplore possibilities of error in the laying of the cornerstone, the construction or the grahapravēsam. The Ācāris and the Brahmins came out clean from the test. Finally, by means of systematic elimination, it was decided that all the misfortune had resulted from a serious incompatibility between the horoscopes of Aravandi and the house. The extreme incompatibility between Aravandi's kuṇam (as indexed in his horoscope) and the kuṇam of the house affected Aravandi's putti to such an extent that it in turn affected his heart and drove him to his death. Similarly, the house was affected by Aravandi's incompatible kuṇam and its kuṇam was irremediably altered.

Accan Pūcāri, one of the local diviners, told me that if Aravandi had but sold his house in time, or even if he had left it within six months' time, he would have saved his fortune and he would have lived according to his horoscope. Furthermore, Accan maintained, the house itself could have been successfully occupied by someone else. Sadaya Kavuṇṭān, a second diviner, disagreed.

> You may say so regarding Aravandi and his wealth. The man would have lived. The woman [his wife] would have gotten better long ago. That much I shall accept. As for the house, that's another story. If it is harmed at such a tender age, it is destroyed. That goes for any house. Take my house. It is of age [*muttal*]. Even if Yaman [the god of death] himself comes and spends a few days there, nothing will happen. It will stand like a rock. What do you think its age is? Seventy-five years old.
>
> Aravaṇṭi Piḷḷai avan cottayumpatti appaṭi collunka. manucan polacciruppān. pomapalayum eppōvē koṇamākiyiruppā. atu nān ottuokkirēn. Vīṭu atu vēra kata. inta paruvattila cēdom naṭantā atu nācamaipōkum. Ita nān enta vīṭṭukkumē colluvēn. en vīṭṭa eṭuttukkanka. atu muttal. Yamanē anka vantu reṇṭoru nāḷ ninnuṭṭu pōnalum onnum naṭakkātu. kallu mātiri nikkum. atukku ettana vayacu teriyunkalā? eṛuvattanci.

Periyasamy Ācāri believed that if only Aravandi had left the house and lived elsewhere while his family remained in the house, nothing would have happened to anyone. However, Periyasamy maintained that he should have left at least before three months had passed. Six months, he felt, was too long a time.

I asked Marimuttu Ācāri if he could unearth from his knowledge of the code book of house construction (*Manayaṭi Sāstiram*) a means for correcting a bad kuṇam in a house once the formative period is past. I suggested that perhaps such a change could be effected by moving a window or a door a few inches (a procedure used to correct certain ills). He replied by saying:

> They say that even if you change a person's *kulam* (clan, *jāti*, etc.), you cannot change his kuṇam. Can you then change the kuṇam of a house by changing a few doors and windows?
>
> Kulattaiyē māttinālum kuṇatta mātta muṭiyātunnu colluvānka. Appa oru jannalayō katavayō māttiratāla oru vīṭṭu kunatta māttalāmā?

Clearly there is consensus on the point that a house has a formative phase during which it is vulnerable to variously influenced changes. There is disagreement, however, as to how long this vulnerability lasts. On the one hand, it is believed that a house deleteriously affected in its tender age (*paruvam*) will have a bad kuṇam permanently. On the other hand, it is believed that a house that is auspicious for the first several years with its first inhabitants will remain essentially auspicious.

Given the permanency of the kuṇam of the house after the formative period and the critical nature of the impact of these kunams on the inhabitants, it is understandable that much anxiety is experienced by house owners until they know for sure that their house is compatible with themselves. Great concern is also felt by the owners of neighboring houses, which are also affected by the kuṇam of the new house. Let me illustrate this point by relating the story of the effect of Thevaraya's house on its neighbors.

While the residents of Thevaraya's house prospered, every house on which the shadow of his house fell began to gradually fall into disrepair while the inhabitants slid into debt and poverty. Almost every affected neighbor had a theory to explain this strange phenomenon. Those who were bold enough to voice their opinion against the much-loved and charitable Thevaraya told me that though Thevaraya was generous and kind on the exterior, he was a jealous and bitter man inside. "And that is why," it was said, "whichever house his house looks at, that house is ruined" ("Anta vīṭu enta vīṭṭa pātticcō anta vīṭu nācamāp-pōkum"). Others thought that the residents of the affected houses were envious of Thevaraya's success, and this envy (*porāmai*) and the resulting bitterness (*manakkacappu*) brought debt and poverty upon them. In the words of one informant, "Their suffering was brought upon them by the burning [envy] in their own stomachs" ("ivanka vaitteric-calāla uṇṭāna vētanai itu").

Most pertinent to the present thesis, however, were opinions that did not involve the residents of any of the houses but which spoke of the houses themselves, as if the houses were in some sense the responsible actors.

For example, Andiya Piḷḷai was one of Thevaraya's neighbors whose family life had taken a definite turn for the worse ever since the Thevaraya house was constructed. On the first year after the arrival of the new house, Andiya Piḷḷai lost a son. The second year he lost several thousand rupees in a business venture in timber which eventually went bankrupt. He told me that on the fourth year, his wife was struck with "laziness" (*aluppum cōmbērittanamum*). The fifth year his second daughter lost her husband. Ever since Thevaraya's house was ceremonially opened for habitation, Andiya Piḷḷai claims that his assets have consistently dwindled and his crops have annually been ruined by drought or floods. When we were in Kalappūr, a diviner was called upon to divine the cause and prescribe a cure for his ills. Thevaraya's house was singled out by the diviner as the cause. Among other things, Andiya Piḷḷai was advised to hang a scarecrow on the east side of his house so that Thevaraya's house could see it. "This will cool the evil eye of that house," said the diviner. ("Tēvarāyā vīṭu pākkiramātiri pūccāṇṭiya kiṛakkupakkamā naṭanum. Appa anta vīṭu kaṇṭiśti taṇiyum.")

I was later to ask the diviner how it was possible for a house, which can neither speak, hear, nor think, to have an evil eye and thereby cause harm to other houses near it. An eavesdropper who happened to be another affected neighbor told me that the arrival of Thevaraya's house was like the arrival of Selvaraja Piḷḷai in the village.

Now, Selvaraja Piḷḷai is the leader of one of the two major village factions. His detractors claim that prior to his return to the village in 1958, there had been neither factions nor parties and that all the villagers lived together in peace and harmony. Karuppanna Piḷḷai, who had likened the house of Thevaraya to Selvaraja Piḷḷai, maintained that Selvaraja Piḷḷai, by his very presence, disturbed the tranquillity of the village. I objected, saying that it might be true that Selvaraja Piḷḷai was an evil man who lied, stole, and cheated in his moneylending practices, but "how can we say any.such thing of a house that looks so benign?" The diviner chose to respond to my question by resorting to another analogy.

The diviner likened the arrival of Thevaraya's house to the birth of the third child on a Friday. "The child itself may be healthy, be intelligent, and have all the comforts and wealth it needs, but it is sure to bring ill luck to its parents," he said. "It is the same with this house of Thevaraya." I was acquainted with this belief abut the third child born on a Friday. However, I also knew that there were remedial rituals for this, which included the piercing of one of the child's earlobes. I asked the diviner if any comparable measure could be taken with regard to the house. The diviner said that the ritual he had performed and the scarecrow he had recommended were like the single earring prescribed for the child of ill omen. I objected to the analogy. I told him that when the third child is born on a Friday and consequently brings bad luck to its parents, he treats the child. But when a house such as Thevaraya's brings bad luck to neighboring houses, he treats the affected ones, that is, the neighboring houses, rather than the cause, Thevaraya's house. This point was debated to no good result until Marimuttu Ācāri joined the discussion. He remarked that in the case of a house whose kuṇam is already formed, there is no ritual that can alter the house's kuṇam. Therefore, the only remedy is a symptomatic one, which deals with the evil eye of the house of bad kuṇam. Such a remedy naturally features protecting the affected houses rather than attempting to change the nature of the offending house.

Houses as Persons

It has become apparent that to the Tamil villager, a house is a living being that is conceived in a sexual act, grows, is born, has a horoscope, goes through a formative period comparable to childhood, matures, and attains a stable nature (kuṇam type), interacts in predictable ways with its human occupants and with neighboring houses, and ultimately dies when it is abandoned. A house is a member of the village community. As in the analogy that likened the showy house of Thevaraya to the arrival of the village "big man," Selvaraja Piḷḷai, houses have varying degrees of importance and impact in their communities. Like Selvaraja Pillai, they can loom large and factionalize human neighbors and house neighbors alike, or like the small huts of poor villagers, they can cause very little stir.

Houses also assume the rank of the jāti of their occupants. Hence, houses, too, must observe the rules of status and propriety which govern intercaste relationships. To illustrate this point, let me relate the following incident.

Subbiya, a Kavuṇṭā, is one rung lower than the ANVs in the local caste hierarchy. When Subbiya became wealthy through some spectacularly wise agricultural investments, he decided to buy an east-facing house on the corner of Middle Street and Hospital Road. It was located on an elevated bank four or five feet above the level of the street and several ANV houses that were on the level of the street. His enterprising instinct told him to convert the newly acquired house into a tea shop. The astrologer concurred.

The building was remodeled, and the opening day was scheduled. Two days before the ceremonial opening, Kanda Piḷḷai, an ANV who lived in a west-facing house at street level across from Subbiya's house, raised objections and called a Panchayat meeting.

His first objection was that it was improper for a Kavuṇṭā house to face east (the most auspicious opening) when an ANV house directly across from it faced west.[17] Fortunately, Subbiya had an ANV ally at the meeting, who spoke up on his behalf. (This man was the village munsif to whom Subbiya had loaned Rs. 1,000.) The munsif managed to dismiss this objection on the basis that in other villages, there were east-facing Kavuṇṭā houses across from west-facing ANV houses. Others argued that the Kavuṇṭā's wealth entitled him to own a more auspicious house if he so chose.

Kanda Piḷḷai was furious at this rebuff and raised yet another objection, this one in reference to the elevation of the Kavuṇṭā house. He said,

> Tell me: Is my head and the floor of his shop to be on the same level? Must I apply the dust of his feet on my forehead? Next year he will raise his roof above the temple kōpuram.

> Collu: en talayum avan kaṭattarayum oru maṭṭamā? avan kāl tūciya nān nettiyila pūcanumā? aṭutta varuśam kaṭa kūra kōyil kōpuratta tāṇṭum.

[17]Kandapillai, for want of space to the east, had no choice but to build a west-facing house. For a Kavuṇṭā, with more money and space, to build the more auspicious east-facing house directly across from his "better," the ANV, was to rub in the ANV's lesser financial standing. It was therefore considered uppity on the part of the Kavuṇṭā.

It is not only objected that the feet of the lower-cast Kavuṇṭās are at a higher level than are the heads of the ANVs. The objection implies that the house itself, as a Kavuṇṭā house, is in an improper position vis-à-vis ANV houses. Since villagers liken the floor of a house to its feet and its roof to its head, the Kavuṇṭā house is essentially standing with its feet on the same or higher level than the head (roof) of the ANV house. Such an arrogant stance is predicted to further express itself in the Kavuṇṭā owner raising the roof (head) of his house even above the kōpuram (head) of Kāmācci, the goddess.

This argument proved so persuasive that Kanda Piḷḷai won the day, and Subbiya was ordered at great cost to lower the floor level of his shop to the level of the street.

The analogies that liken the house to the human body are extended by villagers, who refer to the front door of a house as its mouth and the windows as its eyes. This likeness was carried to its logical extreme by Swaminadan who, although considered somewhat eccentric by other villagers, felt that the house, like the human body, had to be periodically purified.

I was in the house of Swaminadan (henceforth S) when his servant boy was washing the house by alternately pouring buckets of water on the floor and sweeping it with a broom made of a bundle of coconut fronds.

S: Do they wash their homes every day in America?

A: No. But they have a machine. It sucks up the dust. They use this once a week.

S: I have seen one of those in Ceylon—in a white man's house. They call it a "vakkum."

A: That is exactly it.

S: Once a week. Yes, tell me, I hear they "go out" [defecate], too, only once a week.

A: That is not quite true. Each one goes to the bathroom according to his own need.

S: So it is not mandatory for one to go out daily?

A: No. But on the average they go out at least once a day.

S: That is not what I have heard. Do they take purgatives?

A: If they need a purgative, they will take one.

S: It is not so in our ūr. We must wash our homes every day. We must go out every day. Twice or thrice a year we must take a purgative and cleanse our stomachs. Likewise, on occasions such as Pongal, New Year, Deepavali, Sivaratri, we must give our house a "special" wash.

A: In this ūr I have not seen anyone but you wash this house daily.

S: Orthopraxy is gone! Allow ten more years. They will go out once a week, like the white man—to the lavatory [*kakūcu*]. This, too, they will build it inside their houses. They have already started doing so.

Just then, the servant boy, a recently hired one, was observed to sweep the water toward the front door.

S: You ass! Take the water that way [pointing toward a rear door]. Do you defecate through your mouth? [Aṭa karuta. Appaṭi koṇṭu pō taṇṇīya. Nī vāyāla tān kakkūcukku pōviya?]

There is yet another dimension to the personlike attributes of houses, their humanlike feelings. This is a tricky issue since, as in the example of Subbiya, his house is considered to be uppity, but this arrogance seems to be a quality of Subbiya expressed through his house and not a quality of the house itself. Similarly, in the case of Thevaraya's house, some informants said that Thevaraya's envy and bitterness resulted in the evil eye of his house. (Recall the statement, "That is why, whichever house his house looks at, that house is ruined"; here the house "looks at" other houses with an evil eye, but the envy is that of Thevaraya himself.) It appears, however, that more is implied here than a metaphoric projection of Thevaraya's nature onto the house. The underlying premise could be that Thevaraya's envious kuṇam had marked the kuṇam of the house in its formative years and that therefore, the house also had an envious kuṇam and thus an evil eye.

It is, however, possible for a house to have a nature (taṉmai and kuṇam) that is independent of that of its owner. Thus, the diviners for Andiya Piḷḷai expressed the view that it was the house itself that had an evil eye, and not Thevaraya himself. Yet the question as to what extent a house is believed to express conscious volition or to merely evidence (passively and without volition) its inner nature (kuṇam) is not clear. Some villagers tend to attribute more volition and conscious feeling to houses than do others. For instance, to PP, houses have humanlike needs for company of both human occupants and neighboring houses. When left alone, like humans they are given to fear and loneliness.

Whatever the level of volition attributed to houses, it is apparent that houses are members of the village, and their feelings, evil eye, and other attributes must be dealt with, even as the feelings and influence of human villagers must be taken into account.

Despite all the ways in which houses seem to be personlike to the villager, it should be noted that houses are not full persons in that their life is derived from their human occupants (specifically from their breath). When houses are abandoned, they die.

Much that has been said about the effort taken by an owner to establish a compatible relationship with his house can be explored in greater depth through the analysis of the case of an ANV house owner, Thevaraya, whose house has been already mentioned with respect to its evil eye.

Thevaraya was an ANV who rose from very humble beginnings to become one of the richest men in his community. The means by which he accumulated wealth, as recalled by his fellow villagers, were not very noble. Nonetheless, that is not held against him, because there is a fundamental assumption prevailing among ANVs that no one can acquire wealth through noble means. Unlike most of his wealthy fellow ANVs, however, Thevaraya became one of the most generous members of his community, and his fame for charitable giving spread beyond the six nāṭus.

Thevaraya's father's sister's son is Kasi Piḷḷai, who is several years older than Thevaraya. According to Kasi, Thevaraya's life may be divided into three phases:

1. His childhood and early youth, when he was poor and worked with Kasi in the fields.
2. His emigration to Sri Lanka, where he started life as a laborer on a tea plantation and gradually rose to become a very wealthy tea plantation owner. During this phase, his mentor was a ruthless labor leader (kankāṇi), who took kickbacks from the laborers he supervised. It is implied that Thevaraya's method of making money was the same as that of his mentor, Ekambaram Kankāṇi (hereafter referred to as EK).
3. His return to India, where he continued to make money. He eschewed his former custom of directly exploiting laborers, however, and instead reinvested his money in "helpful" ventures, such as a pawnshop and a rice mill. This also began his phase of charitable deeds. During this phase he helped many poor ANVs, especially by marrying off their daughters; he built a school and several temples.

Whether Thevaraya himself consciously saw his life in terms of three phases, I do not know. However, I do know that Kasi and Thevaraya were quite close to each other after Thevaraya's return to India, and it is more than likely that Kasi's schematization of Thevaraya's life reflected the way Thevaraya himself perceived the various stages of his life.

When Thevaraya returned to Kalappūr from Sri Lanka, he wished to build himself a two-story house in place of his former hut. He wanted the structure to be the biggest and best house in Kalappūr, a true index of his newly acquired status and wealth. While he was actively planning the construction of this house, he had a dream, the details of which were recalled for me by Thevaraya's wife and Marimuttu Ācāri (who built the house). Thevaraya's wife was able to repeat the details of her husband's dream quite vividly because not only had he related the dream to her but he was also very troubled and sick for several days after the dream. Marimuttu Ācāri recalls the dream because not only did he feature in it, but Thevaraya made him swear to secrecy when he related the dream. This made Marimuttu Ācāri go over the dream several times in his head to find out what was so special about it that would require him to be bound by such secrecy. At the time when he first related the dream to me, he felt that there was little point in preserving its secrecy, since he did not find the dream of any special significance. Later, however, he came to view the dream as a prediction of the misfortunes that were to befall Thevaraya and his family.

Thevaraya's Dream

Thevaraya's mentor, EK, initiates the construction of the proposed house by laying the cornerstone in the southwest corner of the site. Suddenly, all the guests who had been invited to watch the laying of the foundation stone leave. The only ones who remain at the building site are Marimuttu Ācāri, Kasi, EK, and Thevaraya. They decide to continue work on the construction of the house. The ācāri lays the second stone, and EK lays the third, and so on, each one laying alternate stones so that the ācāri lays the even-numbered stones and EK lays the odd-numbered ones. Kasi is seen in the dream as a small boy of about ten years of age, the way Thevaraya remembered him as a playmate in the fields. Kasi helps both the ācāri and EK by carrying baskets filled with a mixture of cement, water, and sand, which is applied between the stones to hold them together. All goes well until the builders have to begin laying the roof. The rules of the code book for house construction (*Manayaṭi Sāstiram*) are vividly displayed on a table. On the one hand, clearly seen in the code book is the rule that the last stone to be laid on the wall before work on the roof is begun must be laid by the ācāri and nobody else. Yet on the other hand, it so happens that the ācāri has been laying even-numbered stones; and if the roof were to be laid on a wall with even-numbered stones, it would entail a violation of the rule of incompletion, and the house would be inauspicious.[18] Unable to solve the dilemma, they postpone the problem of making a decision about it and continue to build the walls higher and higher. Suddenly, Kāmācci, the goddess, appears in her terrible form and stares at Thevaraya with piercing eyes. Thevaraya runs to his elder brother Kasi and finds him to be no longer the little boy helping the ācāri and EK with cement, but an old man, dressed in a sāri. Anxious and out of breath, he asks:

> Elder brother! Elder brother! What shall I do now? Kāmācci has come here to cut off my head. Break down this building! Break it down right away!

> aṇṇē! aṇṇē! nān ippa enna tān seiiratu? Kāmācci vantuṭṭā en talaya veṭṭeratukku. inta kaṭṭiṭatta oṭacciṭu! ippavē oṭacciṭu!

Kasi replies:

> How can I do that, younger brother? I have been your elder brother for seven generations [lit., "head times"]. Do you remember how we used to play the game "I am the leader [also, I am the "head"], You are the Leader?" This picture [pointing to the blueprint of the house] was drawn

[18]It should be noted that in reality, the rule of incompletion does not have anything to do with odd- and even-numbered stones. The problem as posed in the dream is a creative elaboration of the rule of the dreamwork.

in play at that time. I drew it. Do not fear. The house will bring you wealth for many years.

atu eppaṭi ceiyalām tambi? ēṛu talai muraiyā nān ōn aṇṇaṇāiyiruntirukkēn. niyāpakōm irukkā namma veḷaiyāṭina veḷaiyāṭṭu: nī talaivan nān talaivan appaṭiyinnu. appaṭi veḷaiyāṭura pōtu varanca paṭōm itu. Nān varancēn. payappaṭāta innum ettanayō varuśankaḷukku itu onakku celvākku koṇṭu cēttitum.

End of dream.

Dream Analysis

A cultural interpretation of the dream will take us somewhat beneath the manifest content. Let me consider first one level of the analysis.

Kasi's schematization of Thevaraya's life is helpful, and as has been suggested, it is highly probable that Thevaraya himself perceived his own life according to this tripartite scheme. The three phases are signified in the dream by three individuals. His boyhood is signified by Kasi, who is seen as a young lad, a playmate. His middle, Sri Lankan years of upward mobility through unethical means is signified by EK, without whose help Theveraya could neither have become "good" or charitable. Marimuttu, the ācāri, symbolizes a poor but worthy recipient of Thevaraya's charity, standing for all those poor people without whom he could never have practiced his good works of charitable giving. (Marimuttu and his family were special recipients of Thevaraya's generosity.) Kasi, in addition to signifying Thevaraya's boyhood, stands for that element of constancy and continuity from childhood to old age. In fact, Kasi, the boyhood companion, also proved to be Thevaraya's most trusted friend and confidant until Thevaraya's death in April 1976. The unscrupulous, immoral, and exploitative past as well as the reformed, moral, and benevolent present were known to Kasi, and in a sense, he helped bridge these two aspects of Thevaraya's life. Evil past and good present lay stone upon stone to build a house, with neutral Kasi helping to cement the two together.

Another level of interpretation also emerges from the dream. It is clear from the dream and from Thevaraya's stated ambitions that he wished to build the biggest and best house in all of Kalappūr, even as, in accumulating wealth and in dispensing alms, he wished to be the most famous ANV. Yet in building his house, as in building his financial empire, he gave more importance to unscrupulous methods than to an observance of his dharma, or code for conduct, with its attendant karmic consequences. This misplaced priority is symbolized by EK's usurpation of the ācāri's rightful role in laying the odd-numbered stones. The displacement of the ācāri from his central role in laying the odd-numbered stones is a thwarting not only of the dharmic codes of house construction but of the dharma of the ācāri himself, whose duty it is to observe the proper codes. Yet according to village belief, dharma cannot be set aside without causing grave karmic results. One cannot build an auspicious house or a good life if one violates one's dharma. This is symbolized by the dilemma in the construction of the walls. Thevaraya's excessive ambition and misplaced values had set into motion the construction of a grand house, as it did his financial empire, but the house-empire constructed is flawed and cannot come to a happy end. Sheer momentum carries it onward, and Thevaraya's moral weakness in postponing tearing down the structure and building again according to dharmic codes prevents any solution to the problem. In the end, Thevaraya's ambition even violates the proper respect toward the village goddess. His house dares to rear its head above that of the goddess's kōpuram. The goddess retaliates by threatening to cut off Thevaraya's head, of which the house's head is symbolic. She does this because his ambition has no limit; it is unregulated by attention to dharma. Only when Thevaraya's life is threatened does he propose to tear down the structure and begin again.

The interpretation of the rest of the dream relies heavily on five critical concepts borne by five distinct sign vehicles.

1. "*Head*": In the game called "you are the head, I am the head," the word *head* is selected for emphasis in two ways. First, its redundancy helps its conveyance through "noise," as in a Morse code or in communication theory (Cherry 1957: 277). In fact, a triple redundancy is encountered when the word *head* is used somewhat later (see no. 4 below) in the expression "seven lifetimes," which in Tamil is *talai murai*, literally, "head times." Second, the lexeme stands out because there is no such game called "you are the head, I am the head" in an Indian village, and neither Kasi nor Thevaraya recalled ever having played such a game as children.
2. "*Drawing*": In the dream Kasi claims to have "drawn a plan." "To draw" (*varai*) is used interchangeably with "to write" (*eṛutu*) in one context, namely, with respect to God (Kaṭavuḷ) writing (or drawing) man's destiny on his head. A typical sentence would be: "That is his head *writing*. Can one change what God had *drawn*?" ("Atu avan talai eṛuttu. Kaṭavuḷ varancata māttamuṭiyumā?")

   Number one and number two together add up to "head writing," which is what this part of the dream is all about.
3. "*Play*": The "drawing of the plan" is done in "play." The act of head writing performed by God is often described as one of his sports, an act of play, or *līlā*.
4. "*Seven lifetimes*": Kasi is said to have been a brother for seven generations (*ēṛu talai murai*, literally, "seven head times"). This again emphasizes the element of destiny, or karmam, carried over from one lifetime to the next.

5. *Kasi is dressed as a woman*: Fate in South Indian folklore is often called Vitiyamman[19] or Vitiyāyi, both names meaning Goddess or Mother of Fate. In the dream then, it is Kasi, as Vitiyāyi, who draws (writes) the plan (head writing) of and for his brother, Thevaraya.

The extremely troubling message of the dream was that Thevaraya had no option but to build this foreboding house, since fate had indelibly inscribed on his head that this is how it shall be. The final reassurance of Kasi is equivocal. "Do not fear," he says, "it [the house] will bring you wealth for many years." He does not say, however, "all will be well for as long as you live." "Many years" connotes finitude of a prevaricating and unsettling nature, and implies that perhaps there will come a year when all that is well will turn to ill.

After much indecision and anxiety, Thevaraya went ahead and built himself his dream house, if not the house of his dream. EK had nothing to do with it, since he had been dead for over fifteen years by this time. The ācāri had no problem with odd and even numbers or with any of the other codes of his trade. Furthermore, in keeping with Kasi's reassuring words in the dream, Thevaraya continued to prosper.

Yet during our stay in the village, first sickness and then death struck his house. He died; only months later his wife died as well. Then his granddaughter who lived in the house committed suicide. Some villagers thought that these sudden deaths had been caused by a charm hidden under some corner of the house. But those who knew of Thevaraya's dream, particularly the ācāri who built his house, thought otherwise. According to them, it was the house that had caused the deaths. The prophecy had been

[19]I am thankful to A. K. Ramanujan for making me aware of this point by relating to me a Kannada folktale in which Viti as a goddess figures centrally.

fulfilled. Although Thevaraya had had many years of success, prosperity, and fame, in the end, the flaw in his character (that is, his *adharmic* propensity), which had imprinted itself on the house (as symbolized in the flaw in the dream house), had eventually been his undoing. This flaw was his excessive ambition, symbolized in the dream by the house that kept rising higher and higher until it dared to rival even the kōpuram of the Kāmācci temple. Yet according to the dream, his success as well as his punishment were part of a fate written on his head, a fate that he was powerless to change. It was his destiny to build a house that would cause his death, and although in the dream he wished to tear it down and start again, fate, in the form of Kasi, decreed that this was not possible. Thevaraya had to live out his fate, whatever the benefits and punishments it entailed.

Conclusion

It is clear that a house is more than a mere dwelling place. A house is conceived, born, grows up, lives, and interacts very much like human beings do. To explain such a similarity merely by means of a simple theory of psychological projection, by which that which is human and animate is projected onto the inanimate house, is to miss the crucial cultural dimension that sustains a relationship. Furthermore, while structural homology between the human body and the house is culturally perceived, this in itself is not the extent of the relationship between house and inhabitant. Both the house and the inhabitants are constituted of similar substances, which they share and exchange. In tropological terms, while it is tempting to suggest that the person-house relationship is only a metaphoric one, in which resemblances are analogously perceived, it is culturally more veritable to say instead, that the person-house relationship is as a union of a "deindividuated" metonym and a "desymbolized" synecdoche, wherein some significant quality of the one inheres in the totality of the other, a quality that suffuses and constitutes the essential nature of both relata. Houses may not be persons in every last detail, but they come so close to being persons that the likeness cannot be missed.

4
Sexuality Exposed

In this brief chapter we shall consider a particular context in which Tamils might seek to achieve substantial equilibrium in their relationship with other persons. The context is congress. Much has already been written on intercaste relationships, but much elementary ethnographic work is yet to be done on Tamil theories of how male and female jātis relate, particularly when their relationship is a sexual one that involves the exchange of the highly potent transformative substance of *intiriam*.

In Kalappūr, the Brahmin accountant will tell you that the fetus is like a sprout (Tamil *taḷir*), the woman like a field (Skt. *kṣētra*), and the man like a seed (Skt. *bīja*) that is sown. This is old wisdom. Susruta said it, and Caraka said something like it. Sounderam Piḷḷai, the Kalappūran knowledgable in such matters, told me that the Tamil Siddha saint Tirumular said the same thing. In any event, this metaphor is generally accepted by most villagers (including a few women) I talked to. But the Brahmin accountant will go on to tell you that the male seed or semen is called *śukram*, and the female seed is called *ārtava*. The villagers lose interest. They prefer to view the formation of the fetus as resulting from the combination of fluids secreted by the female in her vagina (yōni) during intercourse and the fluids secreted by the male at the same time. These fluids are simply called intiriam.

The health and welfare of the fetus and of the child that is eventually born are believed to depend to a large extent on the compatibility of a couple's intiriam. Compatibility is determined by a whole range of factors: time of congress, planetary influences, location where congress occurred, jāti of male and female, diet of both partners, and so forth. In what follows we shall look at these factors in some detail and develop further the case for substantial compatibility and equilibrium that we have considered in the preceding chapters.

To learn about ārtava, śukram, *ṛtu, dhamanī,* and other Ayurvedic concepts, I might have done well at the feet of the Brahmin accountant. But I couldn't get many other villagers involved in the discourse. It was not because of any jāti barrier that this happened but because most villagers were not quite interested or for that matter convinced by the Brahmin's esoteric explanation of what happened in these quintessential events of fruitful congress. On several occasions a large group of men would gather near the *pipal* tree outside the Brahmin's house to discuss local level politics. But when the conversation turned to theories of procreation, the villagers missed the thread and lost interest.

Fortunately, in Kalappūr there happened to be an ANV named Devaraj who was not only articulate on the subject of sexual union and conception but spoke in an idiom that held the interest and involved the participation of other villagers as well. Although as a member of a maximally transacting caste, his theory favored active sexual transaction rather than minimal transactions and semen retention, his basic ideas about the nature of intiriam and how it mixes or is mismatched in intercourse and conception are similar to the theories of minimally transacting Kalappūr castes, such as the Ācāris, as well as those of the optimally transacting Brahmins.[1] Let me begin with his thoughts on the nature of intiriam. What follows is not an exhaustive study of the topic of sexual intercourse and procreation, but one man's perspective.

The sexual fluid of both males and females is called intiriam. Women have ten times as much intiriam as men; "some women have even one hundred times as much." The intiriam of a male remains qualitatively and quantitatively the same throughout life. The female's intiriam undergoes significant changes both cyclically over each month and over the course of a lifetime. For example, each month a woman's intiriam is contaminated with undistilled blood ten days after and three days before her menstrual period. Her intiriam during this time is said to be without the true essence (*arum cāram*). Quantitatively, the intiriam of the female varies from its peak period four or five years after puberty through its gradual reduction as menopause approaches. While a woman after puberty and before menopause produces quantities of intiriam vastly more than that produced by the male, ten or twelve years after menopause, the woman begins to produce the same amount of intiriam as the male. In time her production falls even below that of a male.

In healthy intercourse, four important processes take place:

1. Excess intiriam is secreted from the systems of both partners into the yōni of the female.
2. A physiologically healthy and controlled mixing of the two secretions takes place inside the yōni.
3. A portion of this mixture, which is a new substance, is reabsorbed into the bloodstream of both partners, and the blood thereby becomes enriched.

[1]For a comment on the typicality of this and other "typical" informants, see the Introduction.

4. The rest of the mixture either forms a fetus or helps nourish the fetus already formed.

I was told by Devaraj that if the male and female are compatible in terms of age and other factors so that the mixture resulting from the combination of the two intiriams is good, then the female reabsorbs four times more fluid from the common pool than does the male. Given that Devaraj is fond of quantitative thinking, I suggested to him, using a quantitative illustration, that since ordinarily females contribute at least ten times as much intiriam as the male to the common pool, if a woman were to take back but four times as much as the male from the common pool, she was in fact being shortchanged. I worded my illustrated question as follows: "If we assume that the female contributes 100 grams of her intiriam and the male, 10 grams, and if from this common pool of 110 grams, the female reabsorbs four times as much as the male, then the amount the girl takes back will be about 88 grams. This means that the girl receives less than what she gives."

Devaraj (henceforth D) agreed with my arithmetic but corrected me for confusing quantities with qualities, numbers with value, which confusion, he indicated, led me to the wrong conclusion. He illustrated his point as follows:

> There is a kind of *vellam* [sugar] made from two kinds of syrups. Both are syrups. But one comes from the coconut palm and the other from the palmyra palm. One ounce of the one syrup is mixed with two ounces of the other. I don't remember the exact proportions, but let us assume that it is two parts of coconut syrup to one part of palmyra syrup. Let us say that each part costs Rs 0.50 each. When the mixture solidifies, it is sugar. And it is sold not for Rs 1.00 [i.e., the total cost of the two syrups] but for Rs 2.00. He who gave the coconut syrup takes Rs 0.75 from the Rs 2.00., and the one who brought the palmyra syrup takes the balance. When I say the one took away more than the other, I mean

that he took Rs 1.25 and that the other took Rs 0.75. But both took more than they originally contributed. What they gave was syrup. What they got was sugar.

(I realized that I had been confusing apples and oranges; that the mixed intirium is of a different order of value than the pure intiriam.)

A. What does all this mean?

D: That both the boy and the girl take away more than they give.

A: But why does the boy take less [i.e., less than the girl takes]?

D: Because he needs less. A woman needs more śakti, and she has the first choice, so to speak, of taking as much intiriam as she needs. What is left is for the boy. When the match is good, what is left is plenty, if not just enough for the boy.

A: Why does a woman need more intiriam mix, or as you said, more *śakti*?

D: Have you seen any man who has the sheer energy to do a fraction of the work that a woman does?[2] And think of the quantity of blood she loses in childbirth and menstruation. One bout of masturbation and a man's tongue

[2]Subramaniam, a Parayan villager, had made the same point some days before quite vividly. He told me how a man's work is limited to sowing and ploughing from sunrise to sunset with a long siesta break in the afternoon. A woman's work begins two hours before the man gets up in getting the breakfast ready. Then she joins him in the field around eight or nine in the morning, runs back around eleven to get lunch ready; after lunch the man sleeps while the woman finds other housework to do and then goes to the field before the man wakes up to start weeding; with the arrival of dusk she goes in search of firewood to kindle the hearth for dinner. When the sun sets, the men gather to shoot the bull, while the women cook the night's meal. After the meal, the men either sleep or engage in idle chatter for a while longer; the women wash the pots, sweep the house, and put the children to bed. As a rule, women retire to bed several hours after the men start snoring.

hangs out. If he makes a habit of it, he goes blind. But a woman—she can do it all her life.

A female of any age can have intercourse with a male of any age and suffer no ill effects from imbalanced mixing of intiriam. However, a man must observe at least three basic rules if the mixing of intiriam is to be conducive to his good health.

First, the age difference between partners must not be greater than twelve years, and the male must always be older than the female. If this rule is violated and the male has intercourse with a female much younger than himself, he will be unable to contain (both qualitatively and quantitatively) the female's intiriam. The result is that the female's intiriam contaminates his system. In order to compensate for the female's overproduction of intiriam, which enters his body, he tries to retain ("hold back") his intiriam in an attempt to neutralize this vast quantity of female intiriam. The young girl, sensing this, retaliates by drawing with "unmatchable force" (*opptra śakti*) every drop of intiriam in his body.

D: You see, the woman thinks like this: "Ah, he is trying to cheat me." And so, like the washerman who split the washing stone in his attempt to remove a stain, she draws out more than he is able to give. What can the old man do? Let it all go out and go, "*Aiyo*! breath! breath! [gasping]."

A: You said that he tries to hold back [*aṭakki piṭi*] the intirium. Do you mean that he tries to control his ejaculation [*intiria veṭippu*, "explosion of semen"]?

D: Are you out of your mind? If he tries that game in his old age, his brains will explode. He tries to withold only after all that [stuff] has leaked out. By the time he tries to hold back, it is finished. And there is nothing that makes a woman madder than that. She goes "shloop," like that, and sucks in everything; that which will have come out in any case and a bit more. What can the old ass do but lie on his back and let his tongue hang out, like a dog.

A: You said, "his brains will explode." What do you mean?

D: I mean he will go mad in a short time.

A: What if he does not hold back but lets go of what has to go?

D: Even if he protects his brains [by doing so], it will show in his body. He might as well start thinking, "Now, how many more days do I have left?"

Devaraj considers Aristotle Onassis's death premature and for no other reason than that Jacqueline Onassis sucked off all his intiriam. Selvaraja Piḷḷai (head of the rival faction in the village) is often cited by Devaraj as similar to Aristotle Onassis. Devaraj attributes Selvaraja Piḷḷai's arthritic knee joints and swollen feet to his having intercourse with very young women. (Selvaraja Piḷḷai is not only noted for his promiscuity; his second wife is thirty-five years his junior.)

When a young boy copulates with an older woman, the process is a little different, but the result is the same: always detrimental to the male. The young boy has a lot to give both in quantity (which is also true of an older man) and in quality. It is strong stuff. The essence of youthful blood. But he cannot afford to lose all this without regaining something from his partner. A young partner has plenty of intiriam to offer and gives of it freely and willingly. "An older woman has to be parsimonious with the little she has. The old bitch always says the final word—when enough is enough—after which no young bull can extract even a drop." So here, too, the male loses intiriam without compensation.

As an example of a younger man having intercourse with an old woman, he cited the case of a classificatory grandson of his who lives in Naga Nallur. This lad was found in the cowshed with his "vēṣṭi up"[3] when he was sixteen. When they searched the haystacks there emerged the neighbor's wife, who was thirty years his senior.

> They whipped the lad and confined him to the house for a few weeks. The woman was sent back to her natal village. But that didn't solve anything for the boy. He took to visiting prostitutes—always older women—and ruined himself. The parents finally found him a wife [at twenty-nine], but he had become sickly and impotent. They did not have children for ten years, and his stupid parents started nagging the daughter-in-law for being barren until finally one day she burst out with the truth about their own son.

The second is that intercourse must not take place when the intiriam of the woman is contaminated by undistilled blood (that is, three days before her period, ten days after, ten months after conception, and ten months after a miscarriage. Miscarriage has serious effects on the composition of a woman's bloodstream in general and on her intiriam in particular. Both blood and intiriam are contaminated by impure particles that are neither pure blood nor pure intiriam. They are a sort of betwixt-and-between type; post-blood, preintiriam.

The consequence of intercourse during an impure period is disease for the male. Devaraj cited diabetes in particular. In his words, "Diabetes has nothing whatsoever to do with sugar. 'Sugar' is a euphemism for the male sex organ. While it is true that diabetes is a sick condition of the blood, it is contracted during intercourse and transmitted to the bloodstream by the penis." When women contract diabetes, he explained, it is because for some reason they cannot rid their own bodies of the impure intiriam.

The third rule is that even as a balanced and regulated diet is important to the maintenance of good health, so is a balanced and regular schedule of sexual intercourse. Ten

[3]The Tamil equivalent of the expression "pants down."

times a month is the optimum rate.[4] Total abstention is as bad for one's health as too much sex.

Devaraj believes that most, if not all Sanyasis and Sadhus who claim to have renounced sex are frauds. "They wait in lonely places to pounce on any straying woman." The same he believes is true of Brahmin temple priests: "They are a bunch of sex-starved, dangerous rogues. The dark rooms, damp halls, and dusty corners of most temples are such that it makes these priests who live there day in and day out think about and look for similar dark chambers, damp halls, and dusty corners under women's saris."

As for the attempt to control intiriam by *yōga*, he had the following to say:

> They say that by doing yōga exercises, man sends his intiriam by way of the kuṇḍalinī to his head and controls it there. I don't believe in that. Of all people, *yōgis* are for this reason the most dangerous. You can't trust them. There was a yōgi a few years ago in the village of Sattanampatti. They kicked him out when they found out that he had intercourse with a Brahmin girl ten times a day. Mind you, ten times! All this talk about the kuṇḍalinī going to the head is nonsense. Even if it does go like that, it can't be good for the head. It is better for it to have stayed right there where it was. There is but one way. Out.

Although Devaraj looked upon the yōgi and his philosophy of extreme seminal retention disparagingly, he nonetheless believed, with the minimally transacting jātis such as the Ācāris, that too much sex or unregulated sex is detrimental to the man's health. However, in Devaraj's opinion, it is extremely difficult for a man to control his intiriam. In his words,

> Ten chaste men out of five hundred males is rare. Two hundred chaste women out of a total of four hundred is

[4]Contrast ANV value of controlled seminal emission with Carstairs's obsessively retentive types (1967: 84).

> common. All this is because man can't control his intiriam. A woman is like a well. You keep drawing from it and it keeps filling. You keep filling it and it keeps its level down. It rarely overflows. The woman has learned to live a controlled life. It is her kuṇam. It comes to her naturally. Man is not like that. It is his kuṇam to go up and down [rise and fall]. It is his *intiriya kūttu* [the comedy of his intiriam].

It should be noted that villagers commonly spoke of women as having greater *kāmam* ("sexual desire") than men. Many of these villagers, however, also said that women generally controlled their *kāmam* better than did men. Yet there were a few villagers who felt that women were the aggressors in most acts of seduction and that this made it doubly hard for the male to limit his sexual activity and thus preserve his health.

The fourth rule, which applies to both males and females, is that only males and females of compatible bodily substance should have sexual intercourse. To Devaraj, one of the major forms of incompatibility is a difference in diet, which, incidentally, also correlates with a difference in caste. Food particles, he believes, float in the blood, and their essence is distilled into the intiriam. A Brahmin who is accustomed to a diet rich in ghee (the essence of all food) has ghee particles in his blood. A Harijan who eats coarse/gross (*koccaiyāna*) food has coarse food particles in his blood. When the essence of these two types of food filters into the intiriam and is mixed in intercourse, the result is an incompatible mixture that is harmful to both partners. In some cases, if the intiriams are highly incompatible, they will not mix at all (like "oil and water") hence rendering the sex act not only unproductive and harmful but infertile (the intiriam must mix for conception to occur).

There are, of course, many other criteria of substance compatibility besides diet. According to Devaraj, four of the eight important poruttams, or points of compatibility, recorded in two persons' horoscopes, namely, linga, yōni, *kuṇa*, and *nāṭi* poruttams, are in fact compatibilities of blood substance. Blood determines the type of yōni and lingam. Blood is also suffused with kuṇam substance. In the case of nāṭi poruttam, the way in which it is expressed in terms of blood substance is rather involved, connected by a series of relationships, with *nāṭi* assuming a wholly physiological meaning, its astrological meaning either lost or subsumed by the physiological one. In Devaraj's view, nāṭi is related to blood.[5]

In astrology, a nāṭi is a record of the horoscope of one's previous life (or lives). There are various centers all over India which are famous for having archives, so to speak, of horoscopes and detailed life histories of many persons' previous incarnations.

This meaning of *nāṭi*, however, plays no part in Devaraj's concept of compatibility of nāṭis. For him, *nāṭi* means pulse. According to Dr. Kannan, the other nāṭi, that is, nāṭi as a record of one's previous incarnations, flows in one's pulse, waiting to be deciphered by a competent Siddha physician. The nāṭi, or pulse, then includes—both semantically and substantially—the astrological nāṭi.

However, the search for the compatibility of two persons' pulses is not an end in itself. It is only a means of detecting the compatibility of two persons' humoral dispositions or humoral compositions.

There are three humors, namely, bile, phlegm, and wind. How does one pulse indicate anything at all about these three humors and their state in a person's system? The Siddha physician's training and skill enable him to distinguish six pulse readings, three in each wrist, instead of just one, which is all a Western physician is trained to distinguish.

The Siddha physician takes a patient's pulse by taking hold of the wrist and placing his index finger nearest the

[5]Devaraj's main source of information on this matter is Dr. Kannan, a Siddha physician whose practice in Tiruchy is patronized by several citizens of Kalappūr. For this reason I shall include herein some statements of clarification I obtained directly from Dr. Kannan himself.

base of the thumb on the inner side of the wrist; his middle finger is placed next to the index finger, and his ring finger is placed next to the middle finger. Each one of the fingers is supposed to sense a different pulse. The index finger senses the pulse that indexes the wind humor; the middle finger, the bile humor; and the ring finger senses the phlegm humor. These three pulses are supposed to pulsate at distinguishably different rates, compared, respectively, to the pace of a chicken's trot, a frog's leap, and a snake's crawling. These time intervals are called *naṭai*. This is not all, however. The naṭais merely help the physician differentiate between the three humoral pulses. Once this is done, he attempts to sense in his fingertips the differential pressures exerted by these rhythmic pulses. The pressure of the pulse is called *eṭai*. By comparing the eṭais of the three humor-indexing pulses in a wrist, the physician is able to determine which humor predominates in a person's system and which humor is inadequate or recessive.

To complicate matters, the same operation is carried out on the other wrist, thereby giving the physician six readings in all. Six readings are necessary, because even though there are only three humors, they are further classified into right-side humors and left-side humors. Thus one has right wind, right bile, and right phlegm as well as left wind, left bile, and left phlegm.

The pulse, then, is but the means for detecting the nature of a person's humors in order to determine his humor type. Once the humor type of two persons is known, it is easy to determine whether or not these two persons are compatible (that is, whether their humor types are compatible). The knowledge of the humoral disposition/composition itself is, however, just the index of the state of yet another series of bodily substances whose compatibility with the corresponding bodily substances of the sexual partner is of importance. These substances are the *tātus* (from Skt. *dhātu*), or body tissues or body fluids.

Each of the six subhumors governs or impels a corresponding body tissue or body fluid, as shown in table 3.

TABLE 3

Nāṭi	*Tātu*
Right wind	Blood
Right bile	Bone
Right phlegm	Flesh
Left wind	Fat/marrow
Left bile	Nerve tissue/skin
Left phlegm	Saliva/serum

Thus we see that by means of a series of indexing relationships, compatibility of pulses (nāṭi) turns out to reveal not merely compatibility of humoral types but even a compatibility of body tissue and fluids.

These unfolding series of relationships may be taken one more step; a step that brings us back to intiriam, namely, the sexual fluids. According to Devaraj's guru, Dr. Kannan, there are seven, not six, body tissues or body fluids. Table 3 represents but six of these with their corresponding humor subtype. The seventh body fluid is intiriam, or sexual fluid. The sexual fluid is constituted of the essence or distillate of all the other six tātus. Thus, in any given emission of sexual fluid, the entire constitution or state of the six body tissues and fluids at that time is substantially and essentially represented.

Thus, nāṭi poruttam is, finally, a concern with compatibility of intiriams, which implies, by its very nature, a concern with compatibilities of other intermediary substances as well, such as humors and the various body tissues.

Conception

In addition to the concern with maintaining the health of the male and female in sexual intercourse is the concern with conceiving and bringing forth a healthy baby. According to village belief, conception occurs when equal portions of the male and female intiriam combine and enter the womb and there begin to take shape. It is essential to conception that the intiriam of male and female mix. If the male and female are not of compatible blood substances, then their intiriams will either mix badly and produce an unhealthy child or they will not mix at all. Hence, the concern with the matching of poruttams before marriage is a concern not only with the well-being of the husband and wife but with their fertility and with the health of their offspring.

Once the intiriam mix enters the womb, if the man's portion of the mixture is denser (*aṭatti*) than the woman's, it settles toward the bottom of the womb and results in a male fetus. If the woman's portion is denser, the fetus will be a girl. As for the formation of the fetus, the male's intiriam goes to form the bones, and the woman's intiriam forms the flesh. The blood is formed from both male and female intiriam.[6]

Many other factors besides compatibility of substance types for the father and mother are important to the development of a healthy fetus. The marriage ritual is scheduled to occur in only the most auspicious months of the year. In general, it is believed that children born in the months of Cittirai (April/May) and Adi (July/August) are either unlucky to themselves or to their parents or to their maternal uncle. For this reason, there is an axiom that says, "Join not in Adi and Aippasi [October/November]" ("Āṭiyilum, Aippaciyilum cērātē"). Even in an auspicious month, the couple's first night together should occur at an auspicious time.

In the chapter on houses, it was discovered that there are certain cardinal points in the house that must be avoided for sexual intercourse. The consequences of conception in each of the eight cardinal directions may be schematically represented as in table 4.

[6]There are, of course, numerous variations on this theme of male and female contributions to the formation of the fetus. This view was that of Devaraj and was also held by a number of other villagers.

TABLE 4

Direction	*Consequence*
North	Children of both sexes will live long lives.
Northeast	Children will have to work hard to succeed.
East	Children of both sexes will have wealth and enemies.
Southeast	Children of both sexes will have bad habits.
South	A male child will be impotent; a female, barren.
Southwest	A male child will be a spy; a female, a harlot.
West	A male child will grow up to be a wise man; a female child, a beauty.
Northwest	Children of both sexes will live in poverty.

Once conception has occurred, there are a number of rules and rituals that govern the development of the fetus during pregnancy. For example, the mother is enjoined to abjure all frightening thoughts and to avoid looking at maimed or deformed creatures. The most critical time for the baby is the moment of birth. At this moment the child enters into a lifelong relationship with the nine planets. As in the case of the birth of the house, the owner of the house, like the parent, can take all due measures to ensure that his creation (the house or infant) will be compatible with himself, but he has little control over the moods of the planetary deities at the moment of birth. Their attitudes when they are summoned to bless the new house or infant have profound effects on the kuṇam and destiny of the new arrival. If the planets are out of sorts at that moment, then the house or child might be unlucky for itself or might cause family illnesses, death, or disaster. To illustrate the quixotic nature of the planets, let me quote a few passages from an interview with Ragunatha Jōsiyar, a village astrologer.

> For man, marriage is most important. That is when we invite all the guests and have them throw rice as *ācīrvātam* [blessing] on the couple after the tāli is tied. For the planets, the birth of a man is what is most important. They are the

only guests at birth. They are the chief guests. Every time a child is born the planets give ācīrvātam. However, this ācīrvātam is not the same [of the same quality] every time. Sometimes this ācīrvātam may be given halfheartedly, and at other times it can even be a curse. You ask me why? I shall tell you.

The planets have their own houses, like you have yours and I have mine. The planets are most comfortable, "cushy" in their own houses. But then can they always stay in their own houses? No. They are obliged to visit the other houses. In some of these other houses they feel as comfortable as they would if they were in their own house, while in other houses they may feel quite uncomfortable and be in a bad mood. Moreover, some of these planets are friends, and others are neutral to each other, while others are archenemies. Now, even if you were comfortably seated in your house, if your enemy sat across from you in his house and looked into your house, it would put you in a bad mood, wouldn't it? The same is true of the planets. One planet's ire may be kindled by its enemy staring it in the face. There are also times when planets are on the move, moving between one house and the next. This is called *peyarcci*.[7] They hate to be disturbed during this time. To be born at such a time is like my stopping Arunasalam Piḷḷai[8] and asking him, "Where are you going?" What will he do? He will curse me. He might even hit me with his umbrella. The planets are the same.

But human beings are born all the time. Man cannot wait until the planets get organized in their favorite niches. And when a child is born, it is the duty of the planets to give ācīrvātam. So each planet will take a handful of rice and throw it at the child like we do at weddings. But depending on whether he is in the right house, an inhospitable house, whether he is on the move, or whether he faces a friend or

[7]Peyarcci is the act of departing, getting up, and leaving. The peyarcci of some planets, such as Saturn and Jupiter, is marked by the performance of elaborate, day-long rituals designed to mitigate the ill effects the moving planet might have on human persons.

[8]A Veḷḷāḷa landlord known for his ill temper.

foe, his ācīrvātam can be a blessing, a curse, or a perfunctory act. Whatever it is, one has to live with it. This is the *annatānam*[9] of the planets. The annatānam that the parents give is not important. That is not going to change the child's kuṇam or life one bit. The annatānam of the planets is what counts. If you get a stomach upset from this annatānam, you will have stomach upsets all your life. One is lucky to find them all happy in their own houses.

It is like this. I need Rs 20. Now, if I were to turn up with this request while you were at my friend's [Chettiya Piḷḷai] house sitting on a rope bed being bitten by bedbugs and burning your tongue by drinking hot tea from an ever-silver [stainless steel] tumbler,[10] you will, of course, give me Rs 20, because you are a *tarmacāli* ["a generous person"] and it is not in your nature to say no. But your heart will curse me [*tiṭṭum*]. And for that reason, that Rs 20 will turn out to be a curse rather than a blessing. I would probably go into the street and there meet Selvaraja Piḷḷai [the money-lender] who would say, "Hey, bring that money here. And where is the interest?" But if I ask you for Rs 20 while you are in your own house, comfortably seated in your easy chair, drinking coffee from a cup and having a "cool heart," you will say, "Why, Rs 20. Here, take Rs 200." And the money you give me will be a true blessing. I will probably invest it in some rice mill and like Thevarayā Piḷḷai, make thousands of rupees in a few months' time.

Postscript

To sum up, when a male and female are brought together in marriage, which is a relationship in which the two are meant to give and receive from each other many bodily substances, chief among which are sexual fluids, a concern

[9]Annatānam, or "the gift of rice." It is the ritual weaning of an infant by feeding him specially prepared rice. The infant is fed in this ritual by his parents.

[10]This allusion comes from Ragunatha Jōsiyar having witnessed me burning my lips while drinking hot coffee from a stainless steel tumbler, which, in South Indian fashion, requires the person to pour the hot liquid directly into his mouth from a height in order to avoid lip contact with the edge of the tumbler.

for compatibility of substances thus exchanged is clearly evidenced. Not only is the health of the sexual partners affected by this exchange, but the fetus formed as a result of the mixing of these fluid substances will be healthy only if these substances are mutually compatible. This concern obviously extends to include extramarital sexual liaisons as well. Such liaisons are especially prone to incompatible mixing of substances with undesirable consequences because more often than not, unlike in marriage, the mutual compatibility of sexual fluids and other bodily substances is not determined by astrology and other means.

When sexual fluids are optimally blended (determined by compatible horoscopes of sexual partners, choice of appropriate times and places for sexual union, and so forth), the marriage is said to be in a state of quiescence, or equilibrium (*amaiti nilai*). Yet, as in the case of the house, it is extremely difficult to effect a perfect optimization of the mixing. There are times in the life of a house when its horoscope may turn out to be incompatible with that of one or more of its inhabitants. Undesirable and unexpected visitors may affect the house adversely and subsequently affect the relationship of house and inhabitant. The same is true of husband and wife. Practical exigencies of life, if not the reality of existence, preclude a completely insulated state. The planets that determine life's ups and downs, its good times and bad times, are forever in motion, continually altering their interplanetary systemic configuration and thereby their effect on the body substances of those born under their power. Thus, even when all due precautions are taken, the ever-shifting universe of which men are a part can undo and negate some of these defenses and upset relationships of compatibility and, ergo, states of equilibrium. One can only be constantly vigilant and do one's best to manipulate the known and anticipatable variables within a defined context in the interest of optimizing equilibrium within one's body, between two bodies (as between husband and wife), and among the several bodies of a household or family. Such manipulations call for a knowledge of, among other things, those formulas that enhance a balanced and harmonious blend of intiriam substance between compatible people at compatible times and in compatible places. When such times and places are most ideal, they are also thought of as being most auspicious (*mukurtamāna*). Astrology is among several sources of knowledge one may turn to, if not to determine the most auspicious, the most compatible, and the most equilibriated, then at least to know and avoid the inauspicious, the incompatible, and the dangerously disequilibriating.

5
Kunams Divined[1]

In the preceding chapters we explored the ways in which persons establish substantial relationships with ūrs, houses, and sexual partners. These relationships involved exchanges of substances which affected the health and well-being of the persons involved in such exchanges. We noted that the kuṇam substance of persons, after the formative years, is highly resistant to change. This permanence of the kuṇam substance is expressed in a number of proverbs, the most common being, You may alter your clan (*kulam*), but you cannot alter your kuṇam (Kulattai mātrinālum kuṇattai mātra muṭiyātu).

Nonetheless, most Tamils also believe that nothing whatsoever in the manifest world is completely resistant to change, and this includes kuṇams. Seen in this light, then, all the proverbs, sayings, and claims about the fixed nature of kuṇams are only intended to convey their *relative*, not absolute immutability. As we have already noted in the history of the ANVs' appropriation of Kalappūr, the famous

[1]A slightly modified version of this chapter has been published as a separate essay in Charles F. Keyes and E. Valentine Daniel, eds., *Karma: An Anthropological Inquiry* (Berkeley, Los Angeles, London: University of California Press, 1983).

false oath was an act significant and powerful enough to change the kuṇam of an ūr̆. As the ANVs see it, the false oath was a very efficacious karmam. But other, less powerful, and less efficacious karmams, or actions, also can and do effect changes in the kuṇams of persons and things. These karmams are aimed at altering small facets or strands of a person's kuṇam. Within a prescribed context and within a defined telic structure, such changes can appear to be important and critical. But in terms of the wider context, the effect of such changes on a person's overall kuṇam substance is minuscule.

This chapter will focus on just such a change; a change in the kuṇam substance of a person which may be insignificant vis-à-vis his kuṇam as a whole but which, nonetheless, becomes important in the context of a specific illness. In broad terms, then, while the previous chapters were about the essential immutability of kuṇams, this chapter explores the dynamics of their limited mutability.

The mutable aspect of the kuṇam substance is the aspect or portion that has to do with hot and cold states. The substances that bring about changes in this aspect of the kuṇam substance are certain kinds of karmam substances. Karmam, or action, is, in fact, substance. I introduce this point here, ex hypothesi, in order to emphasize the fact that the quest continues to be one of establishing substantial compatibility and equilibriated states.

The dynamic interplay between kuṇam and karmam will be explored through the microanalysis of a ritual of divination which I call the ritual of flowers.

The ritual of flowers, a colorful little rite of divination, may be encountered in almost any roadside shrine or temple courtyard all over South India and in the Tamil-speaking areas of Sri Lanka. Even though this rite is very commonplace, it has, by and large, gone uncelebrated, if not unnoticed, by the countless scholars whose interest in things religious and ritualistic has been more than perfunctory. Bishop Gustav Diehl, who has recorded this particular rite, has done so with so little pause that the reader hardly notices it (1956). Not until Brenda Beck's paper on "Colour and Heat in South Indian Ritual" (1969) do we find a serious attempt at understanding the structure and meaning of this rite.

In this chapter I shall attempt to uncover the logic underlying this rite and in so doing will be led to differ with Beck on several points of analysis. While most of these differences are due to the limited nature of the body of data that was available to her, some are due to the different types of questions that we have asked of the same data. In principle, however, her analysis is sound and was my original source of inspiration for studying this ritual more intensively. I shall not engage in a point-for-point comparison and contrast of Beck's analysis with mine, except where such comparisons seem inevitable.

Several cultural concepts are indispensible for an understanding of the analysis of the ritual that is to follow.

Hot and Cold

Hot and Cold Foods

In "Colour and Heat in South Indian Ritual" Beck has provided us with a list of foods classified according to whether they are "hot" or "cold." At least five qualifications have to be made with respect to such a classification.

1. Foods are not lumped into a clearly defined hot or cold category. Rather, they are strung along a hot-cold gradient.
2. The classification of known foods according to hot and cold is not a generalized, translocal, pan-Indian, or pan-South Asian one. Foods that are considered to be cold in one region of India may be thought of as hot in another region, and vice versa. There is a variety of

the plantain fruit known as *āna mālu*, for instance, that is considered hot by the Sinhalese of southern Sri Lanka but cold by some groups of Jaffna Tamils of the island's north.

3. Such variations in the classification of foods according to hot and cold may cut across caste lines in the same locality or village. Buffalo milk, for example, considered hot by the Telugu Brahmins of Kalappūr is thought of as neither too hot nor too cold by the Parayans of the same village.
4. One can even become more centrifocal and say that there is a variation in food classification between one individual and another.
5. Furthermore, there may be a variation in food classification with the same individual from one context to another.

The case of Sunther (discussed in the Introduction), the ANV youth for whom milk was hot rather than cold, as it is to most others, illustrates the person-centeredness of this categorization. The variation according to context with respect to the same individual (no. 5, above) was illustrated to me by a Siddha physician in Tiruchy Town, who maintained that even the same patient who is able to eat a particular food because of its being cold on one day will not be able to eat the very same food on another day, when for one reason or another it will turn out to be hot for him.

Hot and cold are relative concepts; relative to locality, caste, individual, and even time. General criteria for the classification of foods into hot or cold are neither unequivocal nor consistent. The only incontrovertible statement that can be made regarding hot and cold foods is that foreign foods (including Western drugs) or foods whose origin is clearly marked as alien are, without exception, hot. The most pointed example is ice cream, which is thought of as very hot. This example emphasizes the fact that the South Asian concepts of hot and cold have little if anything to do with temperature per se, that is, as we understand it thermometrically.

Hot and Cold Persons

Like foods, persons, too, may be seen to occupy places along a hot-cold gradient. Some have hot bodies, and some have cold ones—once again with the added qualification that cold bodies can become hot and hot ones cold under certain conditions in certain contexts. In general, it may be said, however, that maximally transacting ANVs and the pessimally transacting Parayans have hotter bodies than the optimally transacting Brahmins and the minimally transacting Ācāris, the smiths and carpenters (Marriott 1976). The hot castes, it will be noted, more readily, willingly and customarily eat hot foods than do the cool castes. Here, too, individual variations, such as seen in Sunther, the ANV boy for whom a prescribed diet had to be cooler than even that of a Brahmin or an Ācāri, must be taken into account.

A healthy person, then, is one who maintains an optimum balance between hot and cold. This optimal level, however, is caste specific and even person specific. One's code substance (Marriott 1976), or kuṇam, determines the optimal level.

Hot and Cold Humors and Kuṇams

While the stabilization of the easily disturbed humoral balance is a cumbersome task and calls for constant attention, it is not an impossible one. This is, in fact, the primary preoccupation of a skilled Ayurvedic or Siddha physician.[2] The proportion of humors in a body is alterable by several means, diet and drugs being the most common ones. The

[2]Two of the three major branches of indigenous medical systems practiced in India, the other being Unani. Siddha medicine is confined to the South.

kuṇams, however, are exceedingly stable and cannot be altered as easily as the humors can.

In terms of the physician's concerns and priorities, humors are more directly related to states of illness and health than are kuṇams. Humors, not kuṇams, belong to the diagnostician's and physician's expertise. The physician's primary aim is to get at the humor imbalance, even though he may admit that humors and kuṇams are related and by extension that kuṇams, too, implicate conditions of health and illness, even though less directly.

Of the three humors, bile (pittam) is hot, phlegm (kapam) is cold, and wind (vāyu) is middling, though more often than not tending toward heat. In the village of Kalappūr I was able to compile seventeen disorders attributed to bile, sixteen to wind, and only eight to phlegm. To this list must be added one bodily disorder resulting from the combined malfunctioning of bile and wind, one from that of phlegm and wind, and one from that of phelgm and bile. Of the entire catalog of humor-caused bodily disorders, only eight were seen as having been caused by or resulting in cold-*cum*-sick bodily states. And all eight of these were caused by an imbalance in phlegm. The remaining thirty-seven were associated with heat—either as being caused by or resulting in heat.

On a frequency table drawn up from a sample of ten local nonspecialist diagnosticians who translated illnesses in terms of the humors and hot and cold, the ratio of heat-associated disorders to cold-associated ones was twenty-five to one. About the same ratio held in the case of the Siddha specialist in Tiruchy Town. So according to cultural categories, heat is far more likely to be implicated in causing bodily disorders than is cold.

Both the native physician and the priest performing the divination are concerned with heat and cold. However, while the former is but secondarily concerned with a patient's kuṇam, for the divining priest (in the ritual of flowers), the kuṇam of his patient is of primary importance.

If the priest is at all concerned with humors, it is only in terms of the humors' relationship to the patient's kuṇam. The physician deals with temporary conditions of heat and cold caused by the ever-changing humoral balance and imbalance. The priest is concerned with the more permanent conditions of heat and cold, which are determined not so much by the fluctuating humors as by the relatively permanent kuṇams or dispositions. If one may make a cytogenetic analogy here, it may be said that the priest is interested in genotypy, whereas the physician's primary interest is in phenotypy.[3]

Hot and Cold Processes

Heat is also associated with transformations, most obviously in cooking, but less obviously in initiation rites, life-crises rituals, all manner of rites of passage, and menstruation (especially in a girl's first menstruation), to mention but a few. All these processes involve separation or mixing and transformation of bodily and nonbodily substances.

The following folk poem illustrates the work of heat in a maiden's first menstruation:

potinta tāmarai pūttal kaṇṭu
oṭiyatō mūtupani—alla
katiravan eṛutal kaṇṭu
maraintatō kūren kaṇmaṇi

Tell me, my precious one;
Has the mist run away
Seeing the lotus-bud unfurl,
Or is it the sun's awakening
That has driven him into hiding?

[3]There are several points of congruence between my use of genotype and phenotype and that of Robert LeVine's (1973: 121–124) in spite of LeVine's use of these concepts to explicate personality alone. The analogy will be reconsidered below.

Here, the heat generated by the blossoming (pūttal) of the lotus—symbolic of the vagina and the coming of age—is compared to that generated by the sun. More often, of course, menstrual heat is spoken of in less poetic and more dangerous terms. In any event, it is natural for a girl's first menstruation to be a heat-generating process. Furthermore, in spite of all the danger and vulnerability associated with puberty, it is on the whole a desired change from childhood (*kanni*) to a potentially fertile state (*kumari*), a change that brings a female to the threshold of what Babb aptly describes as "the supreme affirmation of her identity" as a woman and provides her a secure "place in the scheme of things" (Babb 1975: 76).

The house-opening ceremony known as grahapravēsam is yet another example of a transformatory ritual believed to generate a great quantity of heat. This is why Agni is fed cooling ghee in the hōma kuṇṭam ("ritual hearth"); the nine planets are fed cooling watermelons; the ancestral spirits (pitrus) are fed cooling halved limes; and every room in the house is washed with turmeric water, which is considered to be cooling.

Sexual intercourse, another process involving transformation through combining and separating, is described as a heat-caused and heat-generating process. Cold, however, seems to be associated with stabilized, sterile, and nonprocreative states.

Hot and Cold Colors

Hot and cold also have certain colors with which they are ordinarily associated. Black and red are hot, while green and white are usually thought of as cool, and never as hot. Red, in particular, by being associated with heat, is an auspicious color with respect to fertility, procreation, and motherhood—and consequently marriage itself. Thus we find that a Tamil Hindu bride would never consider wearing white, which is an infertile, unpassionate, cold color: a color of widowhood, social disinterest, marginality, and even asceticism. The most popular color of the bridal sāri is red or shades of red. One informant, who had told me that green was a cold color, was asked to explain why a bride was wearing a green sāri. He first explained it away by saying, "Ah! The green brings out the *jarugai* ('gold border'), and gold is a fertile color." After a while he appended, "Well, green, too, is a fertile color: It reminds you of the green fields after the monsoons." White, I might add, does not have any such redeeming iconic or even indexical attribute in the context of a maiden's marriage.

Description of the Ritual of Flowers

This ritual is one of divination in which the temple priest, usually a non-Brahmin priest, or pūcāri, takes six packets made of green leaves. Within three of these are concealed red flowers, and within the other three, white ones. When the supplicant has stated his question to the priest, the priest throws the six packets of concealed flowers on the floor of the temple after reciting a few incomprehensible mantras. When this is done, a bystander, preferably a little girl (or some such marginal individual), is asked to pick one of the packets. The priest then divines the future of the supplicant or that of the subject for whom the ritual is being performed from the color of the flowers found in the packet thus chosen. The divination is phrased either in the form of a direct statement as to what the future holds for the patient or in the form of a conditional statement in which the priest says, "If you do *x* you will reap *y*," which is as much advice to the patient as it is a divination of the future.

In any event, to conclude one's divination from a single throw and pick is rare and may be considered to be the most elementary form of this ritual. More often than not, one or more additional throws are made, and the colors picked are sequentially added onto the color of the first pick before a final judgment is given. The most elaborate form of the ritual allows for a maximum of four throws and four picks. An important point is that when and if the divination is to be made on the basis of more than one pick, there must be a change of colors in the sequence at some point of the ritual. Only then is it deemed possible to answer the question posed for divination.

Red Flowers Equal Heat; White Flowers Equal Cold

We have established the equivalence between red and heat and between white and cold. On the one hand, we saw that red, because it is a warm and fertile color, was auspicious for anything that had to do with marriage. On the other hand, we saw that most illnesses are caused by excessive heat, and therefore, it is only reasonable to assume that white, by being the equivalent of coolness, should be a desired or auspicious color with regard to most illnesses.

Not all illnesses, however, are heat caused; there are some, admittedly a few, that may be caused by cold. For this reason, to group questions presented to the priest for divination into those having to do with illness, as opposed to those having to do with marriage, as Beck seems to imply in her categorization, can be misleading. As we take a closer look at the ritual of flowers it will become evident that a much broader definition of illness than that which Beck employs is warranted. Under such an expanded definition, the protracted unmarried state itself may be said to be a condition of being ill regardless of whether the abnormality of the protracted maidenhood of the patient is the result of an imbalance of the humors, or the result of Mars being in the seventh house, or of some other astrological mishap (which is capable of expressing itself in humoral imbalance, only one of many ways it could become manifest). The physician, as was stated earlier, is concerned with symptoms (such as dysmenorrhea or some such apparent disorder) and the causes that directly underlie them, which causes are invariably related to humoral imbalances. For this reason, for the average native physician, the unmarried state may not be an illness, in the strict sense of that term, unless, of course, there are symptomatic disorders such as the ones mentioned above. For the divining priest, however, the protracted state of maidenhood itself is symptomatic, not necessarily of a relatively superficial phenomenon, such as a humoral imbalance, but of a deeper, undesirable condition of the supplicant's kuṇam. By this broader conception, an abnormally protracted unmarried state becomes tantamount to an illness.

Even if we were to circumscribe our analysis by a narrow definition (a physician's definition) of illness, as Beck has done, and thereby remove marriage from the province of sickness and health, two obvious problems persist in her categorization of questions presented to the diviner in the ritual of flowers. First (as has been already indicated), there are some illnesses, few as they may be, that are caused by cold, and in which instances the warmth of red will be desirable. Thus, to unequivocally identify red (warm) flowers in the ritual as inauspicious with regard to illness is not justified. Second, in the ritual of flowers there are questions presented to the diviner which have nothing whatsoever to do with marriage or illness per se—questions such as "Should I go to Madurai tomorrow?" or "Should I embark upon this new business venture?" and the like. These questions do, however, have something to do with movement and stasis, instability and stability, restlessness and peacefulness, desire and satiation—all these pairs in turn being various expressions of hot and cold.

To return to our flowers, the criterion upon which the auspiciousness of a color is based is whether that color (red or white) is associated with the state that is desirable or not with respect to a particular condition of the subject for whom the ritual is being performed, this condition being determined as either cold or hot.

It is also fallacious to classify illness-related questions, as Beck has explicitly done, as "questions about the end of an undesirable condition existing at present" and to classify marriage-related questions as "those about the occurrence of a desirable event in the future" (Beck 1969: 555). Even if we were to overlook the fact that there are many questions that may be asked of the diviner which have nothing to do with marriage or illness per se and if we were to limit ourselves to Beck's own catalog of marriage- and illness-oriented questions, both classes of questions are at the same time about an undesirable present condition—either an unmarried state or the state of being ill—and about the occurrence of a desirable event in the future: marriage and health, respectively. This brings us back to the way I find to be most satisfactory of classifying the questions presented to the diviner, namely, as questions relating to cold-caused undesirable states and to heat-caused undesirable states.

In its most elementary form, the ritual of flowers consists of a single throw and a single pick. In this form, however, the meanings assigned to the flowers are quite arbitrary and have nothing to do with either hot or cold, being merely the product of the whimsical choice of the moment made by priest or supplicant. After the packages of concealed flowers are thrown on the ground, the supplicant or the priest makes up his mind as to what colored flower, if picked, would be a good omen. In this case, the meaning attributed to any given colored flower is quite arbitrary in every sense of that term, and both de Saussure (1959: 69) and Peirce (2: 307) would have agreed to call the meaning thus constituted symbolic—even a bit unconventionally symbolic.

Most diviners, however, base their divinations on a certain complexly structured logic of signification. This logic is iconic and indexical rather than symbolic. By *iconic* I refer to a signifying relationship in which the representamen and the object are qualitatively alike and which quality renders the representamen fit to be as such. Thus, the redness of the flower in being hot is an icon (representamen) of the hot state of a patient afflicted by a hot disease (object), or a white flower in being cold is an icon of the cold state of an inherently unmarriageable girl.

In the context of the ritual, the flower, be it cold-white or red-hot, may also index the state of the patient. As an indexical sign, the particular flower or flower-sequence qualifies as a sign because of some existential relation or connection to the object it represents, which connection then makes it an appropriate sign for calling attention to that object (see Fitzgerald 1966: 61).

What follows is an analysis of the more elaborate, complex, and specialized iconic-*cum*-indexical mode of the ritual rather than the simple, nonspecialized symbolic form. The analysis of the iconic-indexical itself may be carried out on four levels.

Analysis, Level One

Table 5 displays in outline the colors and their sequences in picks ranging from one to four, which signify either affirmative or negative responses to two kinds of questions. It is quite clear that in the single-pick form of the ritual, the decoding of the colors into their appropriate messages is done in terms of their iconic associations with heat or cold.[4] Thus, to the question regarding a cold-caused undesirable state of being unmarried, a red flower, by its association with heat and fertility, spells out an auspicious answer. A white flower, on the other hand, portends a cold and infertile state, hardly desirable for marriage.

We noted above the inadequacy of Beck's statement that

[4]The divination made from a single pick is not represented in the table since it is completely arbitrary.

TABLE 5
Heat-Caused and Cold-Caused Undesirable States

	Cold-caused Undesirable States				Heat-caused Undesirable States			
	Sample question: Will my daughter be married?				Sample question: Will my son recover from smallpox?			
	Auspicious		*Inauspicious*		*Auspicious*		*Inauspicious*	
Single pick	R			W	W			R
Double pick	RW			WR	WR			RW
				(WW)				(WW)
				(RR)				(RR)
	Karmam complex				*Karmam complex*			
Triple pick (a)[a]	WRR:	Strong	Weak:	WRW	RWW:	Strong	Weak:	RWR
(b)[b]	WWR:	Present	Absent:	WWW	WWR:	Present	Absent:	WWW
	RRW:	Present	Absent:	RRR	RRW:	Present	Absent:	RRR
Quadruple pick[a]	WWRR:	Strong	Weak:	WWRW	RRWW:	Strong	Weak:	RRWR

[a]These throws and picks are called *pūcai palankaṇittal*, or "the evaluation of the strength of the karmam complex."
[b]This throw and pick is called *pūcai kaṇittal*, or "determining the existence of the karmam complex."

classified illness-related questions as "those about the end of an undesirable condition existing at present," and marriage-related questions as ones concerned "about the occurrence of a desirable event in the future." I maintain that all questions, regardless of whether they are marriage-related or illness-related, are about an undesirable present condition and a desirable future one. This is still inadequate, however, in that it fails to be specific; it fails to delineate the sign function and the signifying mechanism involved. Here again, the double sequence form of the ritual enables us to confront this question more squarely than we have done so far.

Do the first and the second flowers in a given sequence in any way stand for past, present, or future? Let us attempt to answer this riddle by looking at our sample hot-state question, in which the supplicant wishes to know whether his son will recover from smallpox, a heat-caused illness. There are three possible ordered pairs for the white-red sequence.

1. *White equals past, and red equals future*: This must be ruled out on the grounds that if red were to symbolize the future, the future is bound to be a hot one and hardly a desirable state for a patient afflicted by smallpox, an illness caused and exacerbated by heat.
2. *White equals present, and red equals future*: This must also be rejected for the same reason that (1) was rejected. Furthermore, to say that white symbolized the present would, at least on the face of it, contradict reality, in which the patient is anything but cool.
3. *White equals past, and red equals present*: This makes little sense when we remember that the whole purpose of this ritual is to divine the future, not so much to know about the past and present, unless, of course, these can shed some light on what might be. Moreover, if in the interest of consistency we were to apply the same rule to questions about marriage, it would be meaningless to speak of a past unmarried state and a

present married one, or vice versa, given that the subject's past and present states are both that of being unmarried. Furthermore, if there were a flower sequence that could meaningfully symbolize the unchanged, unmarried state, it would be a white-white sequence. Yet we have already noted that a nonalternating sequence is disallowed by the ground rules of the ritual, for such a nonalternating sequence is judged null and void.

A clue to this riddle was provided for me by a supplicant named Karuppan, whom I met one day as he was returning after having had the ritual of flowers performed for him.

Karuppan's daughter was twenty-three years old and had failed to secure herself a bridegroom. On this occasion the reading given by the flowers was a good one. The order of colors in a double-throw sequence had been red and then white, an auspicious response to a question related to a cold-caused unstable state. On his way from the temple I asked Karuppan whether this had been the first time he had had the ritual of flowers performed in his behalf.

K: No sir. I've been doing this every January since my girl attained puberty at the age of fourteen.

A: Is this the first time Murugan [his favored deity] has given you a pleasing answer?

K: Oh, no! He has given me the good sign twice before.

A: Then why isn't Janaki married as yet?

K: Man is hasty. Always hasty. Murugan knows the right time. God never fails. It is all written. It is one's *yōkam*. It is one's *viti*.[5] It is one's kuṇam.

A: If it is one's yōkam, then why worry about it? Doesn't viti always fulfill itself?

[5]Both *yōkam* and *viti* can be translated variously as "fate, luck, fortune, destiny."

K: Yes sir. There is viti. But one can always prevent viti from happening or make viti happen [then, quoting a common Tamil proverb]: *Vitiyai matiyāl vellalām*. ["Viti can be conquered by *mati*" ("discernment, judgment, intelligence")]

A: I don't understand.

K: If I had good yōkam and did not try, that good yōkam would never be fulfilled.

A: Can you stop bad viti?

K: Of course I can, provided I do the right karmam [*muraiyāna* karmam].

Then he proceeded to relate the following incident:

> My youngest daughter was fated [*vitikkappaṭṭiruntatu*] to die before she was five. It was in her *jātakam* ["horoscope"] that she was to die of a snakebite. For five years I made vows, visited Kadirgamam [a holy place in South Sri Lanka], and I prayed to Civan and his son, Murugan, and they saved her. He never fails. God never fails. Right effort (*muraiyāna muyatcci*] never fails. After that, her viti changed. Her yōkam changed, and her kuṇam changed.

Two salient conceptual sets emerge from this dialogue. First, viti, yōkam, and kuṇam are used in a roughly interchangeable and equivalent manner connoting relative permanence. Second, right effort (muraiyāna muyatcci), proper action (muraiyāna karmam), and intellect, judgment, and discernment, collectively called *mati*, are used in a roughly paradigmatic manner. It is shown that viti-yōkam-kuṇam can be controlled and directed, suppressed or given expression, by karmam-muyatcci-mati. I am in no way minimizing the differences (semantic or pragmatic) between and among viti, yōkam, and kuṇam, on the one hand, and the differences between and among karmam, muyatcci, and mati, on the other. On a scale of determinism versus indeterminism, viti is most deterministic, yōkam less so, and kuṇam least deterministic of the three. On a scale in which the degree of will, or *cittam*, is the criterion, mati and muyatcci would tend to have greater cittam than would karmam, and so on. Basically, however, there is something that holds the former three members together in contradistinction to the latter three. Viti, yōkam, and kuṇam are primarily states or conditions, whereas karmam, muyatcci, and mati imply action and effort. In the context of the ritual, at least, this is how these terms have been used. Significantly, this duality collapses in different contexts and even at different levels of analysis and exegesis of the ritual. It is only too well known that karmam, for instance, describes both action and state, as in "Have you performed all your karmams?" and in "Poor chap. He has to suffer so much. That is his karmam."

Henceforth, for the sake of convenience I shall refer to viti, yōkam, and kuṇam collectively as the kuṇam complex and to the set of karmam, muyatcci, and mati as the karmam complex.

The kuṇam-complex is believed to be inherent and unalterable in one's lifetime. With the help of the karmam complex, however, one can bring about the realization or the nonrealization of the kunam complex. In other words, the kuṇam complex is potentially fixed and permanent. This potential form can be converted into its kinetic counterpart, however. Such a conversion can be effected only by performing some manner of action upon the kuṇam complex. This action, karmam complex, or "appropriate effort," as Karuppan called it, may take the form of sacrifices, pilgrimages, vows, offerings, pūjās, prayers, or plain old effort (muyatcci).

It is not unusual to hear a Tamil mother bemoaning the fact that her son failed to live up to her ideal by saying, "My son's viti and yōkam was to become a doctor, but alas, he never tried!" In other words, her son's potential yōkam or kuṇam complex was that of becoming a doctor, but he never acted upon it in order to transform it from its potential to its kinetic form.

While action or right effort, or the karmam complex, can aid in the actualization of the kuṇam complex, it can also arrest the fulfillment of an evil kuṇam complex. Thus, the way Karuppan arrested the evil viti of his youngest daughter, who was fated to die of a snakebite at the age of five, was by performing the proper karmam complex.

The duality made here between the kuṇam complex and karmam complex is analogous to the duality that holds between actor and action, product and process, or condition and operation. Am I really justified in making such a distinction? Yes and no. I am afraid that the apparent contradiction is not mine—it is Tamilian; I dare say it is South Asian. It ultimately comes down to a question of levels. As we take a closer look at the structure of this ritual of flowers we shall be able to see both the apparent contradiction and its resolution in an encapsulated form.

I shall continue my analysis of the ritual of flowers at the level in which the duality between the karmam complex and the kuṇam complex is maintained. I shall return later to the level in which this duality is neutralized.

My hypothesis about and a response to what we called the riddle of how the first and second flowers corresponded to the periods of time is that the flowers do not, in a simple one-to-one correspondence, symbolize past, present, or future. What the flowers in fact do is signify one's kuṇam complex and one's karmam complex. The two complexes, as has been established, are different in both form and kind, analytically and semeiotically at the level we are now considering. One is a state, the other is a process; one is a condition, the other is an instrument that is intended to act upon that condition. How is this duality signified by the ritual of flowers? The answer is quite clear. As you may recall, according to the rules by which the ritual is performed, *the colors must alternate*. The difference in color between the first and second flower is what establishes this distinction between the kuṇam complex and the karmam complex.

The first flower picked, I hypothesize, is one's kuṇam complex, which is, admittedly, an inherent, inalienable state. In the most elementary form of the ritual, in which only one pick is made, the color of the flower picked is iconically related to the "complexion" of the subject's kuṇam complex as either hot or cold. In response to a question regarding a cold-caused undesirable state, a red flower is auspicious because it signifies a potentially favorable kuṇam complex, suitable for marriage. The same would be true for the auspicious white flower picked in response to the question regarding a heat-caused undesirable condition, such as being afflicted with smallpox.

Earlier, I equated the kuṇam complex with genotypy. One could, however, conceive of equating the kuṇam complex with the cryptotype in Whorf's opposition of phenotype to cryptotype (1956: 105) or substitute terms such as *unmanifest, covert, latent*, and so forth as the analogue of the kuṇam complex. Instead, I have chosen the word *genotypy* as it contrasts with *phenotypy* because I wish to stress the cultural idea of the kuṇam complex's relative permanence and immutability, which are indeed the qualities and attributes of genotypy.

The analogy's appropriateness becomes even more meaningful when we focus on the priest and his aim in the context of the ritual. What, in fact, the priest is interested in finding out in this ritual of divination is the relatively permanent genotype of his subject. Phenotypy is only of secondary importance to him. An unmarried girl may eat cold foods because it is believed that cold foods do keep one's passions under control, and the control of one's passions is tantamount to preserving one's chastity. These cold foods, prescribed by cultural edicts, parental advice, or even a physician's counsel, are intended to address themselves to the girl's phenotypy, real or imagined, potential or actual. The priest, however, is interested in finding out whether or not, regardless of phenotypic expressions, the genotype (the kuṇam complex) itself is such that it destines the girl to live a cold, unfertile, and/or unmarried life.

If a white flower is picked up when the question "Will my son recover from smallpox?" is asked, the message conveyed by the flower may be paraphrased as follows: "Fear not. Even though your son is 'phenotypically' hot and sick, his 'genotype' is cool. Therefore, his chances of recovery are good."

The second flower in the double-pick sequence adds on to the message of the first. The second flower, however, does not indicate the state of the subject through its iconicity to either hot or cold, as did the first flower—at least not at the level of the sign function we are dealing with at the moment. Its only function here is to establish its distinctiveness by virtue of its color vis-à-vis the first flower and then to diagram this difference of form and kind into the relationship that holds between the kuṇam complex and the karmam complex. In other words, what is established is this: even as the second flower is different from the first, so is the karmam complex different from the kuṇam complex. That is not all, though. In establishing this difference, the second flower also acknowledges the fact that the karmam complex does exist, that the patient or supplicant has made some significant effort or performed some significant action, whether to repress or express a preexisting kuṇam complex.

Thus the red-white sequence relating to a question regarding a cold-caused unstable state, such as a protracted unmarried state, is auspicious, because not only does the first (red) flower signify a potentially good hot kuṇam complex with respect to marriage but there is a second flower that signifies the existence of a karmam complex needed to bring about the kuṇam complex's fulfillment.

What of the white-red sequence with respect to a cold-caused unstable state, which our table tells us is an inauspicious sequence? Here, too, the first color, in this case white, establishes the fact that the kuṇam complex of the subject is a cold one and therefore not suited for a happy married life or even marriage itself. The second flower, by being different from the first, establishes the presence of the karmam complex. The karmam complex, however, is not adequate or sufficient for preventing the fulfillment or the persistence of the inauspicious cold kuṇam complex. In Hindu culture (as alluded to earlier in our discussion on kuṇams), evil and decadence are taken to be the normal and the expected, whereas goodness and virtue call for great effort to create and sustain. The tendency of the phenomenal world is to devolve rather than evolve; the bias is toward degeneration rather than creation. In such a world, the intensity, if you will, of the karmam complex needed to arrest or suppress the activation of an evil kuṇam complex must be double that of the karmam complex required to effect the expression of a good kuṇam complex.

This argument was illustrated to me by the priest by the following example:

> Take my rice fields. I sow high-quality, Kaṇṇaki [a modern, high-yield crop] paddy. Now nobody can deny that in each and every one of those seeds, there is the best, *pakka*, rice plant. But without the monsoons and the expensive chemical fertilizers, nothing will come out of those seeds. Take that field over there. All those weeds. Belongs to that lazy Paṇṭāram.[6] I saw him weed it once. Just once. And he thought that was it. That was enough. But look how the weeds have grown. A jungle. Without any help. No fertilizer, no water. Just the Paṇṭāram's laziness. You've got to weed fields like that not just once but several times. Must use chemical weed killers, too. It is hard to make good paddy grow, I grant you. But it is twice as hard to keep weeds from growing.

When we consider the more elaborate forms of the ritual of

[6]Temple assistants, a non-Brahmin caste of priests.

flowers, this argument will be clearly substantiated by the structure of the ritual itself; suffice it to note for now that a single red flower is not adequate to contain the inauspiciousness signified by a single white flower.

A nonalternating sequence of red-red or white-white is called *pūcaittavaru* (an abortive ritual), because the second flower fails to indicate the presence of the karmam complex, whether the supplicant has performed sacrifices, vows, or whatever. Insofar as the flowers fail to acknowledge his efforts and actions, the flowers are thought to "lie."

Therefore, the throwing and picking is repeated two or more times until the colors alternate. If, however, after several throws, the colors persist in repeating themselves, then either the supplicant is said to be lying about having performed the various rites, vows, and sacrifices he claims to have performed or else it is determined that the actions performed to date are not significant, are insufficient or irrelevant.[7]

Once I witnessed the priest make ten attempts before he finally obtained an alternating color sequence. He was so persistent on that occasion because the supplicant had come to the priest previously with the same problem, and the priest had prescribed a course of offerings and rituals that the priest himself administered or performed over a period of time. This foreclosed the escape route of declaring to the supplicant that he was lying about having performed the prescribed course of action.

The Triple-Pick Sequence

The analysis thus far has centered on divination arising from only two picks. But it so happens that if an auspicious sequence is not picked up in the first two throws, one, or even two, additional throws will be made. The triple-pick

[7]The expression most often used is *karmam palikkavillai*, which is translated as "karmam has not borne fruit."

sequence belongs to two subtypes, namely, (1) a third throw following an alternating inauspicious sequence, and (2) a third throw following a nonalternating inauspicious sequence. Let us take these one at a time.

When a third throw is made in order to add on to an inauspicious alternating color series, the purpose of this throw is described as pūcai palankaṇittal. Literally, this means the evaluation of the fruits of *pūcai*. *Pūcai* here refers to what we have called the karmam complex, which includes pilgrimages, offerings, along with any other efforts that have been made for the purpose of bringing about the fulfillment of a good kuṇam complex or the suppression of a bad kuṇam complex, as the case may be. The temple priest, with a certain amount of etymological error, translated *pūcai palaṇkanittal* as "the evaluation or gauging of the strength of the rituals performed," that is, the gauging of the strength of the karmam complex. In any event, the essential meaning is retained, whether the "strength" or the "fruits" of the ritual enter our translation. In fact, the folk etymology as given by the priest is culturally more meaningful than the true etymology.

In the third flower, then, one attempts to discover whether sufficient effort has been expended in order to prevent the fulfillment of a bad kuṇam complex. If in regard to a marriage-related question—or more generally, a question posed in connection with a cold-caused unstable state—an initially inauspicious sequence of white-red is followed by a red in the third pick, the second red adds to the existing red (which has already signified the existence of a certain amount of karmam complex) and strengthens it, so to speak. Thus, a white-red-red sequence indicates not only the presence of a bad kuṇam complex in the white but also the presence of a reinforced karmam complex signified by the double red. From this the priest is able to conclude that the expression of the potentially bad kuṇam complex, realization will be effectively obstructed so that the patient will achieve his or her goal, which can be realized only in the absence of cold. If the third pick yields a white flower, however, giving a sequence of white-red-white, then the last flower, in being different from the second pick, weakens the already existing but inadequate karmam complex, in the words of one of my informants, "boring a hole through the wall of a dike that is already too weak to contain the waters of the monsoon rains." This sequence would assuredly result in the fulfillment of a bad kuṇam complex caused by a cold state. The argument for heat-caused unstable states is the same when the color sequence is reversed.

When a third pick is made in order to add on to an unalternating sequence of two picks of red-red or white-white, this pick's purpose is described as pūcai kaṇittal. Here the purpose is not to gauge the strength of an already existing karmam complex, as in the case of pūcai palan-kaṇittal, but rather to see whether or not karmam complex exists at all. If in the third throw a different color of flower is picked and added on to the first two isochromatic flowers, then the third flower is said to acknowledge that some kind of effort has been made toward solving the crisis in question. Yet if the color sequence fails to change even after three throws, then this sequence is interpreted as indicating the absence of karmam complex, or else the flowers are said to lie, and the whole ritual is repeated. More often than not, a red-red-red or a white-white-white sequence is considered to indicate conclusively that as of that moment, there is no reason to believe that the patient's problem will be solved.

Relative to the conclusively negative response derived from the triple unchanging sequence, both red-red-white and white-white-red are positive. Only the red-red-white sequence, however, is unequivocally positive with respect to questions relating to cold-caused unstable states, whereas the white-white-red is still ambiguous and requires a fourth pick whose color will add to the existing sequence before a final judgment is given. This is so because, as has been argued, it is believed that a stronger karmam complex is required to contain a bad kuṇam complex than to bring about the realization of a good kuṇam complex. Accordingly, the purpose of the fourth and final pick is also described as pūcai palankaṇittal, which the folk-etymological translation renders roughly as "assessing or gauging the strength of ritual effort [karmam complex] expended."

Before we move on to the final pick I shall make one more point regarding an unchanging sequence obtained in the first two throws. Unlike the white-red-red or red-white-white sequences, in which the third flower, in its similarity to the second one, reinforces the meaning of the second flower (implying a strengthening of the karmam complex), in a red-red-white or a white-white-red sequence, the second flower, by being the same color as the first, in no way implies an intensification, or doubling, of the kuṇam complex that the first flower establishes. Two initial consecutive reds or whites are considered the same as a single red or a single white, respectively.

I came to this conclusion after the following experience. When the priest and I, with pencil and paper in hand, were discussing and diagramming the various possible sequences in this divination rite, a very curious thing happened. We would begin to consider, for example, a red-red sequence. He would explain that "a red flower follows a red flower. Now I make another throw and the little girl picks a white flower. Now we have a red-white sequence." Or again, when discussing a white-white sequence, "Ah—first pick white, second pick also white. But third pick is red! Now what does this white-red sequence mean?" I kept correcting him by saying, "you mean a red-red-white sequence" or "you mean a white-white-red sequence." He would simply nod his head in agreement and then carry on as usual, repeating the omission of the "red-red" or the "white-white" part.

Frustrated, I confronted him squarely with his persistent and obvious (to me) omission. In an absolutely irritated tone he told me, "Yes, red-red-white or red-white: it is the same. White-white-red or white-red: it is the same." This was in keeping with the divination itself, in which the priest considered a red-white positive response to be identical to a red-red-white positive response and a white-red response to be identical to a white-white-red sequence.

The Quadruple-Pick Sequence

The sequence that is subjected to a last addition is a white-white-red or a red-red-white sequence, if either one of these does not spell out a conclusively positive response. If we were to take the white-white-red sequence as the one obtained in response to a question posed regarding a cold-caused illness, and if to this sequence another red is added as a fourth, the double red establishes the existence of a karmam complex sufficiently strong to contain the inherently unfavorable cold kuṇam complex. A fourth, white flower, contrastingly, would imply the presence of a weak karmam complex, inadequate for the containment of the unfavorable cold kuṇam complex.

Analysis, Level Two—"Blood in Milk and Milk in Blood"

In the analysis thus far, the distinctiveness of the karmam complex as opposed to the kuṇam complex has been seen as one of the first requirements of the ritual of flowers. This requirement was met by the syntax of alternating colors.

But there is another level—once again, a level of analysis generated by the ethnographic data.

The priest and I were discussing a question about an unmarried girl whose condition (to repeat) was believed to be the result of a cold state. On that morning, the sequence in a double-throw form of the ritual had been an auspicious red-white, indicating that her kuṇam complex was inherently hot, despite the conclusion one might arrive at from the external evidence of her protracted unmarried state, and also that there was sufficient karmam complex to bring about the expression of this favored kuṇam complex. The priest also indicated that the girl's body was "warm" (*ye-tuvetuppānatu*) rather than "hot" (*cūṭu*) and that this was good. I questioned him as to what he meant by "warm." His response was:

Priest: What do you get when you add a pint of milk to twenty pints of blood?

A: What?

Priest: Pink [*iḷancivappu*]. And that is warm [*iḷancūṭu*].

A: But you just said that red is the best color for an unmarried girl, because it meant that she was fertile and hot for marriage. And so pink must mean that she is less fertile and does not have as much heat for marriage as she would have had if the color had been more pure red.

Priest: Yes. But too much heat itself could prevent marriage from being successful. That was the matter with this girl's mother, who had three miscarriages, because of too much heat in her womb, before her first son survived. And that is also why you see married men running around emaciated. Their wives have very hot bodies [*trēkankaḷ*].

A: If that were the case then, red-white should be as good as white-red. So why did you consider white-red as bad in this case?

Priest: Is it the same to pour a pint of milk into twenty pints of blood as it is to pour a pint of blood into twenty pints of milk? Well, that's the difference.

When I reread my notes after returning from the field, this "pinking" factor at least initially seemed to throw a spoke in the wheel of my first-level analysis, in which action is clearly differentiated from actor and his bodily state. I could not, however, discard the analysis at that level, because there was sufficient evidence to support it.

The question, then, is this: Are we to present both analyses of the ritual as they are and leave them as contradictions? I think not. The resolution is that at one level the karmam complex (effort, pilgrimages, offerings, prayers, vows, and so on) is differentiated from the kuṇam complex (the actor's bodily state, his yōkam, his fate). Yet the moment it is thus differentiated, action becomes conjoined with actor, altering the actor's kunam complex. This establishes in a capsular form the much-evidenced action-actor identity principle in Hindu culture.

Ever since Arnold van Gennep (1908) identified the tripartite structure of rites of passage, anthropologists have built upon and elaborated this basic structure and in so doing have brought many relevant and interesting details of ritual out from the shadows. Van Gennep's significant work was anticipated in his contemporaries' essay on sacrifice (Hubert and Mauss 1898) and continues to find creative elaboration in one of the more imaginative anthropologists of our time, Victor Turner (1969, 1974; Turner and Turner 1978). Hubert and Mauss's work on sacrifice and Turner's work on Ndembu ritual center on sets of rituals that have symbolic representations of all three phases of the processual form. That is, the preliminal, liminal, and postliminal phases are symbolically enacted or portrayed in the rituals they have studied.

I believe that the ritual of flowers is also a processual ritual in that it signifies a transformation of state. The ritual of flowers is distinctive, however, in that it represents but two parts, or phases, of the ritual process. The first color, as has been noted, reveals the patient's kuṇam complex, and the second color (and the colors that follow the second) reveals the presence and nature of the patient's karmam complex. These two may be said to correspond structurally to the preliminal and the liminal phases, respectively. Then comes the crucial twist of the processual rite. The limen is conjoined with the preliminal to form something new, a postliminal state. The postliminal, however, need not be signified in any way comparable to the distinctly enacted or symbolically represented tripartite forms described by Turner and van Gennep, among others, because in Tamil culture, the union of the preliminal and liminal is itself considered to be a postliminal state and is therefore in no need of signification as such; it thereby implies the actor-action identity not present in most non-Indian ritual modes or cultural systems.

Elsewhere (1973) I have given a number of examples of this Tamil variation of the ritual process, but I did not have an adequate explanation for its peculiarity. I called these rites "implicatory" because the presence of the limen, I held, implied that the postliminal state would follow and that the signification of this last state in the ritual process was deemed superfluous by the cultural logic and was therefore omitted by the Tamils. Now, however, I am convinced that all these rituals that displayed the same structure were, in fact, consonant with the culture at large, in which the action-actor identity is stressed.

Let us at this point reconsider our treatment of that territorial unit the ūr, in which we noted that "frontiers" or "threshold" more aptly describes the territorial limits (ellai) in question than does the concept of a linear boundary. If we were to metaphorically transport this distinction into our discussion of limens, then limens, too, in the rituals of Tamils may be better understood as frontiers in the ritual process. Frontiers, unlike boundaries, are not merely distinct and sui generis entities; frontiers are integrated with what they bound. This is what gives ūr ellais or ūr frontiers a fluid and elusive quality. To extend the geographical metaphor, limens in Tamil rituals of process do not stand for a no-man's-land, as do boundaries; they belong, as do frontiers. This, in effect, is what Tambiah means when he speaks of boundaries "overflowing" (1973).

This brings us to a very important point regarding our understanding of the way in which Tamils perceive this coalescence of actor and action in the concluding phase of the ritual. I have hitherto referred to the "karmam complex" because I wished to emphasize the complex of ideas that surrounds the concept of action (karmam, muyatcci, and mati). The word *complex,* however, confers an abstract quality on karmam. To the Tamil, karmam as action is not solely abstract. It is a substance, even as kuṇams are substances. This substantial aspect of karmam is clearly indicated in the pūcāri's milk-into-blood analogy. Here the effect of karmam (action) or kuṇam substance (actor) is likened to the "mixing" of two substances, milk and blood, which flow into each other and create a new substance, that is, the transformed substance of the person. The analogy of karmam as milk, a substance, and of the mixing itself reveals the Tamil's perception of the kuṇam-karmam interaction as the mixing of two substances.

The milk-into-blood analogy, however, leaves the impression that karmic substance is something external to the body substance, which in being introduced into the body substance then combines with the kuṇam substance. Karmam substance, however, is not external to the body, as is made clear in several Indian philosophical traditions. The analogy of karmam as *pala,* or fruit, is most clearly made in Jainism (Jaini 1980: 217–238) but also occurs in several Hindu traditions, including Śaiva Siddhānta. When a given karmam or karmic residue is activated, realized, or experienced, so to speak, it is said to have come to fruition, or to have ripened (*palikkum* or *paṛukkum*). Following the Upaniṣhads, Śaiva Siddhānta also locates karmic residue in the second innermost body (of the five bodies), known as the *kañjuga śarīram,* encased by the body sheath, called the *vijñāna maya kośam.*[8] Karmam is thus an integral part of the body substance, a part of one of the innermost bodies, to be

[8]See chapter 7 for a more detailed discussion of the body sheath theory.

precise, ripening at its own, predetermined rate, moving toward final realization.

One last snag remains. With respect to the actor-action identity or the identity of the kuṇam complex and karmam complex: all that the ritual shows is that a given action alters or becomes a part of the actor in some measure after the said actor has performed the said action. The actor-action identity has two components, however. To phrase it simply, we may say that

1. An actor is what he is because of what he does.
2. An actor does what he does because of what he is (see also Marriott 1976: 109, 110).

The ritual discussed thus far substantiates only the first half of this claim. I believe, however, that I have evidence to support the claim that what actors will do is predetermined by what they are.

The following incident happened not in the village in which we carried out fieldwork but in another village near the Kaveri River, where I had gone to collect data on the same ritual of divination. The priest in this village asked me if I wanted something divined. As a matter of fact, I did want to know the future of my wife's chronic intestinal condition, which had been incorrigible from the first day of our arrival in India. Most intestinal disorders are considered to be heat caused, and my wife's disorder, as diagnosed by this priest, was no exception. The flowers were thrown on the ground, and the picks were made. The order was white and then red.

Priest: Good. There is no problem. She will be well. Your prayers will be answered. Only do keep your vows.

A: [I told him that I had neither prayed nor made any vows.] All I've done is fold my hands and wait.

Priest: It doesn't matter. The flowers show that good karmam exists and that you will do good karmam. It is

> in your head writing. That is what these flowers show. Maybe this supplication to the flowers itself is it. It was in your head writing, otherwise why would you have come here in the first place?

The second flower, then, need not signify only an action that has been performed or one that is being performed; it records even a potential action, an action that will be executed. Most appropriate is the analogy to a genetic template, in which the temporal dimension is also coded. In other words, the second half of the proposition relating to actor-action identity—that a person does what he does because of what he is—is also established.

Analysis, Level Three

At the onset of the description of the ritual of flowers I chose to focus on what I called the iconic-indexical form or mode of the ritual and distinguished it from the simpler and purely symbolic form. From then onward I have variously referred to the sign vehicles involved as icons, indexes, and at times merely as signs; correspondingly, I have called the signifying mechanisms iconic, indexical, iconic-indexical, or more generally, signification. This apparent overfastidiousness has not been without a purpose, a purpose that goes beyond the classification and labeling of categories of signs.

A given culture may well be a symbolic system, in the Schneiderian as well as the Peircean sense of *symbolic*. As indicated in the Introduction, however, within the system so defined, within the culture, for and among those interpretants who or which make the relationship between object and representamen meaningful, further subsystems of significations may be identifiable. Minimally, the three basic sign types or significant modes, namely, the symbolic, the indexical, and the iconic, are operative in a culture. To rephrase this, cultural reality may present itself symbolically, indexically, or iconically to individuals and groups of individuals in that culture and in different contexts.

When seen from the outside the context of the ritual and from outside the culture, the signs employed in the ritual of flowers are symbolic, that is, general, conventional, and arbitrary. From this perspective, there is neither isomorphism, likeness, and identity, or spatiotemporal contiguity between sign (a particular-colored flower) and object (a state of being hot or cold). A semeiotic analysis or cultural description that is merely symbolic fails to convey how signs or a system of signs achieves its significant effect, how it succeeds in being emotionally and cognitively persuasive.

Within the ritual context, to the involved and informed participants in the ritual, the relationship between a white or a red flower and a cold or a hot patient is an indexical one, a contiguous and causally necessary one. Even more interesting from the point of view of South Asian culture in general is the fact that the relationship is also iconic, a characteristic that we have encountered in the previous chapters as well.

Before examining the place and purpose of iconicity in this ritual in particular and in the culture in general, let us spell out further some of the indexical functions present in the ritual of flowers. It ought to be self-evident that for any rite of divination to be worthy of its name, its major operational signs must be predominantly indexical, in that the purpose of the divination is to index, to point at, to direct one's attention toward something concealed in space and time (or both). From a cultural point of view, the signs focused on during divination are no less causally linked to its object than is acidity to the blushing of blue litmus or a chemical's reaction to a given pathogen in a blood test. Thus, the particular affliction of a patient, be it smallpox or an unmarried state, indexes the presence of an excess of heat or cold, as the case may be. For as an indexical sign, it is a "representamen which fulfills the function of a representamen by virtue of a character which it could not have if its object did not exist" (Peirce 5: 73). To emphasize, the relationship between hot and cold to affliction may not appear to those of us who are members of the "culture of science" to be anything like the relationship of litmus paper to acidity. For us, the former is merely symbolic and the latter indubitably indexical. However, for those who share Tamil culture, for those steeped in its world view, the indexical mode of meaning pragmatically gives the sign in question significance.

Another prominant indexical function we have encountered in the ritual of divination is what we have called the "pinking" effect. Pinking was seen to index a corresponding warmth of the patient's kuṇam.

The crucial role that indexical signs play in the ritual of divination is what makes the whole ritual cognitively persuasive and affectively plausible for those who practice and partake in it. The clothing of our conception, to paraphrase Geertz (1973: 90), with an aura of factuality so as to make the moods and motivations seem uniquely realistic is possible only because of indexical signs.

To the role played by indexical signs in the construction of cultural reality must be added the role played by iconicity. My hypothesis is that in South Asia the iconic function occupies a place of privilege in the construction of reality. This should come as no surprise given the pervasive hold that its dominant nondualistic cosmology has on so many facets of its culture. (See E. V. Daniel 1983*a* and 1983*b*; S. Daniel 1983; K. David 1977; Inden 1976; Inden and Nicholas 1977; Marriott and Inden 1974.) If, indeed, ultimate reality and ultimate truth are to be found in the oneness of all things, it is not difficult to see that everything is an icon of everything else, given that icons are signs that act as signs by virtue of the fact that they share some quality with the object they represent. However, in this highly differentiated phenomenal world of *māyā* and dualism, the fact of iconicity is concealed under ignorance. "Ritual," however, is one of the domains in which the truth of iconicity is pointedly hinted at. The very truth of ritual in South Asia is constituted to a large extent in and through iconicity.

At the most general level of similarity, where the "shared quality" of iconicity is an abstract set of correspondences, we find iconicity expressed through the rule of alternating colors. By this rule, it is required that the second flower be different in color from the first, so that the difference between the kuṇam complex and the karmam complex can be established. This is an instance in which the overtly emphasized signifying relationship is iconic, or diagrammatic (Peirce 2.282). That is, the shift from red to white or from white to red diagrams the shift from actor to action, from kuṇam complex to karmam complex. In Lévi-Strauss's succinct formula, "it is not the resemblances but the differences that resemble each other" (1963: 77).

Iconicity, however, operates at a less abstract and more immediate level as well in the ritual of flowers. We saw how a given color indexed a corresponding kuṇam type, either hot or cold. Yet, red as an icon of hot is hot, and white as an icon of cold is cold. Thus, while a red flower functions as an index of heat just as does a natural symptom (that is, smallpox indexes the hot state of the patient), it also functions as an icon in that it, in being red and hot, exhibits a "likeness" to the sick, hot patient. This commonly shared *quality* enables it to function as an iconic sign. Once again, in the pinking effect described by the priest, in addition to the indexical function already discussed, an iconic function is operant. The quality of warmth that is shared between "pink" and a warm kuṇam makes the relationship between sign and object an inherently iconic one.

To recapitulate the semeiotic involved here, then, we find that iconicity along with indexicality play crucial, I dare say indispensable, functions in making the ritual of divination real and convincing, on the one hand, and preeminently and characteristically cultural (South Asian), on the other.

Past, Present, and Future Reconsidered

It is now clear that the flowers do say something about one's past, present, and future. They do not, however, have a simple one-to-one correspondence, such as first flower, past; second flower, future; and so on. These flowers, through a process of iconicity and indexicality, indicate that one's past is part of one's present, that one's present and past together will be one's future, and that these transformations and transportations, as it were, of past into present and present into future are carried out by the cultural mechanism of the mutual identity that obtains between the kuṇam complex and karmam complex, establishing the dictum that "a person is what he does and he does what he is."

One Last Detail

At the beginning of this chapter, I dissented from the position that the questions posed to the diviner are to be classified as merely either marriage related or illness related. Ethnographic facts indicate that a wide range of questions are entertained. Table 6 contains a sample.
The clearcut cases are (2), (3), and (4). Two and (4) are the sample questions we considered in our analysis; (3), too, insofar as it is held that asthma is caused by a phlegmatic imbalance, specifically requires a red kuṇam complex or body state to be favorable.

If a question such as (1) is asked, the priest will as a rule require the subject to elaborate and then diagnose the illness as caused either by heat or by cold. In my experience,

TABLE 6

Questions	Positive Response
1. Will my son be well?	W, WR, RWW, RRWW
2. Will my daughter recover from smallpox?	W, WR, RWW, RRWW
3. Will my mother's asthma get better?	R, RW, WRR, WWRR
4. Will my daughter be married this year?	R, RW, WRR, WWRR
5. Should I go on this journey?	?
6. Should I accept this new job?	One of the sequences, not both.
7. Will I recover my lost sheep?	W, WR, RWW, RRWW
8. Should my son marry this girl?	Either sequence

however, when the priest is not sure how to categorize the question according to the humor theory or when he considers the supplicant's social status too insignificant for him to spend time probing for details, he will merely assume that the illness is heat caused—as most illnesses are—and then decide on W, WR, and RWW sequences as the auspicious ones.

Five, too, would normally call for an elaboration, and more often than not, the purpose of the journey will be given. In one instance, a certain supplicant did not wish to divulge the purpose of his proposed journey for fear that some of his fellow villagers might create trouble if they knew. On this occasion the positive sequence decided upon was the W, WR, RWW, and RRWW sequences. The priest later explained to me that whatever reason impels the supplicant to go on this journey, it must be so that he may acquire a greater peace of mind than he presently has, and for this reason a white sequence is good, since his present state of perturbation indicates that there is a lot of heat resulting from and causing his restlessness. The W, WR, RWW, and RRWW sequences for question (7) are decided upon as the auspicious ones for the same reason as in (5), because the recovery will restore peace of mind.

Six and (8) present the widest room for interpretation. If the priest decides that the new job is intended to bring prosperity and indicates the leaving behind of a job that was nonproductive, humdrum, and routine, then he would choose the R, RW, WRR, and WWRR sequences as the desired ones. If, however, the present job is causing the supplicant restlessness and a lack of peace of mind, the WR, RWW, and RRWW sequences will be chosen as the auspicious ones.

Question (8) would also call for more information. A knowledge of the girl should help. If she has a reputation of being a *koṇṭi māṭu* (that is, a cow or an ox that has not been trained to be docile and obedient to man's commands; a grown oxen or cow that is skitterish like a calf), then a W, WR, RWW, and RRWW sequence will be an affirmative response forecasting that once married, she will settle down. Yet if the girl is known to have an astrological anomaly, such as Mars in the seventh house (*cevvāi tōśam*), indicating infertility, then the R, RW, WRR, and WWRR sequences would assure the supplicant that in fact, after marriage, a red, hot, and fertile life is destined for the girl. Not all astrological anomalies are nullified or modified by the R, RW, WRR, and WWRR sequence, however. If, for instance, the ascendant falls in the *trimsamsa* or the one-thirtieth division of a sign, it speaks of an adulterous nature—excessive heat. In this case, a W, WR, RWW, and RRWW sequence will be the favored one.

In discussing question (8), the priest gave me an example. On a rare occasion he had found himself at a loss when he was asked to divine the answer, because it so happened that the boy in question was madly in love with the girl. "He was literally a madman [pittan]. But unfortunately, the girl had *cevvāi tōśam*, foreshadowing widowhood." He expressed his predicament in song:

pacukkoṇṭiyillā cevvāiyaṭā
tiru nīr varta trēkamaṭā

kāḷai kontaṛappuṇṇōtalayum
kontaḷamē kontaḷam nāṭutaṭā

A rough translation goes like this:

Mars is ominous for this tame cow
Whose body is covered with holy ashes
The bull, restlessness personified, roams
Like a fire with a raging wound
Searching for her locks to singe

The problem is, as you see, a difficult one. If he decided on a W, WR, RWW, and RRWW sequence, it would be good for the boy and his heat-caused state of "running around like a restless bull and raging fire with a wound in it," but it certainly would not suit the girl, who did not need to be told by the flowers, too, that she was going to be cold and infertile, something she already knew from her horoscope. An R, RW, WRR, and WWRR sequence would have been good news for the girl, promising her escape from her horoscope—but what good will it do the boy if he is going to remain unsatiated after marriage?

The priest solved the problem by first deciding whom he should treat as patient, the boy or the girl. He decided upon the boy because the boy's father was the supplicant. The sequence turned out to be W, WR, RWW, and RRWW, so he gave his blessing and go ahead for the marriage. "The two have been married now for six years and have five sons. The horoscope was obviously wrong. But, then, it still could be right, and she could become a widow."

Summary

The ritual of flowers is a problem-specific and person-specific ritual aimed at divining a person's past, present, and future at the same time. This is done by identifying the kuṇam complex and the karmam complex and then collapsing the two to form a new kuṇam complex. Stated differently, the ritual of flowers helps identify the quality of one's kuṇam substance vis-à-vis its hot-cold aspect. Furthermore, it helps in identifying the qualitative state, the fruition or nonfruition of karmam substance. When karmam substance is ripened, it is fully incorporated into the kunam substance, intrinsically altering the kuṇam substance for better or for worse.

The red and white flowers, through their iconic and indexical relationship with hot and cold body states, are able to respond to a wide array of questions about sickness and health. The concepts of sickness and health, however, must be understood in their broadest sense, according to which, even being overly anxious or worried about something is to be ill.

Excessive heat or excessive cold, on the phenotypic level, is caused by the three humors. The perfect humoral balance is peculiar to person and time. Any deviation from this perfect, or ideal, balance results in either a heat-caused or a cold-caused bodily disorder. These disorders, however, caused by the ever-fluctuating humors, are no occasion for serious concern, unless, of course, it is discovered through the ritual of flowers that the patient's kuṇam substance itself is isomorphic or sympathetic in some measure and conducive to the apparent disorders attributed to the humors, for this would indicate that the condition of the patient is more or less permanent and genotypic rather than merely phenotypic.

The signifying mechanism in the ritual of flowers operates most overtly by means of the indexical function. Yet, the iconic relationship between the various signs and their objects is unmistakably present and is certainly at the surface of the consciousness of the participants. Of all three functions, the symbolic mode is least clearly represented to the consciousness of the interpretants.

Finally, there is considerable room for creative manipulation and interpretation on the part of the priest. Therefore, the choices he makes can only be understood contextually and pragmatically.

PART II

Toward Equipoise

6
A Theoretical Interlude

"Understanding a culture in its own terms" has been appropriated with such earnestness by certain schools of cultural anthropologists that to them it has become almost a creed. Such a creed, to say the least, is a zealous overstatement of a reality that is far more complicated than the believer will admit. Carried to its logical extreme, this concept neutralizes anthropology as anthropology. Understanding a culture *for* its own terms is perhaps a more truthful and realistic enterprise.[1] This does not exclude the possibility of understanding, at one time or another, certain aspects of the culture in its own terms. Any field-worker worthy of the name must have on various occasions felt so intimately a part of what was going on that he or she could not have reflected on the experience even had he or she tried—at least not until much later. There was a time in the field when I had as good a command of the genealogical records of certain ANV kōttirams as did a few elders who specialized in genealogy, and on more than one occasion I was called upon to partake in discussions pertaining to

[1] I thank Lee Schlesinger for introducing me to this significant distinction (personal communication).

certain marriage proposals or dowry arrangements. On some of these occasions, discussions and disagreements would get so heated that passions would rise, especially with respect to property exchange. It didn't take long for my own passions to rise and fall with such cultural appropriateness, in perfect sympathy with the deliberate schemes and the unreasonable (as well as reasonable) emotions of the family whose concerns I had made mine; that dowry, for instance, was no longer a mere academic matter but one of tradition, principle, wit, vengeance, honor, shame, culture, and reality—so much so that my Brahmin field assistant once felt obliged to remind me that I was not an ANV, after all. These moments are moments of understanding a culture in its own terms. However, no cultural account or interpretive account is possible from within these moments of perfect iconicity.[2]

Anthropologizing becomes possible only because a certain measure of aniconicity between object (the native's web of signification) and representamen (the anthropologist's own web of signification, which attempts to tie in with that of the native) is possible. This aniconicity or difference makes significance possible. Without difference there can be no sign. This much is old wisdom for semeiologists, at least since de Saussure and Peirce. The interpretive account of a culture contained in these pages is in itself a sign, albeit a very complex sign, and owes its significance to its inherent structure of difference.

Insofar as I claim to have understood the culture in which I have studied, I have understood it in my own terms, even though some of them, if not most of them, have been intimately and immensely informed and affected by the culture's "own terms" because of my having entered into a deferential dialogue with my informants. This is why I also claim, in Lee Schlesinger's words, to have understood this culture for its own terms.

[2]See my treatment of the iconic First in the Introduction.

The terms in my understanding that I have jealously preserved throughout this study derive from my view of what constitutes culture. This view, as I have indicated in the Introduction, is a semeiotic one that holds that a culture is a loosely integrated system of signs created dialogically in the communicative act between an anthropologist and his informants. Given the semeiotic emphasis of this entire study, if one were to identify the locus classicus of this definition of culture, it would be the sign. The sign, we have seen, is constituted of three irreducible correlates: the representamen, the object, and the interpretant. These were also called Firsts, Seconds, and Thirds. These are relational terms, logical terms in which each subsequent term must presuppose the antecedent term(s), but the antecedent(s) need not presuppose the subsequent one(s). We went on to find that even as the sign itself was triadically constituted, signification, too, occurred in three modes, called iconic, indexical, and symbolic. In any given event of signification, one mode may become dominant at the expense of the others. Within the sign types, iconicity is a relative First, indexicality a relative Second, and the symbol, a relative Third.

The relative Firstness, Secondness, and Thirdness of icons, indexes, and symbols, respectively, may be understood developmentally as well. For reasons of simplicity, consider the example of a child's learning the meaning of a word. (This is not to imply that children learn a language by learning words. More than likely this is not the case, and more recently Western linguistics has begun to recognize that words are learned in the contexts of sentences, a piece of wisdom that Indian grammarians have had at least since Pāṇini [Staal 1979]. For our purposes, the substitution of *sentence* for *word* will not alter the basic point being made here.) If the Peircean hypothesis is correct, as I believe it to be, a child's first apperception of the sounds of a word or the mere utterance of these sounds occurs for the sake of its "quality." The word *apple,* when first apperceived or uttered, is not done so because the referential connection is made between sound and object. It begins as a mere savoring of phonetic quality. Repeated presentation of sound and object creates "preindexical" contiguity. Actual learning, however, or the first significant link between sound *s*, and object *o*, begins only when the similarity (iconicity) between s^1 and o^1, and s^2 and o^2, and s^3 and o^3, and so on, are made. Until then the various pairs of s's and o's remain isolated dyads. The first significant link begins, then, with the recognition of resemblances or iconicity between and among these pairs. Then the child may go on boldly to the indexical application of pointing to a particular o and calling it an s. This is to know that o and s are tokens of types of o and s. When the child attempts to extend *apple* to an orange and is corrected, not only is the lesson of iconicity and indexicality drummed in but also the child begins to learn the limitations imposed by convention, or the symbolic aspect of language. As we move away from childhood, the symbolic function of learning becomes so preeminent that the indexical and iconic precursors in learning hold but a fleeting moment's reign in an adult's awareness. The misguided approach to equating learning with naming is a consequence of the imposition on teaching of an awareness dominated by the symbolic function.

At the cost of dangerously simplifying the learning process (and not wanting to digress far enough to amplify and strengthen the Peircean theory), I have attempted to show why and how icon, index, and symbol are related to one another as First, Second, and Third, respectively. This brief excursion, however, will serve to relate this pervasively and persistently constituted semeiotic to the task of interpretation at hand.

I have said that ultimately, I have understood the culture I studied in my own terms. Yet I qualified this statement by saying that these terms of mine were informed, to a large measure, by the privilege of having been iconically linked with the web of signification that my native informants had "naturally" spun. This has made it possible for me to say as well that I have understood this culture for its own terms. What, however, of the doggedly persistent core that constitutes my "terms of understanding"? The triadically constituted semeiotic sign and its trimodal signification? Do I have any reason to claim that this core, too, has been *informed* by native categories, by native symbolic constructs?

Had there been an indigenous theory of signs, my problem might have been simplified. Of course, there are probably more than one highly reflected-upon theories of meaning and theories of signs in the classical tradition of India. Interest in these theories among Indologists has been only recent, and accessible secondary sources on these theories are yet to become readily available. Even if there were such works, however, and even if I were a Sanskritist with direct access to the primary sources, I cannot presuppose that these theories would have any bearing on the unsystematized notions of signification found among the folks I studied. Anthony Good's finding that the so-called *jajmāni* system (from Skt. *yajamāna*) has little or nothing to do with Tamil cultural categories is a case in point (1982). What we do have is considerable evidence that were we to attribute the existence of a systematic semeiotic to Tamil culture, the dominant or valued mode of representation tends to be away from the symbol and toward iconicity. The reason for this is the regnancy of the significance of "coded substance" in the culture. Coded substance in Tamil culture, like gravity in physics, pulls all other signs toward itself. Quite clearly, the defining feature of the iconic sign, its capacity to represent through sharing of qualities, which can range anywhere from isomorphism up to identity with the object, makes it the most preferred of representative possibilities in the culture. Elsewhere (1983*b*) I show that in Siddha medical practice (and presumably in Ayurvedic practice as well) both diagnosis and treatment rely almost exclusively on iconicity (the sharing of pulses between physician and patient when the physician reads a pulse; the shared qualities between a drug and the patient's body substance ["homeopathy"]; the shared attributes between an invading quasi-pathogen or humor and the body that receives these; the iconicity between an ecological niche, a particular humor, and a particular drug [see also Zimmermann 1978]). By contrast, Western biomedicine relies almost exclusively on indexical (cause and effect, allopathy) and symbolic ("somatization") modes of representation.

In the absence of a systematically developed, indigenously formulated semeiosis, and until such semeiosis is made available through further intensive fieldwork as well as relevant textual research, I must build up evidence for my hypothesis with regard to the culturally preferred semeiotic gradient by seeing whether there are parallel processes in the culture outside the strict domain of signs. I do think that I have such a domain in the field experience recorded in chapter 7. The domain I speak of is that of the acquisition of knowledge.

In chapter 7, apart from bringing the substance theory to an all-encompassing denouement, I attempt to examine my village informants' views on what knowledge is and what processes are involved in its acquisition. This theory of knowledge is far more explicit in the ethnographic material than the theory of signs I have hypothesized for the ethnographic data of the four preceding chapters. By juxtaposing this indigenous theory of knowledge against Peirce's theory of knowledge as expressed through his three phenomenological categories, I will show how the former, though ex pressible in almost identical terms, is processually the inverse of the latter. Given that Peirce's phenomenological categories are taken to be the generative of his semeiotic categories, it becomes even more reasonable for us to believe that a similar (though inverted) set of phenomenological-*cum*-epistemological categories in the Tamil cultural context should generate a similar (but inverted) set of semeiotic categories as well.

7
Equilibrium Regained

We opened this study in the Introduction with a parochial variant of the Sāṅkhya creation myth in which the creative process was seen also as a degenerative process. According to the myth, this generative-degenerative process was triggered by the disturbance of a state of perfect equilibrium and equipoise. This myth opened the curtains to reveal a culture and life of a people endlessly and obsessively concerned with establishing, if not restoring, equilibriated-*cum*-compatible relationships between themselves and other entities of the phenomenal universe, such as ūr, house, and sexual partner, as well as with establishing and preserving substantial equilibrium within their own bodies, between kuṇam and karmam, bile and wind. The opening anecdote in chapter 2 was about the ANV expatriate gentleman who returned to his natal village (conda ūr) to make arrangements for his son's visit. This event introduced a subdominant theme of this study, namely, that of self-knowledge, which theme in fact may be seen as an inseparable corollary to the theme of compatible and equilibriated substances. I now turn to this theme.

Knowledge about "the other" and knowledge about

"oneself" may appear to be different and distinct. In the Tamil world view, however, knowledge about the other, or object knowledge, is but an extension of self-knowledge. This double-edged knowledge can be acquired in two ways. In Tamil, the first mode of acquisition of knowledge is called *iṇaippāl arital*, and the second is known as *pakuppāl arital*. *Iṇaippu* means join, unite, coalesce, to be alike, connection, copulation, sameness, and so forth. *Iṇaippāl arital*, then, means to know by establishing relationships of unity, sameness, coalescence, to know by connecting, joining, and so on. We may approximately translate this kind of knowledge as "synthetic" knowledge. In pakuppāl arital, the root *paku* means many, divide, distribute, apportion, allot, classify. Thus, pakuppāl arital is to know by dividing, classifying—in short, by making distinctions. We may render this kind of knowledge as "analytic" knowledge.

If the goal of synthetic knowledge is to discover the self in the other or to know the self by getting to know in the other that which is also in the self, then analytic knowledge aims at knowing the self by knowing that which is in the object that is *not* in the self. The former seeks to find that which is common between self and other and the latter seeks to distinguish the self from the other by noting how differently they are constituted.

Both synthetic knowledge and analytic knowledge place object knowledge at the service of self-knowledge, but synthetic knowledge distinguishes itself from analytic knowledge in that it aims at the incorporation of object knowledge by self-knowledge, or conversely, its aim is to expand self-knowledge so that it completely consumes object knowledge. At the point at which object knowledge is completely incorporated or engulfed in this manner, not only is there no longer object knowledge, but there is also no longer self-knowledge, which is defined against object knowledge. What remains is pure knowledge (*arivu* or *vidyā*).

According to the Tamil, then, synthetic knowledge may be said to serve self-knowledge (and by extension, knowledge itself) more effectively than does analytic knowledge, even though, paradoxically, this synthetic knowledge culminates in the extinction of self-knowledge itself, which, after all, depends on its opposite, object knowledge, for its epistemic and ontological integrity.

My guru[1] emphasized over and over again that in ordinary life, even as the distinction between self-knowledge (*tannarivu* or *akapporuḷarivu*) and object knowledge (*purapporuḷarivu*) cannot be transcended, so can one not transcend the distinction between synthetic knowledge and analytic knowledge. They are two sides of the same coin.

I believe that among the Tamils, however, the emphasis on and the awareness of synthetic knowledge cannot be missed; that it is valorized (to borrow a term from Louis Dumont) cannot be denied. I believe that this is so because of the central place that substance, in its transactability, transformability, and compatibility, occupies in Indian thought. This fact is best and most frequently exemplified in contexts when strangers meet.

When one stranger wishes to get to know another stranger, the most often employed opener is the question "What is your ūr?" He hopes, of course, that the ūr that is named will be known to him. He hopes not so much to discover that there is something about the ūr that he knows but rather that there is some person already known to him in the named ūr. If such a person is of the same jati, or better still, a kinsman, then he feels that he knows that ūr even better than if the said person is but an acquaintance belonging to another jāti. The underlying principle here is the cultural belief that two kinsmen share more of a common bodily substance than do nonkinsmen of the same jāti, and that nonkinsmen of the same jāti share more of a common bodily substance than do mere acquaintances or friends

[1]The guru referred to here is Krishnaswamy, under whose guidance several of my fellow pilgrims and I prepared ourselves for the pilgrimage (to be described below).

belonging to different jātis. By knowing someone with whom you can lay some claim to shared substance, you may also claim to know the ūr whose substance that person shares, and hence whose substance you, too, share by a transitive-*cum*-substantial logic. This is why Devadas felt he knew Pondicherry when he found out that one of his kinsmen was already living there and had established substantial compatibility with that ūr.

In knowing an ūr synthetically in this manner, you get to know an aspect of yourself "out there," so to speak, and based on the principle of shared substance, that entity out there is an extension of yourself, which is tantamount to saying it is a part of yourself. From this point of view, you may say that in knowing the ūr in this way, your knowledge of yourself has been synthetically extended. It is in this sense, then, that object knowledge and self-knowledge are seen as corollaries, if not one and the same thing; at the same time, in the synthetic mode of its acquisition, the object is incorporated into the self.

In keeping with my guru's emphasis on the inseparability of the synthetic from the analytic and the object from the self, we have seen that Tamils, despite what they valorize, are nonetheless preoccupied if not obsessed with making finer and finer distinctions between their own substance and other substances, such as those of an ūr, a house, and so forth. By making such distinctions, a Tamil strives to maintain substantial compatibility and equilibrium. Yet equilibriated states are continually disturbed when substances move around. Everything in the manifest world is in flux, calling for incessant vigilance and effort to restore what is lost or disturbed. Insofar as such efforts are motivated by an inferior, analytic knowledge which is sustained by the making of distinctions and categories, however, they can only be exhausting and endless. There comes a point when one realizes this fact and seeks a way out.

In the pilgrimage I am about to describe, several of the pilgrims with whom I walked a grueling forty miles had reached such a point, either on their own or through the teachings of the guru. As a pilgrim the discontented person sets himself a new goal, a goal to move away from differentiated knowledge and differentiatable substance to knowledge of the undifferentiated ātman in terms of the essential unity of all substance. With this knowledge, the endless striving for relationships of compatibility has no relevance, since substance is once more undifferentiated and in perfect equilibrium. As will be demonstrated, this kind of knowledge is experienced rather than apprehended. The pilgrimage itself is a ritual, a karmam—a very powerful and efficacious karmam at that—that seeks to generate this kind of knowing experience, which is expected to help the pilgrim to eventually obtain perfect knowledge, or vidyā.

Given that the value of anthropology lies in its contribution to cross-cultural understanding, I wish to compare the cultural attitude toward knowledge and the knowing process that one encounters among Tamil Hindus with that extant in the West. This exercise is not intended to minimize the variations encountered in both traditions: India has its Pāṇinis as much as the West has its Bergsons. Even here, however, one cannot miss the synthetic quality of Pāṇini's grammar, even as one cannot miss the analyticity of Bergson.

In order to represent, for purposes of contrast, the valorized epistemology of the West, I have chosen as its representative the views of C. S. Peirce. The choice is not a capricious one. First, Peirce's theory of knowledge, as embodied in his three phenomenological categories, is directly related to his semeiotic categories, dealt with extensively throughout Part I. In the interest of continuity, then, it is only reasonable that with respect to "knowledge," I should, once again, explore the appropriateness of Peirce's views. Second, I believe that the link between a Tamil theory of knowledge and Peirce's epistemology is even more overt than that which relates his semeiosis with a hypothesized Tamil theory of signs. By arguing backward, so to speak, I wish to imply that the link between the systematically formulated Peircean semeiotic and the unsystematized Tamil semeiotic is a closer one than might have been initially imagined. Third, Peirce's view of knowledge and the systematic acquisition of it is *broadly* representative of Western commonsensical as well as philosophical traditions. In other contexts and for other purposes, the differences between Peirce and Descartes, Peirce and Locke, or Peirce and Kant may be quite remarkable, acute, and crucial as well. Yet for the purpose at hand, the purpose of establishing a broad epistemological gradient or directionality, these differences do not matter. In fact, the learning theories of such psychologists as Jean Piaget and George Kelly (to mention the two whose writings I am most acquainted with) turn out to be Peircean orthodoxy.

Peirce's phenomenological categories most lucidly sketch the epistemological value structure of Western rationality. By virtue of their being descriptively and analytically so precise and sensitive, the categories also turn out to be equally fine accounts of the Hindu knowing process, albeit in its inverted form. Furthermore, Peirce's categories lend themselves in many ways (again though as an inversion) to capture the knowing process as *experienced* in the pilgrimage itself. For these reasons I shall elucidate Peirce's categories at some length, for in grasping Peirce's categories one can also begin to grasp, in anticipation, intellectually (though inversely) that which is intended to be grasped empathetically in the description of the pilgrim's experience which follows.

One of Peirce's least obscure accounts of his three categories can be found in his Lowell lectures. He starts with a general formulation of them: "My view is that there are three modes of being, and [I] hold that we can directly observe them in elements of whatever is at any time before the mind in any way. They are the being of positive qualitative possibility, the being of actual fact, and the being of law that will govern in the future" (1.23).

The being of positive qualitative possibility is what he calls Firstness; the being of actual fact is Secondness, and the being of law is Thirdness.

Let us take up the three categories in detail by beginning with Firstness. Firstness, in other words, is the felt quality of experience *in toto*—present, immediate, uncategorized, prereflective, the manifold of sensuous impressions (in Kantian terms) before thought, either analytical or synthetic, has taken place. In Peirce's words, Firstness is "what the world was to Adam on the day he opened his eyes, before he had drawn any distinctions, or had become conscious of his own existence" (1.357).

In one of the most forceful and elegantly constructed passages, Peirce goes on to describe Firstness as "that which is first, fresh, new, original, spontaneous, free, vivid, conscious, and evanescent. Only remember that every description of it must be false to it." He insists that "the First has to be present and immediate so as not to be a Second to a representation. It must be fresh and new, for if old, it is a second to its former state" (1.357). Insofar as it is vivid and conscious, "it avoids being the object of some sensation. It precedes all synthesis and all determination. It has no unity and no parts. It cannot be articulately thought. Assert it and it has already lost its characteristic innocence; for assertion always implies a denial of something else. Stop to think of it and it has flown" (1.357).

Firstness is not an abstraction. That the sky appears to us positively now as blue before we make any judgment may not be apparent to every mind. Peirce maintained that at least it was not apparent to Hegel. "When anything is present to the mind," he wrote in 1903, "the first and simplest character to be noted in it is its presentness or immediacy" (5.44). So far, Peirce's Firstness is not unlike Hegel's sense of immediacy. Peirce and Hegel part company, however, when Hegel makes immediacy an abstraction. To use a well-known example from the *Phenomenology of Mind*, the *now* that is nighttime becomes the *now* that is day. As nighttime it is not day; as daytime it is not night. Thus far the now, or pure immediacy temporally viewed, is not immediate but something mediated for Hegel, determined through and by means of the fact that something else, namely day or night, is not. It is for Hegel a universal, so immediacy in its presentness becomes an abstraction.

This was not so for Peirce. What is present to the mind is present immediacy—the present "is just what it is regardless of the absent, regardless of the past and future. It is such, as it is, utterly ignoring everything else. Consequently it cannot be abstracted" (5.44).

For obvious reasons, "Firstness is the most elusive of Peirce's categories, since it signifies the thing in itself, or that primary limit to our thought which can never be conceptually grasped in its original state" (1.357—Stearns 1952: 199). Firstness "is identifiable with feeling before the latter has been introspected and has thereby undergone change" (Stearns 1952; see also 1.303 and 1.304). "Firstness is fresh, free, and pregnant with variety" (1.302). Peirce's Firstness has much in common with Turner's communitas and liminality, despite liminality's specifically sociological implications and derivatives (Turner 1967). In this commonness lies much of communitas's and liminality's allure as well as elusiveness, which have moved its admirers to respect and its detractors to skepticism.

Beyond a category of being, however, "Firstness possesses a 'may-be' character which nonetheless still belongs to the mere idea unrealized" (1.304). The ideal First is then identified by Peirce as "quite singular and quite out of consciousness" (5.311) and as possessing a "may-be" quality or as "a mere idea unrealized" (1.342). In other words, Firstness is not merely a mode of being, but it is a mode of becoming. Now let us move on to Peirce's Secondness.

Stearns gleans from several passages of Peirce scattered among his *Collected Papers* the essential characteristics of the category of Firstness, and she highlights them quite lucidly, saying:

> If Firstness for Peirce has the status of a dream, a quality in itself unanchored to any laws, being a mere "may-be," fugitive and evanescent. Secondness on the other hand represents the encounter with hard fact (1.324; 6.95), the undeniable shock of contact with the outer world (1.334–336). Secondness is the category of effort, of struggle and resistance (1.320, 322, 284); it is the category of existence become manifest or indeed possible. . . . [It is] only in the polarity of Secondness that Self and Not-Self becomes precipitated out against each other. (1.324; Stearns 1952: 201)

There is a real world, a sensuous, reactant world, independent of thought although thinkable, which is characterized by Secondness. It is the area of daily existence, where we come up against obstacles that will not give way to our fancies, against actualities that resist and oppose one another, where for every action there is an equal and opposite reaction. Such is the world of existent fact; such is the nature of existence. To exist is not to be perceived but to stand against another, take a place, oppose bodies, resist and react, to belong to a time and a place.

Here is an example given by Peirce, which, in addition to being an illustration of Secondness, serves as a surprising revelation of his capacity for slapstick humor: "Let the universe be an evolution of Pure Reason if you will. Yet if, while you are walking in the street reflecting upon how everything is the pure distillate of Reason, a man carrying a heavy pole suddenly pokes you in the small of the back, that moment of brute fact is Secondness" (5–45). The moment of reaction that follows the encounter between the agent and patient, pole and polee, if you will, the moment of resistance, in short, the moment of "brute fact," before any sort of third medium or any sort of law of action enters the picture—that moment is the moment of Secondness.

Thirdness is the most subtle of Peirce's conceptions. Thirdness is the element of the "general" in our experience. In Stearn's rephrasing of Peirce,

> the category of Thirdness is above all the category of mediation. Without it we may suppose that Firstness and Secondness as quality and event would remain completely out of significant relation to each other. Thirdness is the factor of final causation which manifests itself as a "gentle force" bringing together in a certain measure all that which without it must remain in arbitrary and unmediated opposition. Thirdness cannot in fact have any being apart from Firstness and Secondness. It exists in its role of mediation alone (5.121), and yet as general and as significant it always transcends that which it mediates. It goes beyond the actual instances to signify still other conceivable instances to which it may refer in the future. In terms of Peirce's conception of Thirdness we may understand the "general" as of the nature of rule, or better still, a habitual mode of behavior, a directive tendency which has meaning in relation to its instances to which still others could be substituted. (Stearns 1952: 203)

Its power is its ability to predict, and its strength is its generalizability; its essence—to phrase it in terms of social anthropology—is its structure, and its anchor is in culture viewed in Schneiderian terms as a system of symbols and meanings.

These are Peirce's triadic categories in outline. Now let us consider his epistemology, defined here as the "knowing process." The pilgrimage is an exploration and exercise in epistemology. It is also an exploration of cosmology, even as Peirce's categories explore the evolution of the cosmos. For the Hindu pilgrim, the explorations in epistemology and cosmology are conjoined in an autological quest, the quest after the answer to the question "Who am I?"

Ideally for Peirce, and intrinsic to the nature of the phaneron,[2] both cosmos and knowledge, matter and reason, fact and value, body and mind,[3] evolved from Firstness to Thirdness. The synechistic[4] arrow points in the direction of a perfectly rational system. In terms of social structural organization, the synechistic tendency is toward greater social integration, greater specialization of roles, and greater limitation on the possible varieties of individual behavior. Progress, for Peirce, results "from every individual merging his individuality in sympathy with his neighbor's" (6.6294).[5] Peirce's ideal of Thirdness is to be achieved only when impulse and spontaneity give way to custom and then to law, law being a function of reasoned habit. Victor Turner, in his several studies on the ritual process, observed that the movement from communitas to societas, or from liminality to structure, was characterized by a movement from the "ludic" to the "ergic" (1974: 221–223; Turner and Turner 1978: 35–37). Peirce's Thirdness is Turner's ergic, sans its encounter with resistance. For Peirce, development, like knowledge, essentially involves a limitation of possibilities. In his words, "There is a tendency, as action is repeated again and again to approximate indefinitely toward the perfection of that fixed character, which would be marked by the entire absence of self-reproach. The more closely this is appreciated, the less room for self-control there will be" (5.418). Peirce, however, is also aware here of the increasingly confining and self-alienating direction of his epistemology and cosmology. One cannot miss the echo of Weber's tyranny of bureaucratization, Durkheim's anomie, Marx's alienation,

[2]The phaneron is understood by Peirce as all that appears to the mind and wherein the mind itself is part of that appearance (1.280–287).

[3]Peirce's anti-Cartesian writings, especially with respect to Cartesian dualism, are well known. The Hindu, I am convinced, will take the side of Peirce in treating matter as effete mind (6.25).

[4]Synechism is defined as "the doctrine that all that exists is continuous" (1.172).

[5]For this and other parallels between Peirce's Pragmaticism and Marxism, see Karl-Otto Apel's *Charles S. Peirce: From Pragmatism to Pragmaticism*.

and even de Tocqueville's apprehensions about a totally individualistic egalitarian society. For this reason, Peirce does a double take. He provides his Thirdness with a crucial ingredient, namely, that of indeterminacy or chance, which he called tychism. The modal nature of Firstness is that of logical possibility; the modal nature of Secondness is actual fact; but the modal nature of Thirdness is that future conditional that must be regarded as a real potentiality both in our experience and in nature itself. The doctrine of Thirdness is, then, an assertion that the imaginative freedom has its roots in the habit-taking character of the universe itself. But this habit taking is never so final that it does not permit exceptions; indeed, a new and fruitful tendency may arise. The "general" is, in fact, in the process of growth through its instances; it does not bind them but receives its implementation to a greater or lesser extent through them.

The Hindu pilgrim is less optimistic about Thirdness and its aspect of tychism. In Thirdness he discovers the exaltation of that form of knowledge, namely, analytic knowledge, that his culture at its core devalues. He finds Thirdness and analytic knowledge binding, since this type of knowledge emphasizes the discontinuity of his substance and the substance of his ūr, house, kinsmen, and so on through its incessant concern with the categorization and ranking of substances. To him, the emphasis on rules, laws, theories, categories, distinctions that are a part of Thirdness is the very kind of "knowledge" that alienates him from a true synthetic knowledge of the oneness and continuity of all substance. Therefore, he must strive to move away from the world of theories and laws, through Secondness, which dissolves the rules and theories that classify "the other" into just one other (in the case of the pilgrimage, *pain*), which looms out against the self, to Firstness, where the "other" is experienced in such immediacy that it is no longer clear where self ends and other begins. Firstness, is beyond all self and other distinctions, even beyond the mediacy of perception. In Firstness, the pilgrim leaves behind his temporal, differentiated identity and exists only as the ātman, a pure, unmanifest, and undifferentiated form of substance. It is no longer meaningful to speak of self or other or of perception, since there are no distinct entities to perceive. Knowledge in this state is synthetic knowledge at its most complete, where one knows the self through having incorporated the other so completely that there is no longer any self or other. Incorporative, substantial oneness is then Firstness—*pūrṇa vidyā*—pure knowledge.

Now I will turn to the pilgrimage itself, an exercise in the progressive and processual acquisition of knowledge and the corresponding shedding of ignorance. Less abstractly, its purpose is to visit Lord Ayyappan, who sits upon a mountain, known as Sabari Malai, located amid the hills of central Kerala in southwest India.

Lord Ayyappan, as legend has it, was born to Śiva and Viṣṇu, two major sectarian deities of India. How was Ayyappan born to two male deities? Well, Viṣṇu was not quite male when this happened. There was (I am making a very long story very short) a buffalo demoness who had received a very dangerous boon from Brahma, the creator. The boon was that she could not be killed by anyone born from the union of male and female. With this boon in hand, the demoness went about wreaking havoc on everything in her path. She overthrew Indra's *tevalōkam* ("heavens, abode of the gods"), captured the earth in one day, and exalted the netherworlds to such dizzy heights of power that the whole universe trembled at her footstep. So one day, Indra went to Śiva and Viṣṇu for help. As a result, Viṣṇu took on the form of Mohini, a beautiful female, and then proceeded to bathe in the river that flowed by the place where Śiva was meditating under a tree. Struck by this beauty incarnate who Śiva saw "clinging to her dripping silk wrap," Śiva's semen "sprang like an arrow from his lingam [phallus] and impregnated Viṣṇu in his Mohini-*rūpa*, or Mohini form. Nine months later, Ayyappan was born. To make a shortened story shorter yet, Ayyappan, being the son of male and male, was not subject to Brahma's boon and so was able to slay the awful demoness. Yet no sooner had the demoness fallen to the ground dead then she rose again, reincarnated as the most beautiful maiden. While the young Ayyappan stood there beauty-struck, the young goddess thanked him for redeeming her from her terrible previous birth and expressed her wish to marry him. Ayyappan knew that it was his *karma* ("fate") to marry her, but he also had other promises to keep. So being the son of clever Śiva and tricky Viṣṇu, he made a conditional promise. He said, "on whichever year a virgin pilgrim does not come to Sabari Hill to worship me, on that year I shall marry you." The goddess in turn made her solemn vow to wait, even if it took forever. So to this day, the god and goddess are waiting on their respective hills in their respective shrines. An examination of Lord Ayyappan's iconic representation or the abundance of lithographs of this deity will reveal his very interesting squatting position. The weight of his body rests on his toes, and his knees are held up by a strap at an odd angle. One pilgrim assured me that if I were ever to be struck by an unvanquishable ithyphallic condition, all I had to do was to get into the Ayyappan position and I would be assured of flaccid relief. In any event, it has worked for Lord Ayyappan for the last seven or eight centuries.

In 1976, I, in my small way, as one among thousands of other "virgin pilgrims," helped Ayyappan preserve his bachelorhood. In Tamil Nadu and Kerala, Lord Ayyappan has become the lord of celibacy par excellence. Consequently, only those who have taken a strict vow to celibacy can approach his shrine. No females, except the nonmenstruating kind—prepubertal and postmenopausal—are allowed on this pilgrimage.

The pilgrimage to Sabari Malai is seasonal—between December 15 and January 15. Preparations for the pilgrimage are elaborate; it is probably one of the most elaborate of any pilgrimage in India. Among these preparations are several vows of austerity that must be taken forty-five to sixty days prior to beginning the journey. These austerities involve: no sex, no shoes or sandals, no more garments than two changes of vēṣṭis, which must not be in any color other than black, blue, or ocher, no meat or eggs, no intoxicating beverages, no meals in other people's homes, three baths a day, three pūjās a day, as many visits to as many temples as possible, giving of alms, no losing of one's temper, no verbal, physical, or mental abuse toward others, no violence (even toward the smallest of insects), no sleeping on beds or mattresses but only on a mat or on the bare floor, no unclean thoughts (mainly sexual), avoidance of the company of any woman (be she your wife, mother, sister, or stranger) and so on.

During the forty-five to sixty days from the day the vow is taken to the day of the trip to Sabari Malai, the pilgrim begins to be weaned away from society. In our village, for instance, everyone addressed us as "Swami," and we in turn addressed everybody else as "Ayyappa Swami." In other words, everybody became an Ayyappan for us. Our external appearance—the wearing of a black, blue, or ocher vēṣṭi and holy ashes across our chests and foreheads, along with the consecrated beaded necklace—marked us as not belonging to the social order of the village. None can command an Ayyappan pilgrim, however lowly the pilgrim may be, in the caste structure. Everyone knew that we abstained from sex, and that made us very powerful in the eyes of the villagers, for our curse, if we were to curse, would stick.

On the eve of the pilgrimage, the pilgrims undergo an initiation rite in one of the local temples, in which a two-pouched cloth bag called the *iru muṭi* (literally, "double crown") is placed on each pilgrim's head in such a way that the waist of the bag rests on the head, with one pouch suspended in front of the head and other behind. The pouch in front contains coconuts, ghee, camphor, turmeric, joss sticks, and other offertory items intended for the deity. The other pouch contains the pilgrim's own provisions for eating and sleeping. While this rite on the eve of the pilgrim's departure is called the iru muṭi rite, it contains within it, besides the placing of the iru muṭi on the pilgrim's head, several subrituals. Important among these is a miniature death ritual, which friends and kinsmen of the pilgrims perform by throwing three handfuls of raw rice into one of the pouches of the iru muṭi. This is not unlike the throwing of rice on a corpse before it is taken to be cremated. By this act, friends and kinsmen symbolically complete their duties toward one who is renouncing the world and shall henceforth be as good as dead.

After the iru muṭi was placed on our heads, we left the shrine by walking backward until we reached the temple courtyard. At this point we were stopped and told to turn around three times, even as a corpse is turned around three times on its way to the crematorium. After the third turn we faced the "wilderness," that is, away from the temple. We continued to stand in this position while our friends, kinsmen, and almost anybody and everybody who happened to be in the temple or was passing by in the street came and prostrated before each one of us in order to gain merit by this very act. They were cautioned not to touch us, however, lest we be polluted, and our power be too much for them to bear. While all this prostrating went on, the pilgrim was expected to look straight ahead; by no means was he allowed to turn around to look at what he is about to leave behind. After all the people gathered there had worshipped us to their hearts' content, our pilgrimage began in earnest.

There were seven of us in our group, and we traveled to Kerala by car until we reached a place called Eru Meli. (In days gone by, pilgrims must have done the entire trip on foot. But in these times, given the practical difficulties of getting leave and so forth, one has little choice but to travel the two-hundred-odd miles to the base of the hill, Eru Meli, by automobile or bus.) On our way, of course, we visited every single temple of any importance, especially temples of the goddesses, in order to obtain from them śakti, or power, that would sustain us throughout the arduous walk from Eru Meli to Sabari Malai.

Eru Meli was the actual starting point of our pilgrimage, from which the forty-seven-mile trek to Sabari Malai began. The forty-seven-mile footpath is not by any means the most direct route. There are two other paths to Sabari Malai, one a six-mile track and another a nineteen-mile track, both these being easier, safer, and shorter than our forty-seven-mile route, which winds its way through forests infested with elephants, bears, leopards, and all manner of creepy-crawly creatures, and, of course, very many less dangerous beasts and a few rather pleasant ones—birds, squirrels, and butterflies. The path is circuitous and goes up and down several hills before it gets to Sabari Malai. But our path, though less traveled, was special, because it is the very path that Lord Ayyappan walked on his way to Sabari. By sharing in this historical experience of our Lord, we became special pilgrims, Ayyappans in the true sense; for our efforts we gained special rewards and privileges when we got to the getting place.

When we got to Eru Meli it was about one in the afternoon, and thousands of pilgrims were gathered in groups around temporarily constructed hearths or a guru or a *bhajan* leader. There were stalls in Eru Meli where commercial activities were as spirited as those seen in the bazaars of big cities, but here an atmosphere of festivity reigned. Pilgrims and merchants alike seemed caught up in a spirit of freedom and celebration. The atmosphere seemed somewhat like that of the second novena in the fiesta of three kings described by Victor Turner (1974: 194): "It stressed the commercial and festive aspects of the total situation which contained three major foci in space and time. These were solemnity, festivity and trade, all three representing types of the liminal disengagement from day to day participation in structural role playing and status incumbency."

After we had laid our loads down, taking great care to place our iru muṭis on a special sacred mat, we proceeded toward the stream to perform our first ritual of the day. This was none other than ritual defecation and urination. We were to rid ourselves, to the best of our ability, of the contents of our bowels and bladder, which belonged to a world we were leaving behind. To me and to many other pilgrims—most of whom were urban, middle-class individuals—this was quite a liminal experience. We had never done this in public before, in the company of ritual defecators to the right, left, front, and back, each only two feet away, solemnly doing his thing while precariously perched on two felled tree trunks thrown over trenches, with no walls around nor roof above.

Following this sublime rite, we walked up a little hill to a small shrine, where we proceeded to daub one another with multicolored powdered dyes. It is true that my fellow villagers had not addressed me as "sir" for over sixty-odd days, ever since we jointly took our vows and became Ayyappa pilgrims. There still remained, however, a vestige of a deferential attitude in their behavior toward me, as a guest and as a foreigner. I seemed to receive special treatment in so many subtle ways, even though such treatment was forbidden by the spirit of the pilgrimage. Yet as my fellow pilgrims-*cum*-fellow villagers, several of them belonging to lower jātis, began to paint colored spots all over my face and body, I saw a new glow light up their faces. I was being transformed, and the last residue of social differences of rank and status was beginning to disappear even as my features were being creatively disfigured and transformed. They all broke out in laughter, and so did I when I finished painting their faces and bodies.

Following our transformation into brightly spotted, new individuals, we were given a tree branch. With this green branch in hand, the group broke into song, and we danced in circles to the rhythm of the drums. We proceeded down the street, still dancing, still singing, "Swāmi tintakattom, Ayyappa tintakattom." This is believed to be a song sung by Ayyappa and his hunters returning with the day's booty. Singing and dancing, we worked our way down to the Islamic shrine and tomb of the Muslim saint Vāvar.

A combination of legend and history traces the entry of this Islamic figure into the Ayyappan cult to around the eleventh or twelfth century. It is believed that Ayyappan is a variant, or transform, of the sentinel deity, Aiyanar. Aiyanar is seen in Tamil villages to this day, mounted on a horse and armed with bow and arrow (Dumont 1959). Krishna Chaitanya (1972) speculates that the early occupants of Kerala were migrant groups that made their way through the mountain passes of the Western Ghats. Quite clearly, the biggest obstacles facing these early settlers were the thick jungles and dangerous wildlife. As a consequence, the sentinal deity of the plains village was transformed into Ayyappa, who was no longer a warrior mounted on a steed but a hunter whose hunting pack consisted of tigers.

In the eleventh century, the Chera empire began to disintegrate in its wars with the Cholas, and the Pandya kings of the east extended their rule over many parts of the country, west of the Ghats. The famous marauding and plundering Maravar tribes increased the frequency and intensity of their forays into the plains of Kerala, taking advantage of the absence of a strong and integrating kingship. On one of these pillaging expeditions, the Maravars captured a princess from the small kingdom of Pantalam, located in central Kerala. This princess, the story goes, was rescued by a Brahmin youth and taken to a refuge near Sabari hill. There they were married, and she gave birth to a princely child, who it is believed was Ayyappan incarnate. The boy was schooled by his father in the rigors of the spiritual as well as the martial life. When he reappeared in the king's court, the king of Pantalam instantly recognized the lad to be his long-lost sister's son and commissioned him to be the captain of his army.[6]

In another variant of the legend, a childless king and queen are said to have been led to a place in the forest where the baby Ayyappan had been laid to rest by Viṣṇu. The royal couple adopted the child and raised him to be a great warrior.[7]

Regardless of which legend we choose, it is reasonable to assume that there was a famous captain of the army in the little kingdom of Pantalam. It is also a fact that while Maravar plunderers spoiled from the east, the coastal regions of Kerala had to contend with Arab seafaring traders and pirates. The most famous of these pirates was one named Vāvar. The young Ayyappan is said to have engaged in military combat with Vāvar and to have successfully subjugated him and his army. The vanquished turned devotee and most-favored lieutenant of Ayyappan, whose powers were by now recognized to be divine. With Vāvar's assistance, Ayyappan put an end to Maravar incursions, and peace and prosperity were restored to Pantalam. In time Ayyappan disappeared into his retreat in the hills of Sabari. Vāvar, the Islamic Arab, died and was entombed in Eru Meli, at the foot of Sabari. National hero, traditional deity, and Muslim saint all combine to give the Ayyappa cult its fascinating syncretistic quality. Of sociological and cultural importance is the fact that the shrine of Vāvar, like Sabari Malai itself, provides a place where all distinctions, including religious ones, are broken down. It is also worthy of note that a local Muslim festival known as *koṭikūttu*, celebrated in the Kanjiramattam mosque, takes place on the

[6]This version of Ayyappan's incarnation on earth may be found, among other places, in Krishna Chaitanya's *Kerala* (1972) and in *Sabarimalai and Its Sastha* by P. T. Thomas (1973).

[7]This version is favored by most of the Tamil writers. See, for instance, E. V. Pillai (1974), T. K. Muthuswamy Sastrigal (1972), and the popular booklet in English by Pyyappan, *Lord Ayyappan the Dharma Sasta* (1973).

day that the stellar configuration known as *makaram* makes its appearance in the sky (in late December or early January). This is also the same day that the *makara viḷakku* festival is celebrated on Sabari Malai by Ayyappan pilgrims (see Menon 1979: 174).

At the Islamic shrine of Vāvar, my fellow pilgrims broke coconuts and worshipped Allah in the way they knew best. Some also offered gifts to a follower of Vāvar, a member of the Vaipur Muzaliar clan (P. T. Thomas 1973: 11; Menon 1979: 170). Suddenly a pilgrim (who I later came to know was a Christian) broke into song. He had rendered into song the devotional poems of the ninth-century Śaiva saint Māṇikkavācakar. I did not know at that time that Māṇikkavācakar's *Tiruvācakam* was the source of his songs, and at that time I wasn't able to tape them. I did hear the following refrain, in modern Tamil, however, which was repeated at intervals, between the singing of the ninth-century lyrical poems:

> inku matiyāṭuvōm
> nām veriyāṭuvōm
> pittan pittan pōl
> uruṇṭāṭuvōm
> inku pārpārillai
> kēḷvi kētpārillai
> Civananpil mūṛki
> ontrākuvōm

Fellow pilgrims soon caught onto the refrain and sang along with the singer. In order to provide the reader with the kind of poems that were sung on this occasion and with an idea of the devotional intensity contained and conveyed by these poems, I provide the following translation of a selection of lines from the *Tiruvācakam*. From my notes, it is at least clear that most of the poems sung were selections from the same section in the *Tiruvācakam* from which the following translation was wrought, and the following verse(s) were indeed sung by our Ayyappa devotee:

> He grabbed me
> lest I go astray
>
> Wax before an unspent fire,
> mind melted,
> body trembled.
>
> I bowed, I wept,
> danced, cried aloud,
> I sang, and I praised him.
>
> Unyielding, as they say,
> as an elephant's jaw
> or a woman's grasp,
> was love's unrelenting
> seizure.
>
> Love pierced me
> like a nail
> driven into a green tree.
>
> Overflowing, I tossed
> like a sea,
>
> heart growing tender,
> body shivering
>
> while the world called me Demon!
> and laughed at me,
>
> I left shame behind,
> took as an ornament the mockery of the local folk.
> Unswerving, I lost my cleverness in the bewilderment
> of ecstasy.[8]

[8]*Tiruvācakam*, 4: 59–70, in Ramanujan 1981: 118–119.

Refrain followed verse, refrain followed verse, until he was drowned out by the chorus that he sparked, and communitas prevailed.

By about four that afternoon, after our first ritual bath in which we washed our bodies free of the dyes, we ate a hurried and frugal lunch, sharing our food with whomever happened to be near us, with no distinction between Brahmin and Parayan, Nayar and Turumban. If the Maharashtrian pilgrimage described by Karve stopped short of intercaste commensalism, among Ayyappans no caste distinctions remained for caste commensalism to be practiced (Karve 1962: 19). I am somewhat ashamed to admit that I was the only pilgrim who jealously guarded his precious little boiled water, for reasons you will soon appreciate. After our meal of steamed farina, we solemnly placed our iru muṭis on our heads and started on the long and arduous trek of forty-five miles.

Unfortunately for the pilgrim traveling between sunrise and sunset, the forest area flanking the path has been subjected to much deforestation, thereby exposing the weary pilgrim to the scorching sun. The selective deforestation, needless to say, was carried out by the Kerala government, whose best of intentions was to make it easier for the pilgrim. The path was either covered by sharp-edged stones and gravel or by the softest and finest earth. It so happened that there were very few round, smooth stones on which the traveler might have placed his tender bare feet, thereby avoiding the piercing of jagged stone edges. The areas covered by soft earth would have been so very welcome, if only the path had not been exposed to the direct sun. As it was, this soil merely absorbed and retained the heat of the sun and blistered the soles of the pilgrims' feet, which had already been lacerated and made tender by the stone-strewn pathway. Given the choice between the stony path and the soft earth, one invariably feels that the kind of path one happens not to be walking on at any given moment is preferable to that on which one happens to be walking. The same is true of the ascents and descents. The track to Sabari takes one up four steep hills and down two steep descents. When one is climbing up the hill, one's feet long for the alternative—the descent; when one descends, one's feet long for the ascent.

The mountain track involves as well the crossing of two rivers and two or three streams. The icy-cold water flowing over sore and blistered feet gives pleasure—this being the only physically pleasurable experience of the entire pilgrimage, besides the physical relief experienced when one lies under a shady tree to rest or is free to quench the thirst with cool, clear water. Experienced pilgrims dissuade one from indulging in any one of these pleasures for too long. Soaking the feet in the stream softens the callouses on soles, hastening the blistering process and correspondingly retarding the healing process. Resting too long under a tree allows the limbs and muscles to set and become stiff, so that the recommencement of the walk becomes extremely difficult and painful. According to local medical theories, to drink plentiful cool water when the body is hot from walking in the sun can result in the sudden cooling and contraction of the stomach and intestines, causing colics. I had my own germ theory, which kept me away from the same cool water.

Even though many pilgrims make the trip at a more leisurely pace (that is, in three to four days), getting to the Sabari shrine as soon as possible is highly valued because it calls for great physical exertion on behalf of the Lord and indicates a burning desire on the part of the devotee to get to His feet without being distracted by the comforts of rest and other activities en route. If there is one single sensation that predominates over all other sensations, in terms of sheer intensity and quantity, it is the sensation of pain. The aim of the pilgrim is to conquer pain and also to conquer all other less intense sensations with pain. These less intense sensations are (as gathered from fellow pilgrims): disgust, hate, frustration, irritation, anger, hunger, thirst, lust, joy, peace, and compassion. In this pilgrimage, the sensation of love (I use the term *sensation* instead of *emotion*, because the Tamil equivalent, *uṇarcci*, stresses the relationship between the feeling and the sensory organ, which relationship I wish to maintain) may be so called only insofar as it is associated with the love for Ayyappan. This sensation of love, it is believed, must gradually build up, so that when pain has conquered all other sensations, pain itself will be conquered by love. Eventually, however, "love itself when grown to its fullest dimensions must burst or swallow itself so that at the point of union with the Lord, no sensation should exist, even that of love." These were the words of the leader of our group of pilgrims.

I will omit the details of the pilgrimage itself: the number of stations on the way, the various shrines, the sacred topography, the holy baths, the beggars, the mythology, and much more. Before bringing this chapter to a close, however, I will elucidate the connection already hinted at between Peirce's categories and the pilgrim's progress.

For Peirce, Thirdness was the realm of law, and laws in their most develped forms not merely describe and determine but also predict. Not unlike Peirce's being of Thirdness, the Hindu villager's life is fraught with attempts to predict and with experiences in prediction; he is preoccupied in devising, if not discovering, laws of a general order which will determine and describe his personal existence. One might even go so far as to say that the Hindu is obsessed with prediction. The bhajans (devotional singing) and *pracankams* (sermons) that we attended during our sixty days of preparation were concerned as much with predictions about what we could expect on the pilgrimage as with stories of the life of Lord Ayyappan.

During the Sabari Hill pilgrimage's preparatory phase, when I asked pilgrims why they were going on this pilgrimage, their responses were many. Some (exceptionally few) said that they were going to obtain mental peace; others expected some material gain from Lord Ayyappan upon the successful completion of the pilgrimage; still others said it was a miniexperience in moṭcam ["liberation, heaven"], and so on. The pilgrimage itself, however, was an exercise in prediction and thus an exercise in Thirdness. The level of abstraction that each pilgrim built into his predictions varied, but prediction was invariably present. Never was there a doubt that the anticipated result would be obtained if the rite (the pilgrimage) were performed correctly. The effect, the boon, gift, or moṭcam, was encoded in the cause (the pilgrimage) itself, and therefore the question of doubt did not arise.

On the first night, I talked to a group of Brahmin pilgrims who were convinced that the pilgrimage was a path to salvation. I asked them whether they considered this *bhakti* ("devotion"), karma ("action"), or *jñāna* ("knowledge") *mārga* ("path"). After much discussion and debate it was generally agreed that all three paths to salvation—the paths of devotion, action, and knowledge—were present herein and that with the progression of the pilgrimage, all three modes were going to increase before the pilgrim finally merged with the Lord. Discussions with many others brought agreement on this point. It became evident that there was little use in speaking of devotion, action, and wisdom as distinct alternatives as far as this pilgrimage was concerned. Over and over again the point was made that there could not be devotion without knowledge or knowledge without devotion; nor could there be devotion and knowledge together in the absence of action, which was what the entire pilgrimage was about.

Since I had recently become interested in the "knowing" process, I made it a point to discuss with pilgrims what they really meant by "knowledge" and "to know." On the first evening, before the commencement of our walk up the hill, our discussion on the subject of knowledge went off particularly well; and it became noteworthy that many responses emphasized the predictive aspect of knowledge or knowing. Some sample responses are:

First Informant (henceforth Inf.): I say that I know someone when I've seen him once and can tell you what he looks like. The better I know him the more detailed my description of him will be for you to recognize him when you see him for the first time. [Note the predictive aspect.]

Second Inf.: I say I know Ayyappa Swami because I know that he will grant me my prayer.

Third Inf.: Knowledge is to know the purpose of something.

A.: And what is the purpose of this pilgrimage?

Third Inf.: For me it is to experience mōtcam. For someone else it can be something else. Once you know you are doing this [the pilgrimage], that in itself is knowledge. [Note the mutual immanence of cause and effect.]

There were two responses, however, that were to prove quintessential to my understanding of the pilgrim's progress and the knowing process. The first came from a blacksmith who was treated by the others as the least sensible and most inarticulate of the group. After he listened to my lengthy interview with the others, he turned to me and said: "You know only about all our knowledg[es]. You have come here with us only to try and know how we know, but *you* really don't know. You don't have knowledge. Not even as much as I have . . . even though you know what each and every one of us knows." He seemed to indicate that I, who had "meta-knowledge," or the most abstract kind of knowledge, in fact had the least knowledge.

The second piece of information that I was to find most enlightening and which prepared me to anticipate what I was to subsequently inquire about was given to me by an old Brahmin who had been privy to the first three responses above, and of informants with many other similar responses. When this Brahmin found himself alone with me he told me:

> They [referring to the informants] now think that they know, because they all expect a certain result. This is knowledge of a certain sort, which I don't deny. But you will see this knowledge get sharper as we progress and the walking gets rougher. They'll even say, "I don't know why I came on this pilgrimage." But when you hear them say things like that, don't think that they really do not have knowledge. On the contrary, it is then that they will be beginning to really acquire knowledge.

Insofar as we treat the progress of the pilgrimage as a progressive process in the acquisition of knowledge, we shall find that Peirce's Secondness follows his Thirdness, and not vice versa. Let us briefly turn to Peirce's own exposition of the category of Secondness.

An explanation of Secondness must consist mainly in directing attention to it—an ostensive definition, for Secondness lacks the "genuine" generality of Thirdness and even the "negative" generality of Firstness. However, of the three categories, the

> practical exigencies of life render Secondness the most prominent. . . . This is not a conception, nor is it a peculiar quality. It is an experience. It comes out most fully in the shock of reaction between ego and non-ego. It is there, the double consciousness of effort and resistance. That is something which cannot properly be conceived. For to conceive it is to generalize it; and to generalize it is to miss altogether the hereness and the nowness which is its essence. (8.266)

Secondness may be illustrated by the following excerpts from my diary.

My first holy bath

The water of this tank was holy, very holy, or so everyone said. This tank was nothing more than a bunded area, a hole really, the size of which was no larger than a standard swimming pool. Water trickled into this tank from a stream, which pilgrims used for what is euphemistically referred to in Tamil as washing one's feet, after the said stream's shores had been used as a latrine by the same pilgrims. When there was more water than the tank could contain, water flowed over the western bund and continued on its downward course.

Thousands of pilgrims were in the tank, and several times that many were either drying themselves with their towels or else waiting to enter the water. I entered the pool, toe tips first, wishing that this was all only a bad dream. The water was not more than four feet deep. I crept through the praying, spitting, dipping, dripping, nose-blowing pilgrims, trying to find an area that had the least number of human beings per square foot. My futile search was interrupted by a Brahmin pilgrim who informed me with a smile that the water was so much cleaner than last year this time. My unspoken response was, "You mean to say that you are going through this a second time? How could you?" But my spoken response was, "But it is so filthy!" "You mustn't say such things," he advised, "this water is cuttam [Skt. *sudda*, "pure"]. Call out the names of Ayyappa and immerse yourself. You will receive His *aruḷ* [grace]."

I held my nose, shut my eyes, tucked in my lips between my teeth, counted one, two, and three, gurgled the name of Ayyappā in my throat, and immersed myself in the holy water that refreshed the thousands around me, the millions that preceded me in ages past, and the millions that were likely to follow me in years to come. As I came out of the water, a pilgrim on my left called out to another pilgrim, "Ayyappā, Ayyappā!" [On this pilgrimage, once the vows have been taken, the pilgrim addresses everyone else as Ayyappā.] Failing to draw the attention of the second, he prefixed the name of Ayyappā with a "Dr.," yelling, "Dr.

Ayyappā! Dr. Ayyappā! Look!" The pilgrim who was being called was briskly massaging his scalp with his fingertips, periodically dipping them into the water as if the latter were some precious hair lotion divinely prescribed for his gathering baldness. So he is a doctor, I thought. He finally heard his friend's call and turned around to face his friend. With a grin sparkling in the sunlight, the friend raised his holy black veṣṭi, which he had been rinsing in the holier water, and held it up for the doctor, saying, "Look!" Strands of lumpy phlegm of pilgrims who had cleansed their lungs and throats by expectorating into the water outside were seen clinging to the fabric. "It is all the grace of Ayyappā," was the doctor's only response. I felt the question "How do you mean, Dr. Ayyappā?" feebly rise in my throat, which, however, was instantly choked down by a gagging sensation that forcefully arose antiperistaltically from the pit of my stomach. The doctor's friend received the doctor's advice with a pious "Śaranam Ayyappā" (translated "Ayyappā, my refuge") and returned to rinsing his véṣṭi. Another joked about not having to use starch on the véṣṭis washed in this holy tank. The doctor returned to massaging his scanty scalp, and I scrambled out of the water as fast as I could, lest I retch into a public bathing pool and pollute it. As I neared the edge, all other sensations disappeared; there were no other pilgrims, there was no pilgrimage, there was no fieldwork, there was no dissertation to be written, there was no pride, no hate, no love, no animosity, no admiration, no resentment—there was nothing except me and the phlegmy water around me.

My second holy bath

The river was called Aṛudā. The water that flowed in it was, according to mythology, the tears of the goddess. In all, over 100,000 pilgrims were either bathing, about to bathe, or had just finished bathing in the river. The rocky/gravelly shores were covered with squatters in the morning twilight. It would have taken an acrobat to tiptoe his way through the piles of human excrement, which seemed to be as numerous as the stones and pebbles that covered the shores. I was of half a mind to turn back, to hide, to vanish into the mist, to do something or anything else besides having to take my holy bath. But there was no way out or around. Pilgrim pressure was indefatigable. I felt as if thousands of eyes were fixed on me and me alone, to see that I did not escape. I sludged and slid my way into the water and quickly immersed myself but once and returned to the river bank feeling helplessly filthy. I fetched my comb from my knapsack and let it slide through my dripping hair. I looked at the comb and saw something brown adhering to its teeth. I lifted the comb to my nose. It stank of night soil. For a few moments, which in fact seemed like forever, nothing else existed besides me and the world outside me. This world, however, was not differentiated into pilgrims, a river, trees, stones, huts, campfires, or any other sensation that reached the five senses. The world outside was reduced to a oneness: It was all shit! And I was the only "other" existing apart from this world, acutely and painfully sensitive to its brutal force on all my senses.

My climb up Aṛudā hill

The hill was steep. The path was so straight and so long that it seemed like a modified version of Jacob's ladder. When I lifted up my eyes to see if I could see the end or at least the point where the climb ended and the descent was to begin, all I saw were heads and heads and more heads of the crawling throng of pilgrims who had gone ahead of me. They had accomplished so much! Could I possibly equal them, I wondered. I felt so feeble at the very sight and thought of the task. With me was a group of pilgrims which responded in unison to a leader's recitative chanting of praises to Ayyappan. We were all familiar with the 108 "recitative calls" and their appropriate "recitative responses."

It was tacitly agreed that group leaders [or Guruswāmies, as they were called here] were to carry out the recitative calls, and the others were expected to respond. There was no hard and fast rule as to the sequence in which the 108 stanzas had to be recited. However, frequent repetition of the same line by a Guruswāmy indicated limited knowledge, bad memory, or a lack of familiarity with the verses. A perfect reciter would repeat a line but once in fifteen to twenty lines. The lines thus repeated tended to belong to the first five lines, indicating that when memory failed reciters tended to go back to the lines that were first committed to memory, in somewhat of a Jakobsonian fashion.

The pattern in the recitation changed as the climb progressed. These changes may be noted to occur in several stages.

First stage

1. The leaders of the various groups led the recitation, and the followers responded to the call of their respective Guruswāmies.
2. The lines were recited loudly, clearly, and energetically.
3. The members of each group walked together, around their leader.
4. When one group overtook another, each group leader shouted out his recitative call so that his call would not be drowned out by the call of the other leader, and also so that the members of his group could shout out the recitative response appropriate to that call and not to the call of the Guruswāmy of another group.
5. The pace of walking was relatively constant and maintained an approximate rhythm with the recitation.

Second stage

1. The Guruswāmy gave up reciting the call, which duty was assumed by another member of the group (usu-

ally one who tended to be more aggressive than the rest), and the leader joined the others in reciting the responses instead of leading with calls.

2. The substitute leader's call continued to be loud and clear because of its newness, but the responses were beginning to dim.
3. The group continued to stay together. A slight increase in spacing was beginning to be observed, however.
4. The pace of walking slowed down but continued constant.

Third stage

1. The call was recited by various members of the group, each one calling only for short periods, with long lulls in between when one caller stopped and another assumed the calling.
2. The calls and responses were less loud and not as clear, because the pilgrims were beginning to run out of breath.
3. Repetition became more frequent, a line among the first five familiar lines being repeated every fifteen lines or oftener.
4. The distance between members of the group began to increase even further, which resulted in many members falling outside the sound area of their caller and lagging into the sound area of another caller belonging to a strange group. This drifting resulted in the breaking up of the group and a state of affairs in which everyone was willing to respond to any caller, regardless of whether or not the caller belonged to the respondent's own group.
5. The pace of walking became extremely erratic; "staggering" would be an apt description.

Fourth stage

1. The distinction between call lines and response lines was lost. Often the caller cried out response lines, and the responders replied with call lines.
2. Calls and responses sounded more like feeble cries for help.
3. The group split up into pairs of individuals, with one calling and the other responding, neither one knowing or, for that matter, caring whether what he recited was the call or the response.

Fifth stage

1. Individuals tended to pick out a single line, regardless of whether it was a call line or a response line, regardless of whether anybody called or responded; they merely kept repeating the same line over and over again.
2. The most common line recited was either the call or the response of stanza one, so that each on his own was gasping out the call, "Oh Lord! Oh Lord!" or "Ayyappō, Ayyappō . . ."

This final stage, or phase of physical and emotional reduction and exhaustion is another example, I believe, of Peirce's category of Secondness. In the words of one pilgrim who reflected on this phase of the climb, "there is nothing else I knew, heard, or felt. I was too tired to feel tired. All I heard was my voice calling out, "Ayyappō, Ayyappō, Ayyappō." Nothing else existed except my call and I. This was when I began to know my Lord in the true sense. And then I realized how little I knew him when I took the short six-mile trek last year." To know through Secondness is to become acutely aware that there is nothing else besides yourself and that one other sensation coming from the exterior, which makes you acutely aware of yourself as against that "other."

Secondness is once again illustrated in the pilgrim's experience of pain in his climb down the hill called Kari Malai (the mountain of elephants). The path here is rough and rugged, covered with root stumps and sharp-edged stones. At the beginning of this trek one experiments in mini-exercises of Thirdness. One says to oneself, "If I place my foot in such and such a manner at such and such an angle, the pain will be minimized." Or one plans and schemes how one should dodge the roots and rocks. One tells oneself, "I shall walk on this side or that" or "Look! There's a patch of grass. Let me go and walk on that. It will make my feet feel good, even though the patch is only three feet long." During this phase, one is able to differentiate between the pain caused by the blisters under one's toenails and those on one's heels. Then again, one is able to distinguish between the pain caused by blisters, wherever they happen to be, and the pain arising from strained calf muscles and tendons. One knows or speculates that if one places one's leg at such and such an angle on such and such a surface of one's foot, the pain in one's knee will be alleviated. The headache caused by the heat of the noon sun and the load of the iru muṭi can be distinguished from the pain resulting from the straps of the knapsack biting into one's shoulders. So one adjusts the iru muṭi and the shoulder straps in order to reduce the pain in the head and the shoulders.

Sooner or later, however, all the different kinds of pain begin to merge. You stop predicting. Your knowledge via Thirdness begins to cease to function. It is replaced by Secondness. The experience of *pain* makes one acutely aware of oneself (ego) as the victim, and the outside (undifferentiated as roots, stones, and hot sand) as the pain-causing agent. This again is Secondness.

True to the old Brahmin's prediction, several pilgrims, when asked what or how they felt about the pilgrimage or why they came on it, said that they really did not know or, for that matter, care. Many of these were pilgrims who in their reflective Thirdness had come out with lengthy expositions on the whys and the wherefores of their pilgrimage. Now they ceased to predict. But they still said they loved the Lord. However, all of them said that their predominant—if not sole—sensation was that of pain and that they did not (for the most part) know or care who was around them or what was said. Some of the responses on Secondness I obtained when the weary pilgrims paused to rest. Needless to say, my task was a difficult one, not only because I myself had to extricate myself from the state of Secondness and transport myself to the general level of Thirdness in formulating the questions but also because I had to force my interlocutors out of their own Secondness. Much of what Secondness was about I was to learn later, when aches and pains had been rested and soothed away, from pilgrims who were eager to reflect upon their experiences.

Pain also has an element of Firstness. This is a further step in the direction of knowledge. With time, pain stops having a causative agent, and ego is obscured or snuffed out because it has nothing to contrast itself with or stand against. Ego is no longer a victim, as in Secondness, because the identity of the pain-causing agent is lost. There is a "feeling" of pain, of course, but it is a sensation that has no agent, no tense, and no comparative. One does not know whence the pain came, how it is caused, or whether it is more or less intense than the pain a moment or an hour ago; for there is no before or after. Pain is the only sensation belonging to the eternal present.

Here now is a quote from Peirce about Firstness: "If we imagine that feeling retains its positive character but absolutely loses all relation (and thereby all *vividness*, which is only the sense of shock), it is no longer exactly what we call feeling. It is a mere sense of quality. It is the sort of element that makes *red* to be such as it is, whatever anything else may be" (8.267). If we were to substitute *pain* for Peirce's "red," the definition would still hold, and our point would be made.

As stated earlier, of all the sensations informants talked about, pain was the sensation that was emphasized over and over again, as predominant. Several pilgrims seemed to believe, however, that after a while, pain, having become so intense, began to disappear. In the words of one pilgrim from my village, "At one moment everything is pain. But at the next moment everything is love (*anpu*). Everything is love for the Lord."

Again, this experience of love, I believe, is an experience in Firstness. The old Brahmin (henceforth B) who was with us insisted that the worth of a true devotee is established only when he begins to feel no pain.

A: Must he feel love then?

B. Once pain is conquered, love is there whether you feel it or not.

A: Is this love a special kind of love?

B. It is a love that cannot be contrasted with hate. It has no opposite. No before or after. It was never there before, and yet it was always there. Its existence does not depend on its being felt.

This statement begs to be compared in its simplicity with Peirce's illustration of Firstness containing his favorite example of red: "The mode of being a redness, before anything in the universe was yet red, was nevertheless a positive qualitative possibility. And redness in itself even if it be embodied is something positive *sui generis*. That I call Firstness" (1.25). In the old Brahmin's understanding of love, love, too, is a positive qualitative possibility. Quoting Tirumoolar, the Tamil Siddha poet, the old Brahmin continued to explain the concept of love as follows: "The poet said, 'those who say that love and God are two are ignorant.' True knowledge comes in learning that love is God. As long as the love one talks about is separate from God, that love is contrastable with hate; it has a before and an after. But when Love is God you have nothing to contrast it with."

At the very end of the long and arduous trek, just before the pilgrim reaches the presence of Lord Ayyappan, there are eighteen neatly built steps to climb. Each one of these steps is symbolic. Together they are symbolic of the entire pilgrimage. Taken individually, the eighteen steps stand for the five senses, the three kuṇams, or reals, the eight *rāgas, avidyā,* and vidyā.

The eight rāgas and their approximate English equivalents are as follows: *kāmam* ("lust or desire"), *krōdam* ("jealousy, envy"), *lōbam* ("greed, avarice, stinginess"), *mōham* ("presumptuousness, pride, conceit, recklessness"), *mātsaryam* ("arrogance"), *titikṣa* (whose meaning was unknown to all but whose attempted translation was, "the fixing of one's mind on a single object", or "persistence") and *ḍambam* ("flamboyance" or "showiness"). The pilgrimage, symbolically a progressive movement in the direction of salvation and knowledge, involves and demands the overcoming of these eight rāgas.

The five intiriams, or senses, are the most talked about by the pilgrims of the eighteen entities. It is interesting that the elimination/vanquishing/transcendence/collapsing/coalescing (all these being words used by informants themselves) of the five intiriams is done in a certain sequence. The first to go, so to speak, is the sense of hearing. Here is an excerpt from my field notes.

Inf.: I cease to hear the chatter and talk of those around me. I cease to hear the beggars by the roadside call out. That is why I stopped answering you after Kari Malai. [I found it curious that he knew that I had been speaking to him after Kari Malai but claimed that he still didn't hear me—but I did not press the issue.] I cease to hear even the vendors selling oranges to quench my thirst. I see them, but I don't hear them. All I hear are the recitative lines in praise of Ayyappan.

A: Isn't hearing these recitative lines "hearing"? How can you then claim that you transcend [*mēlōnku*] that particular intiriam?

Inf.: I begin to feel, not hear.

A: Where or how do you feel?

Inf.: All over my body. My skin, my heart, my head, . . . my whole body.

A: You *feel* in your ear?

Inf.: Yes. I feel in my ears, but I do not hear with them.

The argument seemed at first a little strained, overdone, and trapped in contradictions. The informant was a youth of twenty-one, of the Nāiḍu caste and a high school graduate. In my other discussions with him he had always been coherent. I therefore, had enough reason to treat his statements regarding the sense of hearing seriously. Subsequently I was to discover the same pattern in the responses of several other informants. The distinction made was not merely one between hearing and listening. It was generally believed that the ear, as a sense organ, stopped hearing, and began to feel (as a tactile organ would).

The next intiriam to be affected was the sense of smell. With respect to this particular sense, my prize informant was a young Ayyangar Brahmin, a bigot outside the context of the pilgrimage.

Inf.: I stopped smelling things after Aṛudā Nati. [As you will remember, the shores of Aṛudā emit but one odor, strong and clear, that of human excrement.] I could have spent the next night in the gutter. I wouldn't have known the place by its smell. And mind you, this is a great achievement as far as I am concerned. For when I started the journey at Eru Meli, I could smell the foods of all the pilgrims cooking. And you know, I could tell you which was non-Brahmin food, even though all the cooking there was vegetarian. In fact, my sense of smell is so strong that I could tell a non-Brahmin from a Brahmin simply from his body odor. But after Arudā Nati I overcame my sense of smell.

A: Did you not even smell the camphor and incense sticks offered at the various shrines on the way after Arudā?

Inf.: You might say I felt it. I didn't smell it.

The next intiriam to fall under is that of sight. Below is an excerpt from my diary. This experience of mine was supported and corroborated by those of the many fellow pilgrims with whom I talked.

We had walked a mile or so down Arudā Hill. I was overcome by fatigue and felt that I would collapse before long. The blisters on my feet had long since broken and been torn open, and the gravel had begun to cause me excruciating pain by lacerating the tender skin underneath the now nonexistent cuticular layer. The shoulder strap of my knapsack ate into my flesh, and the iru muṭi on my head had just begun to give me a headache, which thumped contrapuntally between temples and medula oblongata. Our pace of walking had been reduced to a crawl now, since there had been somewhat of a traffic jam caused by the falling across our path of an ancient banyan tree. Since the girth of the fallen tree was so massive, no one was able to climb over it and cross over to the other side. Instead, the pilgrims had dug a hole in the ground underneath the fallen tree's trunk, through which we tunneled across. The sun glared at us despotically from a cloudless sky. My response to the recitative calls had become mechanical. I reasoned to

> myself that to open my mouth any more than absolutely necessary would cause dehydration through evaporation of saliva, dehydration which I could not afford, given that my water bottle was now empty. But my eyes were alert, studying every stone, slope, and root stump along my path. Halfway down the hill, something strange happened: I stopped looking. I don't think it would have made any difference if I had been blind. I did not care whether I slipped or stepped on stone or stump. I simply walked on and on, led by an unguided momentum, until the sun had set and darkness had made the leaves of the forest trees indistinguishable against the black night. Only then did I realize how little the light and my sense of sight had mattered.

Informants were not clear about what exactly the sense organ *the mouth* represented. Some thought it indicated taste, while others associated it with speech or the sensation of speech. Most informants tended to believe that the mouth, or *vāi,* referred to both speech and eating, with the emphasis on eating.

If the last six miles to the top of the shrine is climbed as prescribed, the devotee is expected to abstain from all food and drink. Only two of the fifteen pilgrims I observed closely refrained even from quenching their thirst during this last lap of the journey. These two claimed to have temporarily overcome hunger and thirst.

Pilgrims were stricter in their observance of the vow to silence. Obviously, the use of the speech apparatus for reciting praises to Ayyappan was not considered a violation of the vow to silence. When questioned about this apparent discrepancy in the execution of the vow of silence, one informant told me: "By the time I reached the last six miles my tongue began to function in a detached manner. I derived neither pleasure nor pain from it. It went on praising God while I remained silent. I was not aware of the activities of my tongue. It acted on its own without it knowing what it was doing." This was the only informant who was able to formulate his response in such a well-articulated manner. The rest were by and large surprised by the inherent contradiction when it was pointed out to them. The upshot of their responses, however, was that "praises to the Lord are as good as silence." Another informant said, "I feel my tongue move and sounds come out. But I really don't talk. All I do is feel."

The pattern is clear. The four senses of sight, hearing, smell, and taste merge into the fifth sense of touch, or feeling. The organ that receives and reacts to touch or feeling, *uṇarcci*, is called *mei* in Tamil. The word *mei* refers to the entire body or *śarīra* (Skt.). Those schooled in Siddha theories of the body or Siddhanta metaphysics will tell you that *mei* refers only to the two outermost body sheaths, or *kośas*, namely, to the *sūkṣma* and *stūla* śarīrams, and does not include the three inner bodies or body sheaths.

The sense associated with the sense organ known as the mei is called uṇarcci. Uṇarcci may be roughly equated with tactile sensations and is the last sense to be overcome. As has already been indicated, the sensation of pain is the predominant if not the only one that impinges upon the sense of touch. Pain, to begin with, is multiple and differentiated. With time, the various kinds of pain merge into a unitary sensation of pain. This pain persists for some time and is then replaced by numbness (in my case) or the sudden disappearance of pain, with love taking its place (in the case of most of my fellow pilgrims). This "love" is also spoken of as acting upon the mei. Yet the perfect pilgrim must not merely stop feeling pain, he must also stop feeling love. He symbolically does this, in fact, in the final ritual of breaking the coconut filled with ghee and pouring the ghee on the image of Ayyappan. Before we say anything more about this fascinating, ghee-filled coconut, I will elaborate on the term *intiriam*.

If a villager is asked what the five *intriyas* are, he will seriously recite out loud the names of the five senses. If, however, you were to ask a villager what *intiriam* meant, the response would usually be an embarrassed giggle. *Intiriam*, in and of itself, refers most commonly to male and female sexual fluids (usually semen). As is well known and amply documented, for the Indian, semen is the essence of all body substances, even as ghee is the essence of all food substances. Thus, *intiriam*, besides referring to the five senses in general, refers in particular to the sexual fluids, and sexual fluids are associated with sensation par excellence, the essence of all the sensations as well as the sum of all the sensations experienced by the mei. This is why the taboo that demands the strictest observance is the taboo against sexual intercourse. All the other vows of abstinence and austerity are only intended to help the devotee observe the sex taboo; they are ancillary and complementary, not central.

The aim of the pilgrim, then, is to overcome the mei. The transcendence of the mei is the goal with which he begins his pilgrimage, but the actual triumph over the mei must wait for the very last, after all the senses have been overcome.

After having climbed the steps of the eight rāgas and the five intiriams, one has to climb the steps of the three kuṇams, or reals. Pilgrims were able to tell me that the three kuṇams were *tamas* or tāmatam, rajas, and sātvīkam and also what they implied. All that man is is due to the existence of the three kuṇams in different proportions within us. In each human being, the proportion is different. The proportion of the three kuṇams in human beings in general is relatively similar when compared to the corresponding proportions in animals, plants, or any other entity in the phenomenal universe.

In man, tamas is said to cause inaction, lethargy, mental dullness, and base thoughts; *rajas* is physically activating and supplies brute strength; *sātvīkam* causes mental keenness, enlightenment, patience, love, and all other noble qualities.

Pilgrims indicated that before they set out on the pilgrimage, tamas dominated their constitutional being. Physical, mental, and spiritual lethargy dominated their existence. The rise of rajas at the expense of tamas was marked at Eru Meli, when they began to "walk like kings, warriors, and hunters of old" the long and rugged trek to Sabari Hill. (Kings, warriors, and hunters, according to the varṇa āśrama dharma, are believed to be *rajasik* personalities.) After a certain point along the way, when rajas had equalled tamas, the unchecked growth of rajas is prevented by the rise of sātvīkam. Sātvīkam was always there but only in a docile, subdominant state. Sātvīkam was first sparked to action when the decision to make the pilgrimage was taken, but its growth really began only when the five senses became extra sensitive to the bombardment by hitherto unexperienced forces. Sātvīkam reaches its fullness, beyond which its growth is checked, when pain is replaced by love.

What, then, is symbolically represented in the entire pilgrimage as well as by the crossing of the three steps that stand for the three kuṇams is that the three kuṇams are brought into a state of equilibrium and equipoise, as it was "in the beginning," where no one kuṇam is said to have dominated. Only after this state has been achieved is one ready to cross the seventeenth step, symbolizing avidyā.

A clear exposition of the concept of avidyā is a task too great for a short account, such as this, to handle. *Avidyā* may be approximately translated as "ignorance, illusion, lack of knowledge, unenlightenment," and so on—with the emphasis on the qualification *approximate*.

The last and final step, the eighteenth step, is the step of vidyā, that is, all that is opposed to avidyā. "At this point," a pilgrim informed me, "one can truly say that one knows."

These eighteen steps, as I have said, are symbolic. A further elaboration on these eighteen steps makes them more than symbolic, however. It is believed that a pilgrim becomes one with Ayyappan only after he has come on this pilgrimage eighteen plus one times. On his first journey he does two things. First, by symbolically crossing all eighteen steps he symbolically previews what he has to overcome before final union with the Lord. Second, on this first journey, one of the eight rāgas is singled out for permanent annihilation. In the stone of this step lies concealed the specific śakti required to burn a given rāga. On the second year, the śakti inherent in the stone of the second step consumes a second rāga. On every consecutive year, the śakti of a new step is activated and consumes a new rāga or intiriam, or kuṇam, and so on, until on the eighteenth year, vidyā itself is consumed by the śakti of the eighteenth step, making the devotee completely free to fuse with the Lord in permanent union on the nineteenth year. The fact that these eighteen entities are in turn substantially conceptualized is evidenced by devotees' belief that with each consuming step, they lose some weight, appropriate to the given entity's dominance in one's life.

After this eighteenth step of vidyā, or knowledge, is crossed, a simple but important ritual is performed, a ritual that is the climax and fulfillment of the whole pilgrimage.

You will recall that the iru muṭi has two pouches, the rear one of which contains various provisions for the journey. As the pilgrimage progresses, this pouch is gradually depleted of its contents, thereby making a statement that a world with its own material needs is being exhausted, even as it is left behind. The front pouch contains various offertory items for the shrines and deities on the way. The most important and sacred of items contained in this pouch is the ghee-filled coconut that the pilgrim receives when he leaves his village temple after having the death ritual performed for him. This coconut must be protected with the greatest care until the very last. When the pilgrim reaches the deity in his shrine, the coconut is broken and the ghee is poured over the deity. In order to understand the significance of this coconut, we need to understand, in outline, the body-sheath theory, to which we now turn.

The Five Body Sheaths or Bodies (*Pañcamayakośas*)

In everyday language, the word *uṭampu* or *uṭal* refers, in its unmarked sense, to the body as a totality. In its marked sense, uṭampu or uṭal contrasts with *uḷḷuṭampu* or *uḷḷuṭal* ("inner body") or *coppana uṭal* ("dream body"), the former being gross and the latter (inner body, dream body, ethereal body, and so on) being subtle. Villagers will also tell you that the ātman is concealed within the uḷḷuṭampu. Some do know that there are five bodies in all, one inside the other, but rarely, if ever, are they able to name these other bodies, except to say that the three innermost bodies are enclosed by the uṭampu and uḷḷuṭampu and, unlike the last two, are formless.

The Ayyappan pilgrim is instructed on the five bodies or body sheaths in greater detail than is the average villager because of the sacred ghee-filled coconut he carries in the front pouch of his iru muṭi. He knows that this coconut is the symbol of his body, since the coconut, like his body, has five sheaths. The coconut's five sheaths are the outer skin, the husk, the shell, the inner skin, and the kernel. In the very center of the coconut, ghee is poured. As anyone familiar with Hindu dietetics knows, cow's milk is considered to be the essence of all food. By boiling down milk to its essence, one obtains ghee. As an essence it corresponds to man's own essence, his *jīvātmā*, which flows freely with the *paramātmā* ("the universal soul"—the Lord Ayyappan) only when the other body sheaths are torn asunder or broken, as in the case of the coconut which must be broken for the ghee to flow on, over, and with the deity. What follows is a brief account of the five sheaths of the body, starting from the outermost sheath and moving to the center.

Ayyappa pilgrims learn to substitute the Sanskrit word *śarīram* for the Tamil *uṭampu* or *uṭal*. The gross body, or *veḷi uṭampu*, comes to be known as the stūla śarīram. The stūla śarīram is formed through the transformation, evolution, and modification of the five elements (pancca pūta piramā-ṇattāluṇṭākum śarīram). This body has weight and form. The name of a person is attached to this body only as long as it is conjoined with the subtle *uḷḷuṭampu*, also known as the sūkṣma śarīram which it covers (*pōrttal*). The moment the sūkṣma śarīram leaves the stūla śarīram, the latter becomes immobile and is called a *piṇam, cavam,* or *kaṭṭai* ("corpse").

As a sheath, this body is known as the *annamaya kośam*, because it is sustained by *annam* (rice in particular, but food in general).

The *stūla śarīram* is also the body wherein the humors move around. Bodily ailments caused by humors affect the stūla śarīram.

The *uḷḷuṭampu* or coppana uṭal is also known as the sūkṣma śarīram. The sūkṣma śarīram is ensheathed by the annamaya koṣam, and its own sheath is the *prāṇa maya kośam*. This body is also called the *yādanā* śarīram (from *yādanai*, which means pain; it is the body that feels pain because it is the body that undergoes suffering in hell). This body is also known as the *pukaruṭampu* (the body that reacts to or senses praise or fame).

As a sheath it is known as prāṇa maya kośam because it is impelled (*iyakkutal*) to action by the ten *dasavāyus* ("vital airs or vital forces") of which *prāṇan* is the leader. The ten dasavāyus are as follows:

1. Prāṇan impels the heart to beat and the lungs to function.
2. *Abānan* resides slightly behind and below the navel

between anus (*kutam*) and genitals (*kuyyam*) and aids in excretion.

3. *Viyāṇan* resides in the joints of the body and creates fatigue and thirst.
4. *Udānan* resides in the navel and causes the conversion of food into blood by moving through the throat up into the head when it is necessary to promote digestion.
5. *Samāṇan* resides in the nerves and makes digestion pleasurable.
6. *Nāgan* resides in the throat and causes hiccups and yawning and also aids in speech.
7. *Kūrman* resides in the eyes and controls one's waking and sleeping, besides causing horripilation from fear.
8. *Dēvadattan* is that which causes shock on hearing a sudden noise, increases heat with the rise in one's anger, and controls the horripilation associated with pleasurable experiences.
9. *Danajeyan* controls the fattening and thinning processes of one's body.

The sūkṣma śarīram is identical in form to the outer stūla śarīram and even has hair and skin color that are the same as that of the stūla śarīram. The sūkṣma śarīram, however, lacks weight. Furthermore, the organs and the body parts of the sūkṣma śarīram cannot be felt by the sense of touch. Needless to say, "the sūkṣma śarīram also has either male or female genitals, and this is why when a person dies it is said, 'May he or she (as the case may be) reach tevalōkam.' "

In one's waking state the sūkṣma śarīram has to carry the dead weight of the stūla śarīram. Only in the dream state can the sūkṣma śarīram leave the stūla śarīram behind and roam wherever it chooses. When the sūkṣma śarīram leaves the stūla śarīram, even for a moment or two, to wander around in the dream state, the stūla śarīram is a piṇam, or corpse. This is also why the early morning bath on awakening is so important, because it purifies the stūla śarīram, which has become *acuttam* ("impure"), having been a corpse several times during the night.

Paittiyam ("madness") can be caused either by the malfunctioning of the stūla śarīram or of the sūkṣma śarīram. The paittiyam of the stūla śarīram is comparable to Deborah Bhattacharyya's (1977) "deep level *paglāmi*" and is often called *mūḷaikkōḷāru* (literally, "a disturbance or malfunctioning of the brain"). This is a state in which the brain of the stūla śarīram, because of a malformation, disturbs and distorts information sent by the sūkṣma śarīram, causing the person to behave in an irrational or "mad" manner. Certain deliriums during high fevers are also believed to belong to this category. This kind of paittiyam contrasts with that of the sūkṣma śarīram, which is the kind that one gets during spirit or any other kind of possession. "It takes hold of the sūkṣma śarīram," as an informant put it. In such cases the messages for behavior generated by the sūkṣma śarīram are thought of as "crazy" or "irrational" or else merely extraordinary.

The sūkṣma śarīram is also the seat of emotions, such as love and hate. It has desires and preferences. A story is told of a teenage Brahmin girl who was possessed by the spirit (*pēi*) or sūkṣma śarīram of a Naidu woman who happened to have died in an accidental fire in which "her stūla śarīram was burned." Once possessed by the Naidu woman's sūkṣma śarīram, the young Brahmin girl began to demand nonvegetarian foods, as would have the Naidu woman who was used to a nonvegetarian diet.

The sūkṣma śarīram is also a source of *pelam* or śakti. This was seen to be established by the fact that the possessed Brahmin girl was able to carry a heavy pot of water on her hip and another on her head, when before her possession she was able to carry but one small pot of water on her hip.

The five sense organs—the ear, nose, eyes, mouth and mei (body as a tactile organ)—have two aspects each, namely, the gross and the subtle aspects. The gross aspects belong to the stūla śarīram and are called purajnānēntriankaḷ ("outer sensory organs"), and the subtle aspects, which belong to the sūkṣma śarīram, are known as akajnānēntriankaḷ ("inner sensory organs"). The perceptions of the five sensory organs are, in the same order, *ōcai* ("sound"), *maṇam* ("smell"), *uruvam* ("form"), *cuvai* ("taste"), and *uṇarcci* ("tactility").

The five motor organs (*kaṇmēntriankaḷ*) are also divided into external (gross) and internal (subtle) ones, associated with the stūla and śūkṣma śarīrams, respectively. These five motor organs are hands, feet, mouth, anus, and genitals. The actions of the five motor organs are: hands for *koṭai* ("giving"), legs for *naṭai* ("walking"), mouth for *pēccu* ("speech"), anus for *kaṛippu* ("excretion"), and the generative organs for *inpam* ("enjoyment").

During the waking state, the uyir (sometimes called *āvi* or *ātmā*) is in the lalāḍastānam of the sūkṣma śarīram, the lalāḍastānam being located in between the eyebrows. When in this position it is able to link the five senses of the stūla śarīram to the five senses of the sūkṣma śarīram. The seats of the five senses are arranged in such a manner that the ears, eyes, nose, and mouth are in the front, and the locus of the sense of touch is in the back of the head. (Note the sense of touch's special if not unique position, suggesting a possible parallel between this position and the specialness of the intiriam mei in the pilgrimage.) From the lalāḍastānam the uyir is able to control the five senses.

In the dream state, the uyir leaves the lalāḍastānam and moves to the kaṇḍastānam (near the medula oblongata). In this state the sūkṣma śarīram does not have to carry the dead weight of the stūla śarīram with it. Freed from the load of the stūla śarīram, the sūkṣma śarīram can pass through solid matter, such as walls. In this freed state the sūkṣma śarīram is more relaxed than when it is conjoined to the stūla śarīram.

However, deep sleep (*āṛnta tūkkam*) is achieved only when the āvi leaves the kaṇḍastānam and moves to the irutayastānam, located in the chest. While the uyir is in the kaṇḍastānam, the apprehensive powers of the senses are sharpened (viśayikarikkum śakti kūrmaiyākum). *Viśayikarittal* means to cognize, with the added connotation of possession or inheritance derived from the phonetically paradigmatic word *ankikarittal,* which means to possess and/or inherit, also to accept or approve.

When the uyir is in the irutayastānam, this state is called *aviccai nilai* and in fact can be maintained at will only by yogis. In this state cognizance of the five senses is completely neutralized, and only *ajñānam* ("ignorance"), māyai ("illusion"), and *āṇavam* ("pride") remain as the soul's impurities.

The uyir, under appropriate yogic conditions, is able to migrate further down from the chest to the *nābhi,* or navel. Here, prāṇan is cognizant of itself alone (*tannaiyē viśayikarikkum mana nilai; turiya nilai*).

When the uyir moves to the *mūlādāram* (a cakkaram, or nerve plexus in the body, described as a four-petaled lotus [*nānkitaṛ tāmarai*] situated between *kuyyam* ["genitals"] and kutam ["anus"], this state is described as the *turiyātīta nilai.* The mūlādāram was also described to me by our guru in the pilgrimage as the seat of one's orgasm (kāma inpam uccikkum iṭam), especially that experienced in one's early youth—"say, when twelve years of age" (note that Lord Ayyappan was twelve years old when he reached the hill of Sabari). In this state, the uyir may be called ātman or *āttumā,* in the true sense of that word. For here the soul becomes cognizant of the essence, or *māttirai,* of aviccai ("ignorance, illusion, pride").

The word *māttirai,* which I have translated as "essence," is quite enlightening because it indicates a fleeting fraction of a second, a primordial unit, a short vowel; more contemporaneously it also means a capsule or a pill. In one of the Tamil dialects of Sri Lanka, it means a flash of good luck or fortune. The state of turiyātītam, then, is not only one that reveals the "momentariness" and fleeting quality of aviccai, but insofar as it stands for a state in which the soul enters eternal self-apperception, it transforms this fleeting moment into an eternity.

The three innermost bodies are collectively known as *kāraṇa sūkṣma śarīram*, and this is to be distinguished from the ordinary sūkṣma śarīram, or dream body. It is also known as the *puriyaṭṭaga śarīram*. This body cannot be perceived by the five senses and is not impelled or controlled by the twenty-five *tattuvams* ("basic gross substances"). This body is indestructible and knows no beginning or end. This is the body that enters a new yōni each time it is to be reborn. The puriyaṭṭaga śarīram, unlike the sūkṣma śarīram and the stūla śarīram, is formless. This body encases the soul and moves with it from one place to another inside and outside the sūkṣma śarīram. The puriyaṭṭaga śarīram has three body sheaths.

The outermost sheath is known as the *manomayakośam*, because it is the locus of the four intellectual faculties, or the *andakaraṇankaḷ*, which consist of *manam* ("mind") as the leader (hence the name *manomayakośam*), putti ("intellect"), cittam ("will"), and *akankāram* ("primordial power for action"). As a body, it is also known as the *kuṇa śarīram*, because it is here that the three kuṇams are located.

The next innermost body is the *kañjuga śarīram*, whose sheath is known as the vijñānamayakośam. This is the seat of *kālam* ("time"), *niyati* (same as *ūṛvinai*, "destiny," also karmam), *kalai* ("art"), *vittai* ("science"), and *arāham* ("absence of desire").

Finally, the innermost body, enclosing the soul, is known as the *kāraṇa śarīram* and its sheath as the *ānandamayakośam*. This is the seat of vidyā, or knowledge. One attains true *ānandam* ("happiness" or "bliss") when one taps this innermost source of vidyā.

The progression parallel to the yogi's route to self-realization is the pilgrim's attempt to know himself by crossing the eighteen steps and moving inward into and through his five body sheaths, which may be diagrammed for possible comparisons (see figure 4).

With the crossing of the eighteenth step, especially for the eighteenth time, avidyā is vanquished, making the soul free to become one with all that had once been an exterior, an other. In the formulation of the Hindu great tradition, this, as is well known to every beginning student of Indian religions, is seen as the merging of the ātman with the universal soul, or brahman. Such a formulation by humble pilgrims (especially the unschooled ones), though not entirely absent, was certainly not prevalent. Of those pilgrims I walked with and talked with, however, none failed to

Figure 4. The Synthesis of Body Sheaths, Yoga, and the Eighteen Steps

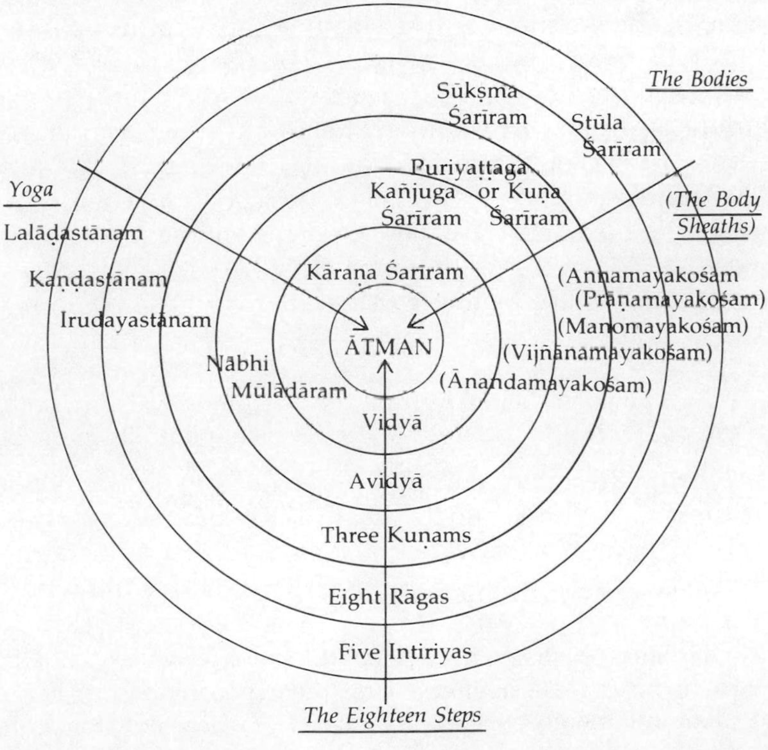

express—even if only in the most inarticulate of ways—the experience of having lost their identity and individuality, even if it had been only for a fleeting moment. This sense of union was often not expressed in words (quite appropriately so) but in states of trance. These moments of loss of self-consciousness and even consciousness were later referred to as the purpose and the highest point of the entire pilgrimage—if not of their entire life. Many expressed the wish that death would have claimed them at that time so that they could have merged with the Lord permanently.

In this final merging, there are no analytic distinctions to separate self from other (Thirdness); no rude consciousness of the other (Secondness). In Firstness the pilgrim is able to know (if not say), "Now I really know." For Peirce, as for the dominant Western tradition he represents, the epistemological movement is from Firstness to Thirdness, from synthetic to analytic knowledge. For the Hindu pilgrim, however, the knowing process moves from Thirdness to Firstness, from analysis to synthesis and then further, to where there is nothing left to know either through analysis or synthesis. This is *pūrṇa* vidyā, perfect knowledge.

This is how our guru described the moment of vidya, which he equated with that moment when the uyir reaches the lalāḍastānam. Note the use of the word *mãttirai* in his description:

> Ajñānam, māyai, āṇavam, ivai mūntrum innilaiyil minnal pōl tōntrum. Immūntru aviccai minnal pōntralla, minnalin māttiraiyentrē kūralām. Atō minnal, itō nān entru colluvatatrkillai. ituvē vittyam. Ituvē jñānam . . . ituvē nittyam.

Which may be translated as:

> Ignorance, illusion, and pride, these three will "appear" like lightning. These three aviccai [their appearance] may be called not merely as lightning but as a "fraction of the time

> taken for lightning to flash." One cannot say, "Behold there! That is lightning" and "Behold here! This is me." Such is wisdom. Such is knowledge. . . . Such is eternity.

When the weary pilgrim approaches the deity, his body is as good as broken and torn, with his senses defeated and rāgas overcome. His three kuṇams are in a state of equilibrium and equipoise. There is nothing left that conceals his true essence or soul.

When the pilgrim descends the eighteen steps on his return to where he will spend the night on the eastern slopes of the hill, he sees a huge bonfire rage to the sky, fed by the shells of the coconuts that were sacrificially broken over the deity. Karma burns itself in its own flames, thereby kindling in the devotee the awareness of his unburnable identity, his soul, which has now become one with the soul of his Lord.

8
A "Différant" Conclusion

I began this study with the aim of writing a cultural account of a culture. David Schneider, who invented for us the concept of a cultural account, unfortunately went on to define culture in terms far more positivistic than are warranted. By defining culture as a system of symbols and meanings, on the one hand he overemphasized the systematicity of culture, and on the other he deemphasized the nonsymbolic semeiotic functions in a culture. In correcting for both of these deficiencies of commission and omission, I argued in favor of a semeiotic cultural account that paid special attention not only to symbols but to indexes and icons as well. Such a semeiotic account is, by definition, also an interpretive account. In adumbrating a further refinement of the structure of signification, a refinement that I only partially employed, I held out the hope that someday someone will be able to write a highly refined and rich semeiotic cultural account, more keenly sensitive to the variety of interpretive possibilities than mine has been. Interpretation itself, I have argued, is a complex sign, and by virtue of its metaphoric structure derives its significant force from the confluence of iconic, indexical, and symbolic functions.

In the introductory chapter I sketched the ten sign types that were generated by Peirce's first taxonomic system. These signs are products of a logical system and were primarily intended to facilitate the analysis of an argument in a logical context. In selectively focusing on the icon, the index, and the symbol, our emphasis has been on the quality of the relationship that inheres between sign, or representamen, and the object for which it stands. These qualities were ones of similarity, contiguity, and convention. Needless to say, the full significance of these qualitative bonds is realized only by virtue of the interpretant completing the triad. In other words, whenever and wherever we stressed an iconic, indexical, or symbolic mode of signification, as the case may have been, there was a tacit acknowledgment of the obvious part the interpretant played in completing the mode in question. However, given the fact that this study claims to be an interpretive account, the interpretant dimension deserves to be highlighted a little more than it has been. The three possible interpretants found in the logical system—the rheme, the dicent sign, and the argument—are not, however, as appropriate in the ethnographic context as they might be in a context of unpacking a logical proposition or argument. In a logical context, the focus is still on the sign: on how the sign represents itself to the interpretant, namely, in the case of the rheme, as a sign of possibility; in the case of the dicent sign, as a sign of fact; or in the case of the argument, as a sign of reason. This system was developed by Peirce in 1904. By 1908, in a letter to Lady Welby (Peirce and Welby 1977: 73–86), Peirce shifts to a more elaborate classification of signs, in which the interpretant is not slighted in favor of the representamen, or sign. In this later typology, Peirce seems to take his definition of the interpretant—the *effect* a sign has on an interpreter—more seriously than he did in the earlier typology. In the interest of brevity and economy, I shall not involve myself in the controversial pursuit of relating the two systems or, for that matter, even in laying out the later system in all its detail. I have chosen, rather, to present to you the three types of interpretants provided for us by Peirce in this system along with the three subtypes of interpretants generated by one of the main types. I do this not as an exercise for its own sake but to reveal the kinds of interpretants that I have implicitly acknowledged in this interpretive account, and with which someone else may choose to structure his or her account more explicitly.

If the interpretant is taken to be the effect of the sign on those for whom it is a sign, interpretants can be classed into three types: immediate, dynamical, and final.

The *immediate interpretant* is defined by Peirce as "the quality of the impression that the sign is *fit* to produce and does not consist in any actual reaction" (8.315). Strictly speaking then, the immediate interpretant, insofar as it does not have any effect on someone or something, is not an interpretant. Rather, it points to the "interpretability [of] a sign before it gets any interpreter" (Peirce and Welby 1977: 111). Thus, when Sounderam Piḷḷai, the famed skinflint of Kalappūr, planted the scarecrow in front of his house, the scarecrow became an immediate interpretant. It was a sign that was predisposed to have the effect of warding off the evil eye, regardless of whether anybody would ever arrive to look at it.

Setting aside the dynamical interpretant for the moment, let us consider the *final interpretant*. The notion of the ultimate opinion of the scientific community figures centrally in any understanding of the final interpretant. The final interpretant is defined as "that which would finally be decided to be the true interpretation if consideration of the matter were carried so far that an ultimate opinion were reached" (8.184). Admittedly, this is a difficult concept, one on which much ink has been spent in attempts to defend and to question its defensibility. It is not in our interest to get embroiled in any extensive controversy over this matter; it suffices to grant that the final interpretant appears "to be the effect the sign finally has, or would have, on the fully developed mind of the scientific community. It is that effect which the sign would finally produce, or have, on the mind of the scientific community were it allowed an indefinite amount of time to investigate" (Almeder 1980: 28).

The *dynamical interpretant* is of greatest value for us as anthropologists. The dynamical interpretant "is the actual effect which the sign determines. . . . It is the direct effect produced by a sign upon the interpreter of it" (4.536). There are three kinds of dynamical interpretants. These are the emotional, the energetic, and the logical; all three are essential for the craft of cultural anthropology. "The first proper significant effect is a feeling produced by it. There is almost always a feeling which we come to interpret as evidence that we comprehend the proper effect of the sign. . . . This "emotional interpretant" as I call it, may amount to much more than the feeling of recognition; and, in some cases, is the only proper significant effect that a sign produces" (5.476).

Several years ago, I read an early draft of the ūr chapter at a South Asia seminar, held at the University of Chicago, on the subject "Persons and Interpersonal Relationships: An Exploration of Indigenous Conceptual Systems." One of the nicest compliments I received after having read the paper was from Prof. Kali Charan Bahl, who said, "This is the first time that I have seen a village ethnography that has created in me a feeling of recognition." Some years ago, Ian Goonetileke, then librarian of the University of Ceylon at Peradeniya, posed the following challenge (which I paraphrase): Assume that there is a house in America furnished with nothing but American furniture and furnishings. Assume that first-generation immigrants from India live in this house, a fact you are unaware of. Assume further that the only odor in the house is the odor of an American meal. Also suppose that none of the regular occupants of the house are present when you enter it. Will you or will you not be able to say whether the regular occupants of the house are first-generation immigrants from India? Both he and I agreed that the probability of our identifying the occupants as Indians in a context such as this was quite high. We had excluded the obvious clues that could lead us to such a conclusion in this imagined experiment. Rather, the inferential means were more than likely to be tacit, largely based on a feeling of recognition of "the organization of space" (to use Goonetileke's phrase). An ANV expatriate who returned to his natal village in India after many years reports of experiencing a feeling of recognition. When pressed to explain why and how, this otherwise articulate man floundered for the appropriate verbal expression and finally settled on, "an inner feeling" (*ullunarcci*). A fellow expatriate attributed this feeling of recognition to the smell of the dry palmyra palm fronds. In all these and in similarly conceivable instances, the feeling of recognition may be traced to a source that is, for the most part, diffuse. Furthermore, to the extent that an inferential process is involved in arriving at such an emotional interpretant, it is a process of abduction.[1]

Unlike induction and deduction, wherein the inferential steps are readily available for cognitive reconstruction, abduction presents itself as a flash of insight, invariably charged with emotion. Whenever the nervous system is disturbed in a complicated way, says Peirce,

> the result is a single harmonious disturbance which I call an emotion. Thus the various sounds made by the instruments of the orchestra strike upon the ear, and the result is a

[1]For a more extensive discussion of abduction, see chaps. 1 and 2 of William H. Davis's *Peirce's Epistemology*; for an ethnographic application of the same subject, see Daniel 1981.

> peculiar musical emotion, quite distinct from the sounds themselves. This emotion is the same as a hypothetic [i.e., an abductive] inference, and every hypothetic inference involves the formation of such an emotion. (Cited in William Davis 1972: 46)

The charge of emotion that accompanies abduction or that is present in the precipitation of an emotional interpretant is not always robust. To be sure, the experience of déjà vu is an instance of an emotional interpretant. The more developed dynamical interpretants must, by definition, be mediated by or built upon an emotional interpretant.

The *energetic interpretant* goes beyond a mere feeling of recognition and impels one to act, to expend effort.

> The performance of a piece of concerted music is a sign. It conveys and is intended to convey, the composer's musical ideas; but these usually consist merely in a series of feelings. If a sign produces any further proper significant effect, it will do so through the mediation of the emotional interpretant, and such further effect will always involve an effort. I call it the energetic interpretant. The effort may be a muscular one, as it is in the case of the command to ground arms; but it is much more usually an exertion upon the Inner World, a mental effort. (5.476)

When a villager is moved to prostrate himself when the deity appears in procession before his house, the significant effect in question is an energetic interpretant. When, after several months in an Indian village and after having sat at several feasts, the anthropologist responds to a hearty meal with a satiated belch, this behavior, by its sheer naturalness in that context, becomes a culturally accepted *energetic interpretant*.

The *logical interpretant* is the meaning of an intellectual concept, something that the emotional and energetic interpretants can never be. The energetic interpretant is a particular act. The logical interpretant is of a general nature. This thesis is a logical interpretant in that it expresses or captures the meaning of the sign (writ large) of the culture it purports to represent. The cultural order is a sign of a general nature. The logical interpretant (this thesis, for instance) strives to express the generality of the sign(s) of culture. Almeder explicates the logical interpretant in the following manner:

> The logical interpretant is not the meaning of the original sign. Rather it expresses, or gives, the same meaning that the original sign expresses. The meaning of the original sign itself, and which is expressed in the logical interpretant, is not itself a sign but rather the habit or Thirdness which the sign itself expresses and which is subsequently expressed in the logical interpretant. This "habit" which is expressed by the sign is the meaning of the sign and Peirce frequently calls it the *ultimate logical interpretant*. (1980: 30)

The ultimate logical interpretant, at least where the human sciences are concerned, will remain an unreachable goal. The flow of human life is such that the best account of it is but a trace of what was. Every logical interpretant of a culture is but an anisomorphic simulacrum of it. The present one is no exception. The logical interpretant of cultural anthropology, by being an integral part of a creative process, is a very special and, I dare say, the finest embodiment of the dynamism of semeiosis. Final interpretants or even ultimate logical interpretants have no place in anthropological inquiry. Anthropological fieldwork tends to begin with every conversation being construed as implicit inquiry. However, as fieldwork matures, it must be transformed in such a way that inquiry becomes "routine conversation" (Rorty 1979: 318).

In the Introduction, we examined the dialogic structure of the sign and argued that in this very structure lay the open-endedness of semeiosis. The anthropological encounter between field-worker and informant itself is an encounter between two worlds of signs, or an encounter between two signs writ large. It is an encounter in which the anthropologist—a composite sign in his own right—seeks out his field of study, including his informants, objectivizes it, and sets himself or his understanding of this object as the representamen of the object. The externalization of yet another sign, the monograph deployed, is the interpretant that opens up the semeiotic process for other signs and other interpretants to understand, and in so doing transforms the original object. All these encounters and juxtapositions between and among representamen (anthropologist), object (informant), and interpretant (the written account) entail a certain play or lack of fit. This play, which constitutes the tychastic dynamism of the sign process, is what Derrida calls *the play of différance*,[2] a quasi-concept that I have considered to be integral to an understanding of culture.

It is time now for us to return, one last time, to the definition of culture with which we opened our study and where we were first introduced to the misspelled neologism *différance*. In that definition we stated that the anthropologist strives to defer to the creativity of his informants and self-consciously reflects upon the différance inherent in this creative product of deference. When Derrida invented this neologism, he intended it to convey, as does the Latin rheme, two distinct significations. The first signifies temporality, as does the English *defer*; the second, spatiality, as the English *differ*.[3]

In our discussion on the dialogistic structure of the sign and the consequent openness of the semeiotic process (and

[2]"Différance" has been adapted from Jacques Derrida's now-famous essay of the same title, which appeared in English in a collection of his essays entitled *"Speech and Phenomena" and Other Essays on Husserl's Theory of Signs* (1973).

[3]It is this spatial dimension of differance that constitutes the core of de Saussure's structural linguistics wherein the focus is on *langue*, understood as a system of "differences without positive terms" (de Saussure 1959: 120). Temporality has no place in the synchronic langue, and by relegating *parole* and diachrony to a place of nonimportance, the temporal dimension of differance falls outside the scope of his consideration.

by extension, the cultural process), we observed that signification could not occur in the absence of difference between representamen and interpretant. We have also observed that this difference, as well as that which obtains between representamen and object on the one hand and interpretant and object on the other, makes interpretation both necessary and possible. In the present study, by self-consciously reflecting on the *spatial* difference that constitutes our interpretation, we were able to identify, among other things, two semeiotic styles, one favoring symbolization, the other favoring iconicity. These "styles," or preferred modes of signification, we found, have implications for phenomena ranging from our different conceptions of village, house, and sex to illness, person, and knowledge. These styles may also be conceptualized as styles of discourse. The relations between these discourses are to be seen as strands in an ongoing conversation, a conversation that does not dogmatically presuppose an epistemological matrix that unites the speakers "but where the hope of agreement is never lost as long as the conversation lasts" (Rorty 1979: 318).

This brings us to the other meaning of différance, the temporally determined, *defer*. In fact, at least in English, *defer* has two meanings: one belonging to the temporal notion of postponement (deferment), at which we have already hinted, and the other to the intransitive verb that means to submit in opinion or judgment; yield with courtesy; be respectful (deference). This meaning is an interesting hybrid of temporal and spatial senses. Among Tamils, deference behavior is signified through a variety of culturally calculated manipulations of space: standing when a superior sits, squatting on one's haunches when the respected one sits on a chair, standing to the side (rather than directly in front) of an elder when speaking to him, sitting on the left of an honored guest at meal, building a house so that it does not exceed the temple tower in height, looking at the ground when walking through an audience of respected elders, not looking a teacher straight in the eye when he castigates you, and so on. Deference (and its obverse) is also conveyed through the manipulation of time: receiving pracātam from the priest after a member of a higher jāti has done so, delaying payment for services rendered, making a petitioner wait "his turn" for bureaucratic services, speaking only when and only after you are spoken to, and so on.

By deferring to the creative input of my Tamil village informants and friends, whose contributions have been greedily assimilated into the interpretive product, I was able to encounter a certain significant construct that kept reappearing in a variety of ethnographic contexts and cultural domains. I have identified this pervasively present construct as a regnant sign in Tamil culture. This regnant sign is characterized by the fact that in all the cultural domains I have considered in this book (and many that I have intentionally left out), a whole array of cultural representations turned out to be representations of a plurality of coded substances and ultimately turned out to be representations of a singular coded substance. Differently stated, in the culture that my Tamil friends and informants helped me create and called their own, coded substance emerged as the hallmark of this creation.

Given the values of our time and the epistemological roots of our discipline, it is tempting to declare with positivistic conceit that this "hallmark" of Tamil culture is indeed the ultimate logical interpretant—or even the final interpretant—of our inquiry. Thankfully, however, the other, purely temporal intention of differance would frustrate any such effort. Constrained by the structuralist prejudice, de Saussure saw the place and play of differance within the sign only in its spatial sense, in langue (de Saussure 1959: 120). For this reason, neither parole nor diachrony occupied the place of importance that langue did in his structural linguistics. The admission of the temporal dimension of différance insists upon the openness of the world, especially the world as constituted by man. Such an admission results in the perpetual deferment of the ultimate or final meaning of any sign.

> The signified concept is never present in itself, in an adequate presence that would refer only to itself. Every concept is necessarily and essentially inscribed in a chain or a system, within which it refers to another and to other concepts, by the systematic play of differences. Such a play, then—différance—is no longer simply a concept, but the possibility of conceptuality, of the conceptual system and process in general. (Derrida 1973: 140)

The pseudonym of the village of which this monograph is a study means "a place of mixed substances." It is of mixed substance in more than one sense. Most dramatically, this mixing began with the false oath of the caste story of the ANVs. Less dramatically but no less significantly, the village is a place of mixed substance in that ideas from the outside world are regularly brought in and blended with the preexisting ones of Kalappūr. Carriers of these ideas range from mendicants, visiting astrologers, Siddha physicians invited for consultation, the doctors and nurses of the local hospital who are trained in Western medicine, hawkers, guests from other villages, ANVs who return from Sri Lanka and Malaysia and a few from such faraway places as England and the United States, to the resident anthropologists. These ideas, too, along with sounds and gazes and so forth, are substances, albeit very subtle, very fluid ones. As have their gross counterparts, however, some of these ideas have mixed well with Kalappūr and Kalappūrans and have proved to be compatible, while others have not.

This interpretive study has been one attempt to capture the cultural imagination in its dynamic flux, to trap the flow and hold it in a moment of introspection. The metaphors of webs, faceted gems, and even molecular clouds are all to one degree or another inadequate. They are attempts at providing a certain measure of fixity, a provisional limitation upon possibilities that has made the crafting of this study possible. To this extent they have been assets, but they are liabilities as well in that they paint a picture of stasis, of imaginative arrest. Such a picture, it must be emphasized, is partial at best. To compensate for this deficiency, I wish to close with an image that was given to me by one of my best informants, Sadaya Kavuṇṭan, which more than any other does justice to the *process* of culture.

Of all my informants in Kalappūr, Sadaya Kavuṇṭan was the most loquacious. He also, more than anyone else, seemed to appreciate my quest despite its diffuseness. He knew that I wanted to study his "culture." In the early days of our encounter, I attempted to describe to him what I meant by "culture." He told me point blank that there was no Tamil equivalent for the concept of culture and that he doubted that such a thing existed among them. His candor drove home the point of the anthropological exercise in general, of its own ethnohistorical and intellectual roots. He was willing, though, to join in *creating* a culture for me. He offered me an approximate Tamil equivalent for the term *culture, cankati. Cankati* means affair, circumstance, news, a matter of interest, and also a secret. My other major informants were continually dragging me off to this ritual and that one. Not so with Sadayan. He was a poet and a teller of stories. He chose to visit me when nothing seemed to happen, in summer afternoons when the temperature hovered around a hundred in the shade; when the only sound to be heard was that of a stray cow trying its halfhearted moo against open space or the crepitation of a dry palm frond submitting to the village mute's footstep in the field. Sadayan would remind me that beneath the stillness of the scene, there was a seething life of gossip and intrigue and a calmer one of myths, dreams, and refreshing recess. He was there to remind me that images of stasis were false and that no cankati could ever be found amid such images.

When the rains come, the village is abruptly unstilled. Static images have no place then. For two years prior to 1974, rain clouds had skirted Kalappūr. In June 1974 (thanks to the auspiciousness of our presence, the villagers said), the monsoons brought torrents. One afternoon that second year, when the showers had briefly paused to allow the village to catch its breath, Sadayan, the man gifted with calmly articulate speech, was beside himself. Silenced by wads of animated words, he beckoned me to come with him. He took me to the edge of a newly formed stream, gashed by the anarchic floodwaters that were rushing in from Kalappūr's northern neighbor, muddying its way through Kalappūr and heading toward the village reservoir. In silence punctuated only by Sadayan's intermittent exclamation, "this is our cankati!" we watched the stream flux and lapse for several hours. Once again, later that year prior to our leaving the field, he took me to see the cankatis of his people. This time the trip was to the village reservoir. The sediment had settled and the water was a deep and transparent green, inviting us to clarify our thoughts against its depth and silence. In its stillness and in its silence, there was movement: the maundering of a thoughtless cloud, the rhythm of farmers leading their oxen home along the bund of the reservoir, the flutter of children throwing grass arrows at one another, the gait of women returning home with pots of water on their hips and heads, the constrained leaps of tongues of fire over which Parayans (drummers) held their drums to stretch them to the desired tone as they prepared to lead a corpse to the crematorium. The dead man, they said, was a victim of witchcraft. The drummers decided that their drums had been sufficiently primed. What began as a flurry of erratic raps on the taut drumskins blended into a parade of rhythmic beats that bounced off the huge tamarind tree at the reservoir's edge, charging the air with their contrapuntal reverberations. The drumming further animated the children's play. One of the grass arrows pierced the water, sending a shiver of reticulate images across its surface. "These are our cankatis," said Sadayan, pointing. "A reticulate of fluid signs," I recorded in my notebook.

The signs that constitute the culture of Kalappūr are fluid. In this respect, the structural metaphors employed in the greater part of this text are provisional and inadequate heuristic devices. The recurrent patterns among these fluid signs we have identified as regnant. Such regnancy, however, does in no way imply a view of Kalappūr as either an isolated or an insulated village, or of Kalappūrans as isolated or insulated individuals. On the contrary, the very meaningful constitution of these regnant signs marks Kalappūr not only as a place that receives ideas and other substances from the outside but also as one that gives. In this sense, then, every Indian village and town with permeable thresholds is a Kalappūr, and every Indian villager is a Kalappūran. In this spirit, I hope that what has been said of Kalappūr and Kalappūrans is not limited to this village and to these villagers alone but may prove compatible with the cultural substance of other villages and towns in other parts of the Indian subcontinent as well.

This chapter is not a conclusion in the strict sense of the term; neither, for that matter, is this book. This study is, as a sign, a fluid buoy marking its own passage through fluid signs. As an interpretation, it is a "différant" one, in the temporal sense of Derrida's neologism; its conclusion, like that of culture, must remain deferred.

Bibliography

Almeder, Robert.
1980 *The Philosophy of Charles S. Peirce*. Totowa, N.J.: Rowman and Littlefield.

Altshuler, Bruce
1982 "Peirce's Theory of Truth and the Revolt Against Realism." *Transactions of the Charles S. Peirce Society* 18, no. 4: 34–56.

Apel, Karl-Otto
1981 *Charles S. Peirce: From Pragmatism to Pragmaticism*. Translated by John Michael Krois. Amherst: University of Massachusetts Press.

Appadurai, Arjun, and Carol Appadurai Breckenridge
1976 "The South Indian Temple: Authority, Honour, and Redistribution." *Contributions to Indian Sociology*, n.s., 10: 187–211.

Austin, J. L.
1962 *How to Do Things with Words*. Edited by J. O. Urmson. Oxford: Oxford University Press.

Ayer, A. J.
1968 *The Origins of Pragmatism*. San Francisco: Freeman, Cooper and Co.

Babb, Lawrence A.
1975 *The Divine Hierarchy: Popular Hinduism in Central India*. New York: Columbia University Press.

Bachelard, Gaston
1964 *The Poetics of Space*. Translated by Maria Jolas. Boston: Beacon Press.

Barnett, Steven A.
1976 "Coconuts and Gold." *Contributions to Indian Sociology* 10: 133–156

Barthes, Roland
1972 *Mythologies*. New York: Hill and Wang.

Beardsley, Monroe C.
1972 "The Metaphorical Twist." In *Essays on Metaphor*, edited by Warren Shibles. Whitewater: University of Wisconsin Press.

Beck, Brenda E. F.
1969 "Colour and Heat in South Indian Ritual." *Man* 4, no. 4: 553–572.
1972 *Peasant Society in Konku: A Study of Right and Left Subcastes in South India*. Vancouver: University of British Columbia Press.
1976 "The Symbolic Merger of Body, Space, and Cosmos in Hindu Tamil Nadu." *Contributions to Indian Sociology* 10, no. 2: 213–243.

Berreman, Gerald D.
1960 "Caste in India and the United States." *American Journal of Sociology* 66, no. 4: 120–127.

Bharathi, Yogi S.
1970 *The Grand Epic of Śaivism*. Tinnevely: South India Siddhanta Works Publishing Society.

Bhattacharyya, Deborah P.
1977 "Madness as Entropy: A Bengali View." Paper presented at Thirteenth Bengali Studies Conference, 6 May 1977, Chicago.

Black, Max
1962 *Models and Metaphors*. Ithaca, N.Y.: Cornell University Press.

Boler, John F.
1963 *Charles Peirce and Scholastic Realism: A Study of Peirce's Realism in Relation to John Duns Scotus*. Seattle: University of Washington Press.

Bouglé, Célestin
1971 *Essays on the Caste System*. Translated by D. F. Pocock. Cambridge: Cambridge University Press.

Bourdieu, Pierre
1972 *Outline of a Theory of Practice*. Translated by Richard Nice. Cambridge: Cambridge University Press.

Carstairs, G. Morris
1967. *The Twice Born*. Bloomington: Indiana University Press.

Carter, Anthony T.
1982 "Hierarchy and the Concept of the Person in Western India." In *Concepts of Person, Kinship, Caste, and Marriage in India*, edited by Ákös Östör, Lina Fruzzetti, and Steven A. Barnett. Cambridge: Harvard University Press.

Chaitanya, Krishna
1972 *Kerala*. New Delhi: National Book Trust, India.

Cherry, Colin

1957 *On Human Communication: A Review, a Survey, and a Criticism*. Cambridge: Massachusetts Institute of Technology Press.

Cohn, Bernard S.

1966 "Regions, Subjective and Objective: Their Relation to the Study of Modern Indian History and Society." In *Symposium on Regions and Regionalism in South Asian Studies: An Exploratory Study*. Duke University Series, monograph no. 6, edited by Robert I. Crane. Durham, N.C.: Duke University Press.

Conklin, H. C.

1955 "Hanunoo Color Categories." *Southwestern Journal of Anthropology* 11: 339–344

D'Andrade, Roy

1976 "A Propositional Analysis of U.S. American Beliefs about Illness." In *Meaning in Anthropology*, edited by Keith H. Basso and Henry A. Selby. Albuquerque: University of New Mexico Press.

Daniel, E. Valentine

1973 "A Penny for the Boatman: A Study of the Rituals of Ceylon Estate Tamils." M. A. thesis, University of Chicago.

1981 "Comment on 'When Rational Men Fall Sick: An Inquiry into Some Assumptions Made by Medical Anthropologists.' " *Culture, Medicine, and Psychiatry* 5, no. 4: 370–373.

1983*a* "Karma: The Uses of an Idea." In *Karma: An Anthropological Inquiry*, edited by C. F. Keyes and E. Valentine Daniel. Berkeley, Los Angeles, London: University of California Press.

1983*b* "The Pulse as an Icon in Siddha Medicine." In *South Asian Systems of Healing*, edited by E. Valentine Daniel and Judy F. Pugh. Contribution to Asian Studies 18: 207–214. Amsterdam: Brill.

Daniel, Sheryl B.

1983 "The Tool Box Approach of the Tamil to the Issues of Moral Responsibility and Human Destiny." In *Karma: An Anthropological Inquiry*, edited by C. F. Keyes and E. Valentine Daniel. Berkeley, Los Angeles, London: University of California Press.

Das, Veena

1974 "On the Categorization of Space in Hindu Ritual." In *Text and Context: The Social Anthropology of Tradition*, edited by Ravindra K. Jain. Philadelphia: Institute for the Study of Human Issues.

1977 *Structure and Cognition: Aspects of Hindu Caste and Ritual*. Bombay: Oxford University Press.

David, Kenneth
1972 "The Bound and the Nonbound: Variations in Social and Cultural Structure in Rural Jaffna, Ceylon." Ph.D. dissertation, University of Chicago.
David, Kenneth, ed.
1977 *The New Wind: Changing Identities in South Asia*. The Hague: Mouton.
Davidson, Donald
1978 "What Metaphors Mean." In *On Metaphor*, edited by Sheldon Sacks. Chicago: University of Chicago Press.
Davis, M.
1976 "A Philosophy of Hindu Rank from Rural West Bengal." *Journal of Asian Studies*, 36, no. 1: 5–24.
Davis, William H.
1972 *Peirce's Epistemology*. The Hague: Nijhoff.
Deacon, Terrence
1978 "Semiotics and Cybernetics: The Relevance of C. S. Peirce." In *Sanity and Signification*, edited by Terrence Deacon. Bellingham: Western Washington University Print Shop.
de Bary, Theodore
1958 *Sources of Indian Tradition*. New York: Columbia University Press.
Dirks, Nicholas
1984(?) *An Ethnohistory of a Little Kingdom*. Cambridge: Cambridge University Press, forthcoming.
Derrida, Jacques
1973 *"Speech and Phenomena" and Other Essays on Husserl's Theory of Signs*. Translated by David B. Allison. Evanston, Ill.: Northwestern University Press.
1976 *Of Grammatology*. Translated by Gayatri Pivak. Baltimore: Johns Hopkins University Press.
de Saussure, Ferdinand
1959 *Course in General Linguistics*. New York: McGraw-Hill Book Co.
Diehl, Carl Gustav
1956 *Instrument and Purpose: Studies on Rites and Rituals in South India*. Lund: Gleerup.
Dumont, Louis
1970 *Homo Hierarchicus: An Essay on the Caste System*. Chicago: University of Chicago Press.
Dumont, Louis, and David Pocock
1959 "Pure and Impure." *Contributions to Indian Sociology* 3: 9–39.
Embree, Ainslie T.
1977 "Frontiers into Boundaries; From the Traditional to the Modern

State." In *Symposium on Regions and Regionalism in South Asian Studies*. Duke University Series, monograph no. 10, edited by Richard G. Fox. Durham, N.C.: Duke University Press.

Fitzgerald, John J.

1966 *Peirce's Theory of Signs as Foundation for Pragmatism*. The Hague: Mouton.

Frake, Charles

1961 "The Diagnosis of Disease among the Subanum of Mindanao." *American Anthropologist* 63, no. 2: 113–132.

1962 "The Ethnographic Study of Cognitive Systems." In *Anthropology and Human Behavior*, edited by Thomas A. Gladwin and William C. Sturtereant. Washington, D.C.: Anthropological Society of Washington.

Fruzzetti, Lina, Ákos Östör, and Steven A. Barnett.

1982 "The Cultural Construction of the Person in Bengal and Tamilnadu." In *Concepts of Person, Kinship, Caste, and Marriage in India*. Edited by Lina Fruzzetti, Ákos Östör, and Steven A. Barnett. Cambridge: Harvard University Press.

Geertz, Clifford

1973 *The Interpretation of Cultures*. New York: Basic Books.

1976 "From a Native's Point of View": On the Nature of Anthropological Understanding." In *Meaning in Anthropology*, edited by Keith H. Basso and Henry A. Selby. Albuquerque: University of New Mexico Press.

Gennep, Arnold van

1908 *The Rites of Passage*. Reprint. London: Routledge and Kegan Paul, 1960.

Good, Anthony

1982 "The Actor and the Act: Categories of Prestation in South India." *Man* 17, no. 1: 23–41.

Goodenough, Ward H.

1956 "Componential Analysis and the Study of Meaning." *Language* 32: 195–216.

1964 *Description and Comparison in Cultural Anthropology*. Chicago: Aldine.

1965 "Yankee Kinship Terminology: A Problem in Componential Analysis." *American Anthropologist* 67, no. 2: 259–287.

Habermas, Jürgen

1979 *Communication and the Evolution of Society*. Translated by T. McCarthy. Boston: Beacon Press.

Hegel, G. W. F.

1910 *Phenomenology of Mind*. Translated by J. B. Baillie. New York: Macmillan Co.

Hesse, Mary

1972 "Scientific Models." In *Essays on Metaphor*, edited by Warren Shibles. Whitewater: University of Wisconsin Press.

Hubert, Henri, and Marcel Mauss

1898 *Sacrifice: Its Nature and Function*. Reprint. Chicago: University of Chicago Press, 1964.

Inden, Ronald B.

1976 *Marriage and Rank in Bengali Culture: A History of Caste and Clan in Middle Period Bengal*. New Delhi: Vikas Publishing House.

Inden, Ronald B., and Ralph Nicholas

1977 *Kinship in Bengali Culture*. Chicago: University of Chicago Press.

Jaini, Padmanabh S.

1980 "Karma and the Problem of Rebirth in Jainism." In *Karma and Rebirth in Classical Indian Traditions*, edited by Wendy D. O'Flaherty. Berkeley, Los Angeles, London: University of California Press.

Jakobson, Roman.

1957 *Shifters, Verbal Categories, and the Russian Verb*. Cambridge: Harvard University Press.

Karve, Irawati

1962 "On the Road: A Maharashtrian Pilgrimage." *Journal of Asian Studies* 22, no. 4: 13–29.

Keesing, Roger M.

1974 "Theories of Culture." *Annual Review of Anthropology* 3: 73–98.

Kemper, Steven E. G.

1979 "Sinhalese Astrology, South Asian Caste Systems, and the Notion of Individuality." *Journal of Asian Studies* 38, no. 3: 477–497.

Kevelson, Roberta

1982 "Peirce's Dialogism Continuous Predicate and Legal Reasoning." *Transactions of the Charles S. Peirce Society* 18, no. 2: 159–176.

Kristeva, Julia

1977 *Polylogue*. Paris: Seuil

Leach, Edmund R.

1954 *Political Systems of Highland Burma*. Boston: Beacon Press.

1962 "Pulleyar and the Lord Buddha: An Aspect of Religious Syncretism in Ceylon." *Psychoanalysis and the Psychoanalytic Review* 59: 81–102.

1976 *Culture and Communication: The Logic by Which Symbols Are Connected*. Cambridge: Cambridge University Press.

LeVine, Robert A.

1973 *Culture, Behavior, and Personality*. Chicago: Aldine.

Lévi-Strauss, Claude

1963 *Totemism*. Boston: Beacon Press.

1966 "The Scope of Anthropology." *Current Anthropology* 7, no. 2: 112–123.

1974 *Tristes Tropiques*. New York: Atheneum.

Marriott, McKim

1976*a* "Hindu Transactions: Diversity Without Dualism." In *Transaction and Meaning: Directions in the Anthropology of Exchange and Symbolic Behavior*, edited by Bruce Kapferer. Philadelphia: Institute for the Study of Human Issues.

1976*b* "Interpreting Indian Society: A Monistic Alternative to Dumont's Dualism." *Journal of Asian Studies* 36, no. 3: 189–195.

Marriott, McKim, and Ronald B. Inden

1974 "Caste Systems." *Encyclopaedia Britannica*, 15th ed., 3: 982–991.

1977 "Toward an Ethnosociology of South Asian Caste Systems." In *The New Wind*, edited by Kenneth David. The Hague: Mouton.

Menon, Sreedhara A.

1979 *Social and Cultural History of Kerala*. New Delhi: Sterling Publishers.

Moffatt, Michael

1979 *An Untouchable Community in South India: Structure and Consensus*. Princeton, N.J.: Princeton University Press.

Olshewsky, Thomas M.

1983 "Peirce's Pragmatic Maxim." *Transactions of the Charles S. Peirce Society* 19, no. 2: 199–210.

Östör, Ákos, Lina Fruzzetti and Steven A. Barnett, eds.

1982 *Concepts of Person, Kinship, Caste, and Marriage in India*. Cambridge: Harvard University Press.

Peirce, Charles S.

1932 *Collected Papers*. Cambridge: Harvard University Press. Vols. 1–6, edited by C. Hartshorne and P. Weiss.

1958 *Collected Papers*. Cambridge: Harvard University Press. Vols. 7–8, edited by Arthur Burks.

1982 *Writings of Charles S. Peirce: A Chronological Edition*. Bloomington: Indiana University Press. Vol. 1, 1857–1866.

Peirce, Charles S., and Victoria Lady Welby

1977 *Semiotic and Significs: The Correspondence between Charles S. Peirce and Victoria Lady Welby*. Edited by Charles S. Hardwick. Bloomington: Indiana University Press.

Pillai, E. V.

1974 *Sri Dharmasastru Sarvasvam*. Tiruvanandapuram: Jeyachandira Book Depot.

Pyyappan
1973 *Lord Ayyappan the Dharma Sasta*. Bombay: Bharata Vidya Bhavan.

Quine, Willard Van Orman.
1960 *Word and Object*. Cambridge: Massachusetts Institute of Technology Press.

Ramanujan, A. K.
1967 *The Interior Landscape*. Bloomington: Indiana University Press.
1981 *Hymns for the Drowning: Poems for Viṣṇu, by Nammālvār*. Translated by A. K. Ramanujan. Princeton, N.J.: Princeton University Press.
1982 "On Woman Saints." In *The Divine Consort: Rādhā and the Goddesses of India*, edited by John Stratton Hawley and Donna Marie Wulff. Berkeley: Berkeley Religious Studies Series.

Ricoeur, Paul
1977 *The Rule of Metaphor*. Translated by Robert Czerny. Toronto: University of Toronto Press.
1978 *The Philosophy of Paul Ricoeur*. Edited by C. E. Reagan and D. Stewart. Boston: Beacon Press.

Rorty, Richard
1979 *Philosophy and the Mirror of Nature*. Princeton, N.J.: Princeton University Press.

Sahlins, Marshall
1976 *Culture and Practical Reason*. Chicago: University of Chicago Press.

Sapir, Edward
1921 *Language: An Introduction to the Study of Speech*. New York: Harcourt, Brace and World.

Sastrigal, T. K. Muthuswamy
1972 *Sri Mahastha and Manikantar*. Madras: Bharati Vijayam Press.

Schneider, David M.
1965 "American Kin Terms and Terms of Kinsmen: A Critique of Goodenough's Componential Analysis of Yankee Kinship Terminology." *American Anthropologist* 67, no. 2: 288–308.
1968 *American Kinship: A Cultural Account*. Englewood Cliffs, N.J.: Prentice-Hall.
1976 "Notes Toward a Theory of Culture." In *Meaning in Anthropology*, edited by Keith H. Basso and Henry A. Selby. Albuquerque: University of New Mexico Press.

Searle, John
1979 "Metaphor." In *Metaphor and Thought*, edited by Andrew Ortnoy. New York: Cambridge University Press.

Short, T. L.
1982 "Life among the Legisigns." *Transactions of the Charles S. Peirce Society* 17, no. 4: 285–310.

Silverstein, Michael
1976 "Shifters, Linguistic Categories, and Cultural Description." In *Meaning in Anthropology*, edited by Keith H. Basso and Henry A. Selby. Albuquerque: University of New Mexico Press.

Singer, Milton
1978 "For a Semiotic Anthropology." In *Sight, Sound, and Sense*, edited by T. A. Sebeok. Bloomington: Indiana University Press.
1980 "Signs of the Self: An Exploration in Semiotic Anthropology." *American Anthropologist* 82, no. 3: 485–507.

Sopher, David E.
1977 "Rohilkhand and Oudh: An Exploration of Social Gradients Across a Political Frontier." In *Symposium on Regions and Regionalism in South Asian Studies*. Duke University Series, monograph no. 10, edited by Richard G. Fox.

Staal, Frits
1979 "Oriental Ideas of the Origin of Language." *Journal of the American Oriental Society*, 99, no. 1: 1–14.

Stanley, John M.
1977 "Special Time, Special Power: The Fluidity of Power in a Popular Hindu Festival." *Journal of Asian Studies* 37, no. 1: 27–43.

Stearns, Isabel S.
1952 "Firstness, Secondness, and Thirdness." In *Studies in the Philosophy of Charles Sanders Peirce*, edited by Philip P. Wiener and Frederick H. Young. Cambridge: Harvard University Press.

Subbarayalu, Y.
1973 *Political Geography of the Chola Country*. Madras: Tamil Nadu State Department of Archaeology.

Tambiah, S. J.
1973 "From Varna to Caste through Mixed Unions." In *The Character of Kinship*, edited by Jack Goody. Cambridge: Cambridge University Press.

Thomas, P. T.
1973 *Sabarimalai and Its Sastha*. Madras: Christian Literature Society.

Trautman, Thomas R.
1980 Review of *Marriage and Rank in Bengali Culture*, by Ronald B. Inden. *Journal of Asian Studies* 39, no. 3: 519–524.

Turner, Victor W.
1967 *The Forest of Symbols*. Ithaca, N.Y.: Cornell University Press.

1969 *The Ritual Process*. Chicago: Aldine.
1974 *Drama, Fields, and Metaphor*. Ithaca, N.Y.: Cornell University Press.

Turner, Victor W., and Edith Turner
1978 *Image and Pilgrimage in Christian Culture*. New York: Columbia University Press.

Wadley, Susan Snow
1975 *Shakti: Power in the Conceptual Structure of Karimpur Religion*. Chicago: Department of Anthropology, University of Chicago.

Wagner, Roy
1981 *The Invention of Culture*. Rev. ed. Chicago: University of Chicago Press.

Wallace, A. F. C., and J. Atkins
1960 "The Meaning of Kinship Terms." *American Anthropologist* 62, no. 1: 58–80.

Watson, James B.
1963 "Caste as a Form of Acculturation." *Southwestern Journal of Anthropology* 19, no. 4: 356–378.

Weber, Max
1949 *The Methodology of the Social Sciences*. Translated and edited by Edward Shils and Henry Finch. New York: Free Press.

Weiss, Paul, and Arthur Burks
1945 "Peirce's Sixty-six Signs." *Journal of Philosophy* 42: 383–388.

White, Hayden
1973 *Metahistory: The Historical Imagination in Nineteenth-Century Europe*. Baltimore: Johns Hopkins University Press.

Whorf, Benjamin Lee
1956 *Language, Thought, and Reality: Selected Writings*. Edited by John B. Carroll. Cambridge: Massachusetts Institute of Technology Press.

Zimmermann, Francis
1978 "From Classic Texts to Learned Practices: Methodological Remarks on the Study of Indian Medicine." *Social Science and Medicine* 12, no. 2b: 97–104.

Index

Designer: UC Press Staff
Compositor: Trend-Western
Printer: Thomson-Shore, Inc.
Binder: John H. Dekker & Sons
Text: Palatino
Display: Palatino